The Last of the Provincials

THE AMERICAN NOVEL, 1915–1925

"Each in his narrow cell forever laid
The rude forefathers of the hamlet sleep."

Books by Maxwell Geismar

AMERICAN MODERNS: From Rebellion to Conformity. A Mid-Century View of Contemporary Fiction

WRITERS IN CRISIS: The American Novel, 1925-1940

THE LAST OF THE PROVINCIALS: The American Novel, 1915-1925

REBELS AND ANCESTORS: The American Novel, 1890-1915

Editor

Thomas Wolfe (Viking Portable Library)

The Whitman Reader (Pocket Book)

The Last of the Provincials

THE AMERICAN NOVEL, 1915-1925

By MAXWELL GEISMAR

H. L. Mencken
Sinclair Lewis
Willa Cather
Sherwood Anderson
F. Scott Fitzgerald

HILL AND WANG · New York

PUBLISHED BY ARRANGEMENT WITH HOUGHTON MIFFLIN COMPANY

LIBRARY OF CONGRESS CATALOG CARD NUMBER: 59-8780

FIRST PAPERBACK EDITION, FEBRUARY 1959

MANUFACTURED IN THE UNITED STATES OF AMERICA
BY THE COLONIAL PRESS INC., CLINTON, MASS.

"Go East, Orphans!"

A short section of the chapter on Sherwood Anderson originally appeared in the *New York Times Sunday Book Review.* The author's thanks are due also to the following individuals and publishing houses for permission to quote illustrative passages in this book: Mrs. Sherwood Anderson, E. E. Cummings, Doubleday and Company, Inc., Messrs. Faber and Faber, Ltd., Harcourt, Brace and Company, Inc., Houghton Mifflin Company, Alfred A. Knopf, Inc., Liveright Publishing Corporation, Random House, Inc., Charles Scribner's Sons, The Viking Press, Inc.

A detailed acknowledgments page is included in the appendix to this book.

Note on a New Edition

I AM GLAD to welcome *Provincials* to a third hardcover printing, and to its first paperback edition. Looking back at this book, after ten years, it may seem that the Author of that earlier time was, like his subjects, imbued with hope and enthusiasm, or somewhat provincial and innocent of spirit himself . . . Yet one returns to these essays with a certain sense of relief, and recognition. After a decade of so-called normalcy, of prosperity and mediocrity, we find ourselves, if we are honest, in a less hopeful frame of mind—a more constrained and threatened stance. The five earlier writers of this volume lived in better times, by and large, and who can do them any further harm? Their posthumous life is in one sense their real life. H. L. Mencken's comic spirit and Sinclair Lewis's satire at its best, or the possessed fantasy of Scott Fitzgerald, the irrevocable serenity of Willa Cather's work, the tender yearning of Sherwood Anderson's: these come back to us now from a brighter orbit of the national spirit.

MAXWELL GEISMAR

Harrison, New York
January 13, 1959.

Preface

THIS IS THE SECOND of a group of books which will deal with the leading American novelists from the Civil War to World War II.

As a whole these books will form a literary record of American thinking over the last century. But the special emphasis of each book will be on the individual studies of the novelists who reflect and also help to form our changing cultural scene.

The general historical pattern of the series is relatively simple. During this period the country changed from an agrarian and provincial society ('the States') to an industrialized urban world power: the U.S.A. This was the end of the young Republic. . . . But the literary temperaments which react to the change—the biographical patterns within the larger historical pattern—are singularly varied and complex. 'The heart has its reasons of which reason knows nothing,' as Pascal said, and it is our purpose to follow the twists and turns of these literary temperaments as closely as possible.

There is also, of course, change within change. The first of these books to be published, *Writers in Crisis,* dealt primarily with the Younger Generation of World War I—the 'Lost Generation'—and chronologically the volume was centered around the nineteen-thirties. The present volume deals mainly with the Middle Generation and is centered around the nineteen-twenties—although, to be sure, writers don't quite live or die according to their historical epoch and most of these studies also will carry us to the edge of our own period.

To open the volume I am using H. L. Mencken as a dominant literary voice of the American twenties, while F. Scott Fitzgerald, as a typical novelist of the decade, will close it. Between these two figures are the studies of the Middle-Generation novelists proper: Sinclair Lewis, Willa Cather, and Sherwood Anderson. In one form or another these figures will present the particular historical motif of the period: the final conquest of the American town, and the values of an older rural life, by the New Economic Order of the industrialized cities. Just as Baltimore's Henry Mencken foreshadows this development most clearly and grimly, so the Sherwood Anderson of Winesburg presents the case fully and finally. Our other authors, too, will have some interesting observations on the change. Right here, with Sinclair Lewis's creation of the Cosmic Bourjoyce, with Willa Cather's journey to the 'well-ordered universe' of the Hospitalières in the Quebec of the early seventeen-hundreds, and with Scott Fitzgerald's establishment on the Côte d'Azur, a shining eastern garden of innocence and grace: right here is the start of all those singular spiritual pilgrimages, those exotic voyages of malaise which were the matrix of our literature in the late nineteen-twenties.

Incidentally, the first two volumes of this series form a unit about strictly contemporary American writing, and I think that between them they include the leading American novelists from 1920 to 1940. Other figures like Theodore Dreiser and Ellen Glasgow will be taken up in the third volume of the series, to be centered around the nineteen-hundreds.

Since the intention of these studies is to present the novelists as completely as possible in their own terms, I have limited the discussion of literary criticism in the text itself. In the appendix, I have listed the main works of the novelists and a selected group of critical studies of them. Similarly, the footnotes are used to indicate historical issues or matters of craft which may illuminate the text but are not strictly essential to it.

I have also included a short summary chapter at the end of the book. But in a way it is misleading to summarize the 'conclusions' of the individual studies of these novelists. The studies are the conclusions.

My thanks are due to the John Simon Guggenheim Foundation for a fellowship awarded to write this book.

MAXWELL GEISMAR

Harrison, NEW YORK, 1947

Contents

Chapter One

H. L. Mencken: ON THE DOCK

◇

1. Happy, Happy Days

2. The Frantic Spectator

3. The Prejudices of Henry Mencken

4. The Gemütlich Superman

5. Coda à la Capitalism

6. Our Theirns and Woulda Hads

Chapter One

H. L. Mencken: ON THE DOCK

1. Happy, Happy Days

'FROM THE BOY SCOUTS, and from home cooking, from Odd Fellows' funerals, from Socialists and from Christians —good Lord, deliver us!' So ran one of his early litanies, and there were other aspects of the native scene circa 1920 toward which he directed the omnipotent gaze——

First, however, a personal word. Henry Louis Mencken was born September 12, 1880, in Baltimore, 'into a family of German extraction, and descended from a line of professors of law and engineering.' As you will see, his view of his own descent is somewhat variable. The early Mencken, under savage attack, and called, among other things, 'an ignorant foreigner of dubious origin, inhabiting the Baltimore ghetto,' bluntly proclaimed his mixture of racial stocks. The later writer asserted he was Anglo and Saxon and 'very little else,' and firmly established an honorable family tree, and a family crest—'a demi-roebuck on a helmet affrontée'—in perhaps the only dull book he ever touched.

As a matter of fact, the background of the local Lucifer *was* eminently respectable; in his later memoirs he admitted he was 'a larva of the comfortable and complacent bourgeoisie.' But we shall examine the nature of those 'happy, happy days,' these last tales of a world without 'psychological, sociological or politico-economic significance': this child's world in a late-Victorian mercantile society, where father came home for his afternoon nap, and mother was beautiful, and the only disturbing sound in the evening was the clomp-clomp of a trotter's scissoring hooves, and even the bad dreams of childhood were, at least in retrospect, benign and fleeting.

Well, there were to be other bad dreams in Henry Mencken's maturity, from which he could not escape. Perhaps he forgot, in his reminiscences (and it is curious that a writer of Mencken's stature should tell us so little about even that world of innocence)—perhaps he forgot about the '100,000 negroes and 200,000 ignorant and superstitious foreigners' who were also in Baltimore, the outlandish and filthy 'Russian-born tailors' or the 'foul, ignorant, thieving' citizens of the Black Belt whom an earlier Mencken had dwelt upon in some length as Baltimore began to yield to the industrial ethos and to 'the frantic efforts of the boosters and boomers.'

Meanwhile, destined to be an engineer himself, he had entered the Baltimore Polytechnic Institute at twelve, and managed to graduate.* He worked for a while in his father's cigar factory, and in 1899 he began reporting for the Baltimore *Morning Herald*. In 1903 he became city editor, and by 1906 chief editor of the *Evening Herald*, and much in demand. He had already published his first and last volume of verse and the little book on Shaw, and, in 1908, he brought out his first major work. *The Philosophy of Friedrich Nietzsche* was a curious opening for the career of a major American critic, possibly the first of such potential stature in our letters since Poe; and a queer sort

* For the biographical details in these studies I am in general indebted to Fred B. Millet's handbook, *Contemporary American Authors.* Wherever possible I have used supplementary sources, in this case Isaac Goldberg's biography, *The Man Mencken.*

of philosophy to be expounded with so much passion and eloquence by a lineal descendant of Paine and Jefferson. Yet it was here, borrowing from the phrases of old Friedrich—'written with sulphuric acid upon tablets of phosphorus'—that Mencken first developed his opinions as well as his style. This precocious Baltimore journalist, formerly cub reporter, ghost writer, and literary handy man, drama critic, columnist, and editorializer: this hard-bitten and professional purveyor of public opinion emerges, in his late twenties, as a full-blown Mencken out of Nietzsche's brow, and for almost another decade there was to be little change in his basic point of view.

There were to be some other changes, though, as H. L. Mencken, along with George Jean Nathan, took over *The Smart Set*. It may be fashionable, at the moment, to deprecate the achievement of 'Mencken and Nathan and God' in this area; it is easy to forget the electrical effect of their work on their period, as well as the gaiety and freshness of their early adventures. There is little doubt that the element of leisure-class snobbism—the esoteric pranks, the fastidious cultivation of their monthly manifestoes—was deliberately heightened to provoke the 'ordinary, dreary, sweating, struggling people of the Republic.' The home life of these two enterprising playboys of the arts: the elaborate bachelor quarters, the boutonnières of blue corn-flowers, the thirty-eight overcoats of all sorts and descriptions as against the selected list of *five* persons, 'so many and no more,' with whom one may carry on social intercourse; not to mention the silk shirts and jeweled scarf pins of these flourishing agnostics and anarchists—in all this, no doubt, there was an element of hyperbole, if not of plain farce.

No, we have no intention here of minimizing the effect of the earlier Mencken as an innovator and a molder of an epoch. . . . But just what *did* happen to this fortunate and powerful critic of the times who reached the height of his career in the midst of a brilliant revival of our letters, a revival which he himself had so largely helped to bring about? How can you account for the rising tension of such a curious rebel: one who is against the old taboos and against the new freedom; who is against the 'dying Anglo-Saxons' and against the flood of 'aliens'; against the capitalist ruling class and even more against the onslaughts of the 'mob'? To some degree, surely, he was the captive of his own aesthetic, and led to the void by his own antics. Yet I believe that this will hardly explain the decisive change in the Mencken of the middle twenties: this key American writer whose first sense of gusto is followed so swiftly by a sense of black despair, and whose goatish prancings draw into a weird dance of death.

What other factors brought Henry Mencken at once to a high point of worldly prestige and to an extreme point of opposition—a point of almost total denial in the midst of both a personal life and an enveloping society which had all the aspects of security and freedom, and even a certain splendor? These too seemed like happy days.

2. *The Frantic Spectator*

To return, then: from the ballot-box and from *Lohengrin,* from women and democracy, the good Lord had already delivered H. L. Mencken.

—But not them from Mencken. In a straightforward manner the apostle of the newest New Freedom mentioned some other irritating aspects of his own place and people at the outset of the American Twenties. Starting with the literary scene for convenience—and convenience often became a necessity in his case—there was Robert Frost, a Whittier without whiskers. And the phosphorescent heresies of William Dean Howells. And the feverish alarums of Paul Elmer More, who was then teaching Sanskrit to the adolescent suffragettes of Bryn Mawr—an enterprise, it was further noted, about as stimulating as setting off fireworks in a blind asylum. What Mencken said about these estimable figures! and what did he not say about Hamlin Garland, the late O. Henry, and the whole desert of American fictioneering, 'at once so populated and so dreary,' and out of which had emerged only one true artist! Dreiser himself was not without minor blemishes. He could be 'flaccid, elephantine, doltish, coarse, dismal, flatulent. . . .' He was still in his intellectual menopause, just as his society was in the transitional state between Christian endeavor and civilization. However, if it was momentarily disconcerting to share in the grace of H. L. Mencken's approval, it was ultimately reassuring. The Hoosier Flatfoot was placed among the immortals—somewhat above Wagner, who had the soul of a *schnorrer*, or Kipling, who was merely a mob-orator, a mouther of inanities, a patriot, a schoolgirl.

So much for the American literati—could one say more for the academicians? One could, and Mencken said it, starting from the kept idealists of the *New Republic* and working up to Messrs. Van Dyke, Sherman, and Phelps *de l'institut Américain*. The latter were an indistinct herd of intellectual eunuchs, of obscure origins, defective education, and elemental tastes. As a matter of fact, the college professor in any form—the university ignoramus, the fat milch cow of wisdom—became a special source of Menckenian grief. 'Learning is there, but not curiosity. A heavy dignity is there, but not genuine respect. . . . Squeezed between the plutocracy on one side and the mob on the other, the *intelligentsia* face the eternal national problem of maintaining their position, of guarding themselves against challenge and attack, of keeping down suspicion.'

Thus Mencken outlined the broad class distinctions that were to form the standard pattern of social thinking in the early twenties: between the plutocracy and the mob the new intelligentsia sought at best a precarious and slippery footing. He went on to analyze the upper half of this cultural pincer movement. What was the true character of the first families of the Republic, the bogus and bugaboo aristocracy toward which every loyal citizen aspired, and which demanded such a fee from the aspirant? For—

> He must exhibit exactly the right social habits, appetites and prejudices, public and private. He must harbor exactly the right political enthusiasms and indignations. He must have a hearty taste for exactly the right sports. His attitude toward the fine arts must be properly tolerant and yet not a shade too eager. He must read and like exactly the right books, pamphlets and public journals. He must put up at the right hotels when he travels. His wife must patronize the right milliners. He himself must stick to the right haberdashery. He must live in the right neighborhood. . . . To hang back, to challenge and dispute, to preach reforms and revolutions—these are crimes against the brummagen Holy Ghost of the order.

Here, obviously, Mencken said,* was no genuine ruling class. On the contrary. 'Imagine a horde of peasants incredibly enriched and with almost infinite power thrust into their hands, and you will have a fair picture of its habitual state of mind.'

And what of the American peasants before they were

* In 'The National Letters,' *Prejudices: Second Series.*

enriched? In *A Book of Burlesques* (1916), in *A Book of Prefaces* (1917), and in these early volumes of *Prejudices* (1919-22),* H. L. Mencken had something to say about this, too—about the inferior classes and the emotions of the mob, upon which the whole comedy, as he saw it, was played. Theoretically the mob was the repository of all political wisdom and virtue. Actually it was the ultimate source of all political power, and the business of keeping it in order must be done discreetly. 'In the main that business consists of keeping alive its deep-seated fears—of strange faces, of unfamiliar ideas, of unhackneyed gestures, of untested liberties and responsibilities. The one permanent emotion of the inferior man is fear.' Was there a brighter side to this grim, and practically Calvinistic emotional predestination at the root of the Menckenian social psychology? In 'The Husbandman' he added an enchanting and almost lyrical exposition of the correlative impulse of the mob: to wit, *envy*. It was the mob's dream to bring the level of civilization everywhere in the Republic down to the mores of Arkansas. It was their secret desire that the code of Kansas and Mississippi, Vermont and Minnesota should be forced upon all of us. 'What I sing, I suppose, is a sort of Utopia'—

> It is a Utopia dreamed by simpler and more virtuous men—by seven millions of Christian bumpkins, far-flung in forty-eight sovereign states. They dream it in their long journeys down the twelve billion furrows of their seven million farms, up hill and down dale in the heat of the day. They dream it behind the egg-stove on Winter nights, their boots off and their socks scorching, Holy Writ in their hands. They dream it as they commune with *Bos taurus, Sus scrofa, Mephitis mephitis,* the Methodist

* The still earlier works of Mencken will be taken up in the fourth section of this study.

> pastor, the Ford agent. It floats before their eyes as they scan the Sears-Roebuck catalogue for horse liniment, porous plasters and Bordeaux mixture; it rises before them when they assemble in their Little Bethels to be instructed in the word of God, the plots of the Pope, the crimes of the atheists and Jews; it transfigures the chautauquan who looms before them with his Great Message. This Utopia haunts and tortures them; they long to make it real. They have tried prayer, and it has failed; now they turn to the secular arm. The dung-fork glitters in the sun as the host prepares to march. . . .

And the upshot of the clash between the enriched peasants and the impoverished peasants—between the insecure supermen and the grasping inferior men, between the quaking blond beasts of Boston and the howling anthropoids of the Hookworm Belt—the upshot of this unceasing and unspeakable struggle was, in brief, American society.

What was left of the Americano? Not, said Mencken, his sense of fair play, or his vaunted efficiency (the average American plumber could not plumb) or his sensuous impulses. In these states, Mencken said, it was impossible to portray the female figure below the clavicle. Maternity, as it was commonly depicted, was scarcely more sexual than playing the piano. Apparently no one in the New World had as yet discovered that the exercise of the reproductive faculty was immensely agreeable.* And even the shy and stagy carnality that characterized the Revolt of the Flesh had its high symbolism and profound uses. 'In so foul a nest of imprisoned and fermenting sex as the United States, plain fornication becomes a mark of relative decency.' †

Did we still cling—like Henry Mencken and his some-

* *Prejudices: Sixth Series.*
† *Prejudices: Second Series.*

what battered optimism—to our instinct for political institutions? American democracy, said Mencken, was the system of government under which the people, having 35,717,342 native-born adult whites to choose from, including thousands who were handsome and many who were wise, had selected a Coolidge to be head of state. Our cultural ideals were those of 'the dissenting pulpit, the public cemetery, the electric sign.' More; our trouble was not really environmental (though he had devoted some passing attention to these matters), but it was biological and immutable. At bottom, we were a mongrel and inferior people, incapable of any spiritual aspiration above that of second-rate English colonials.* Our function, we chose to believe, was to teach and inspire the world. But we were wrong. 'Our function is to amuse the world. We are the Bryan, the Henry Ford, the Billy Sunday among the nations. . . .'

Such was the American cyclorama—or the American cosmology—as it appeared to H. L. Mencken at the outset of the American Twenties, and as it appeared to a generation which, before Mencken, had not discovered just how lost it could be. It was a gruesome prospect and probably it seemed even more gruesome than it was. Had there really been such a void in beautiful letters between Emerson and modern times—a void over which hovered only the immaculate wraith of Howells? Mencken was not averse to using Melville or Whitman as a horrible example of the artist in America, rather than as an example of the artist in America. So with Poe,† who is one of Mencken's chief admirations in these early essays, and who dies 'like a

* *Prejudices: First Series.*

† The influence of Poe on Mencken, extending even into matters of style and vocabulary, probably hasn't been sufficiently noticed. To some degree Mencken's early career parallels that of Ambrose Bierce as the rough and witty literary arbiter of San Francisco in the 1870's. But Bierce, of course, was also directly influenced by Poe.

stray dog' twice in *A Book of Prefaces,* and again, if I am not mistaken, in *Prejudices: First Series.* The desert of American fictioneering was not quite so dreary as herein pictured—but then, like God, or like the Devil, H. L. Mencken could invent deserts when he could not find them, or at any rate he stretched their boundaries considerably.

Moreover, by branding American scholarship either as Charlatanism or as Rabbinism, didn't he, in one stroke, demolish both our native tradition and one of the chief European cultural sources in which, so he argued, our tradition was particularly deficient? And didn't his own philosophical ground consist of a somewhat foggy German mysticism? His view of the Harvard quasi-culture —'by the Oxford manner out of Calvinism'—was somewhat harsh, then, just as his résumé of the New England tradition—which began as a slaughter-house of ideas and finished as a cold-storage plant—was a little strained. As for the South, the Sahara of the Bozart, this so vast a vacuity which had, since the Civil War, produced not a 'single orchestra or a single painting or a single public building of distinction'—perhaps he was himself making a false assumption and jejune conclusion about an area still rich in folk tradition and folk art. In respect to the region of silos, revivals, and saleratus, maybe he underestimated the western circuit-towns that had nourished Douglas and Lincoln. And that dionysian spirit, that joyful acquiescence in life, that philosophy of the *Ja-sager* which Mencken—by Nietzsche out of Schopenhauer—could find nowhere in his own tradition, had been expressed with some finesse, of course, by the Franklin, Jefferson, *et al.,* who were dispensed with in these early volumes.

Mencken liquidated the American past when he initiated the American future. There were some other curious elements in his thinking: a rather slippery logic, a sacrifice of sobriety to the appeal of bravado, for he never hesitated to affirm violently what he had just as violently denied. This skeptic was credulous in the extreme, and the brutal realist was also an incredible sentimentalist. Still worse, there were less obvious and more destructive contradictions in the ipse dixits, ex cathedras, bulls, canons, and papal interdicts of H. L. Mencken. . . . But having created his own 'so vast a vacuity' in which Dreiser alone stood—having hewed out in a few heavy strokes this weird cultural abyss; this man-made or Mencken-made pitfall which was the natural habitat of the early Fitzgerald, Hemingway, and Dos Passos and almost the typical milieu of the early twenties—at any rate Henry Mencken set about to fill the void with his own palpable bulk.

And certainly—while today we see connections between the American twenties and the previous decades which it was considered bad form if not folly to look for in the postwar period—* most certainly there was work to be done by this new prophet with his whips and scorpions and, if all else failed, his boulders. Suppose there was a submerged rotarian in the Baltimore Cassandra? Granted that he plugged George Ade and muffed Ellen Glasgow—and claimed that Lizette Reese had written more 'genuine poetry than all the new poets put together.' All the same he knew who Sandburg and Masters were, and he knew who Hermann Sudermann was, as well as Maeterlinck, Sainte-Beuve, and Macaulay. The Menckenian bludgeoning revived interest in these writers and in a score of others. It focused attention, started searches, awoke the half-alive, and it evoked an outraged clamor in a dozen

* Thus the nineteen-hundreds were hardly so stuffy, the nineties were hardly so vacant: Mencken almost ignores Henry James, as he misses the deeper conflicts of Howells, and passes by Edith Wharton, not to mention Norris, Crane, or Fuller.

American cities;* it put a shroud over the relics of the past and it quickened the blood of the coming age. The function of criticism, Mencken had said in his essay on Conrad, was to beat a drum, and there was no doubt he was beating on one, along with the heads he was knocking together, and while the noise was sometimes excessive, the call to action remained.

'Here,' he said again, apropos of another early idol—Huneker: 'Here, throwing off his critic's black gown, he lays about him right and left, knocking the reigning idols off their perches . . . lambasting on one page and lauding on the next.' And with what celerity did he go and do likewise, this ranting publicist who almost raised journalism to the status of an art! Consider the array of phrases, full-blown, sweet, and caressing, he brought: his critical armamentorium bulging with 'inspired omphalists' and 'academic bunkophagi.' What an appalling line of descent he concocted for the American species, from *homo-boobiens* to *homo stultus!* From *brutum fulmen* to *wiener-schnitzel* he laid waste a dozen tongues to enrich the English language—i.e., the American language—i.e., a language that would actually give the lowdown on American life, and describe the shamans and wowsers† who roamed the Republic. And while the universal order, from the apes to the demigods, took a beating, the Creator Himself—this Cosmic Kaiser, this Divine Schädchen—barely escaped from his passing barbs.

What Mencken did was often so astounding that it was impertinent to think of what he might have done. It could

* In the pages of reputable journals, Mencken was hailed as a weasel, a maggot, a ghoul, a buzzard, a polecat, a howling hyena, a pig, a wasp, and 'one of those little skunks who spread their poison wherever they go.' A general stress was put on his affinity with the lower biological forms, perhaps unfairly so to all concerned. See *Menckeniana, a Schimpflexikon.*

† What is a wowser? What, said Mencken, does it sound like? 'A wowser is a wowser.'

justly be claimed now that the pre-Menckenian literati were as gross and shapeless as Brunhilda. Though the critic admitted he might put the way of saying a thing above the thing said, who else could demonstrate that the Char-Freitag music in *Parsifal* sounded like the setting 'for some lamentable fornication between a Bayreuth baritone seven feet in height and a German soprano weighing at least three hundred pounds'? Who but Mencken could analyze the inspiration of Wagner himself in terms of stenosis, and recall the days when the bard awoke 'full of acidosis and despair'?—Was this the man who viewed music as an absolute, beyond the comprehension of the mob? While Mencken was berating the populace, he was popularizing Culture with a talent that made a Billy Phelps seem like a Byzantine monk. Here the 'infectious gusto' of Huneker became virulent, and incurable. The arts were being democratized by the artist who saw no point to democracy.

For all Henry Mencken's allegiance to the dark and death-enchanted Teutonic mystics, his own early emphasis was fixed on life—and particularly, coming from this defiant Germanophile, on life in America. For all his strong and savage denunciations of his own society, he was a *stamm-vater* of its cultural flowering in the twenties; he was part of the new hope that Van Wyck Brooks was just then expounding in *Letters and Leadership,* and furthermore he was an integral part of the New Freedom he snickered at. (The cultural historian can scarcely afford to omit Mencken's exposé of the blind American optimism that marked the Age of Make-Believe.) Than he, there were few better in presenting the 'whole gross, glittering, excessively dynamic, infinitely grotesque, incredibly stupendous' drama of American life. In fact, he *was* this life—at least as compared with literary 'Humanists' like More and Irving Babbitt. In spite of the abuse that Mencken lavished on his enemies, and the uncertain support he extended to his allies, there was also, as in the case of the only President he could bring himself to admire, a certain charm in his idiocy. Like Teddy Roosevelt, Mencken may have been part comedian and part charlatan, yet: 'He knew how to woo—and not only boobs.'

Was it easy not to be stirred by the fervor of this cynic who mocked at the urge to uplift and abused reformers chiefly? (Notice the Biblical undertones in this traducer of Yaweh and vilifier of the Hebraic prophets.) His expressed rôle was that of the disinterested bystander, his recurrent stress was on 'life as a spectacle'—and on life in the Republic as a circus. Why did he stay on in the United States? 'Why does a man visit the zoo?' The price of the show, moreover, was very reasonable:

> I figure, for example, that my share of the expenses of maintaining the Hon. Mr. Harding in the White House this year will work out to less than 80 cents. Try to think of better sport for the money. . . . The United States Senate will cost me perhaps $11 for the year, but against that expense set the subscription of the Congressional Record, about $15, which, as a journalist, I receive for nothing. For $4 less than nothing I am thus entertained as Solomon never was by his hooch dancers. Col. George Brinton McClellan Harvey costs me but 25 cents a year; I get Nicholas Murray Butler free.

. . . But not often in the annals of the Republic has a spectacle been quite so animated. And seldom in the saga of beautiful letters has a bystander taken quite such a strenuous, nay, almost frenzied part in a spiritual holocaust of the first order. 'It was difficult,' he admitted later, 'even for an American to contemplate the Americans without yielding to something hard to distinguish from moral indignation.' And it was difficult, at times, to distinguish Henry Mencken from something close to an esoteric Teddy Roosevelt or a metaphysical Carrie Nation—this panting spectator and energetic advocate of the immaculate perception who, like his prototypes, carried a big stick, and a hatchet, and also a blunderbuss, and hardly so much walked softly as he trampled and paraded through the jungle of American taboos and false sanctions, accompanied, as it were, by a thousand trumpets. For in Mencken's case, moral indignation was often carried to the point of self-immolation.

Such were the paradoxes which H. L. Mencken cultivated and through which he flourished. He was quite aware, too, of the discrepancies between his rôle and himself; it was the elaboration of his stage presence which sometimes gave the show away. —But as I say, there were less deliberate and less entertaining contradictions in his work. When Mencken became most serious, he was probably not taken seriously enough.

3. *The Prejudices of Henry Mencken*

By 1925 the Puritan Kultur was dead, as H. L. Mencken announced one day, and, to the uninitiated, it might have seemed that the average citizen had taken an odd turn—living as he did in those ratty and unheated studios, gabbling about 'cubism, vorticism, futurism and other such childish follies.' It was indeed a New American that Mencken was describing: one who walked a strait path from Barrow Street to Union Square, whose overt purpose was the overthrow of 'civilization as it existed in the United States,' and whose secret weapon was free verse.

Greenwich Village had come to town, and with it the modern age had burst in all its splendor and terror, from the flappers at Delmonico's to the bohemians of Sauk Center—while a new Babbitt (George F.) was chanting the lyrics of Edna Millay in the glass-enclosed showers of a continent. 'The campaign for birth control,' so Mencken opened his *Prejudices: Fifth Series,* 'takes on the colossal proportions of the war for democracy,' and the most virtuous lady novelists were now writing things that would formerly have made a bartender blush to death. The heirs of Puritanism, the Comstockers, too, were about to be overcome by a veritable geyser of Freudian suppressions. 'When I began reviewing I used to send my review copies, after I had sweated through them, to the Y.M.C.A. Now I send them to a medical college.'

He was not altogether enthusiastic about every manifestation of the sexual revolt in the twenties—

> The venereal diseases are represented to be as widespread, at least in men, as colds in the head, and as lethal as apoplexy or cancer. Great hordes of viragoes patrol the country, instructing schoolgirls in the mechanics of reproduction and their mothers in obstetrics. The lighthearted monogamy which produced all of us is denounced as an infamy comparable to cannibalism. Laws are passed regulating the mating of human beings as if they were horned cattle and converting marriage into a sort of coroner's inquest.

In place of the taboos which had surrounded 'the great physiological farce of sex' there was now a vast running-amok. All that was worth knowing about sex, so Mencken claimed, could be taught to any intelligent boy (or girl?) of sixteen in two hours. . . . Yet this whole revolt of the flesh in American life marked a similar ferment and boiling-over in other crucial areas of a post-war American society. It was obvious to 'every amateur of ghostly pathology' in this Christian realm that the Protestant heresy itself was down with a wasting disease. And with this, what prospects could not be viewed in the golden dawn of a new period? The free body joined hands with a free spirit, the sexual flowering was merely a prelude to cultural flowering

The young literary lions of the Foetal School–E. E. Cummings, Ezra Pound, and T. S. Eliot among them–were cutting capers around the seniors of the Hypoendocrinal School—the Mores, Matthews, and Van Dykes; and the magazine *Broom* had helped to sweep away the aesthetic cobwebs of half a century. Were there certain extremes of revolt here too: from the Freudian necromancy to the occult tosh of the Cézannists? Every New Gallery opened with a new manifesto–although Henry Mencken could find only a series of canvases that appeared to have been painted with asphalt and mayonnaise. All the same, six thousand Little Theatres had come out like a rash on the face of the nation. It was quite clear that Eugene O'Neill was in direct competition with Doctor Baker's Ibsenfabrik at Cambridge; it was almost clear that the contest was over. Even the Sahara of the Bozart trembled on the edge of renascence. The vast vacuity was spawning forth the Caldwells and Faulkners, as well as the Fugitives and Agrarians, and Katherine Anne Porter–was turning out a whole host of Mencken's 'superior people' whose single defect, perhaps, was in their consciousness of superiority.

It was almost comic to find Henry Mencken, hot from denouncing the barren spirit of the American provinces, now complaining about the schools of short-story writing and scenario writing that were swarming in the land, the hundred thousand second-hand Coronas that were rattling and jingling in ten thousand remote and lonely towns. He had to concede* that we were 'the most assiduously literate country in Christendom,' and that our people were reading 'day and night, weekdays and Sundays.' And even earlier† he had concluded that in the face of the dark depression across the water, the literary spectacle on this side had taken on a reassuring and rather exhilarating aspect—that leadership in the arts, and especially in the arts of letters, 'may eventually transfer itself from the eastern shore of the Atlantic to the western shore':

> No longer imitative and timorous, as most of their predecessors were, these youngsters‡ are attempting a first-hand examination of the national scene, and making an effort to represent it in terms that are wholly American. They are the pioneers of a literature that, whatever its defects in the abstract, will at least be a faithful reflection of the national life, that will be more faithful, indeed, in its defects than in its merits. In England the novel subsides into formulae, the drama is submerged in artificialities, and even poetry, despite occasional revolts, moves toward scholarliness and emptiness. But in America, since the war, all three show the artless and superabundant energy of little children. They lack, only too often, manner and urbanity; it is no wonder they are often shocking to pedants. But there is the breath of life in them, and that life is nearer its beginning than its end.

Such a statement deserved to be noticed—if not broadcast through the Republic to the accompaniment of flutes and harps. This was H. L. Mencken amidst sweetness and

* In 'The Fringes of Lovely Letters,' *Prejudices: Fifth Series.*
† In *Prejudices: Fourth Series* (1924).
‡ Youngsters like Lewis, Cather, Cabell, and Hergesheimer.

light. This was The National Scene in a Revised Edition. This was Revelation.

The pronunciamento was not without basis. Never had one age passed into another so swiftly or the polarity of the historical process shown such a faithful magnetism and thesis become antithesis with an equal verve. And the value of the democratic individual could hardly have been demonstrated more effectively than by Mencken himself, the mocker at democracy, the belittler of the individual. The new Joshua trumpeted—to shift the image—and the walls descended with alacrity, and the bricks and mortar of the social arrangement had seldom been so pervious or pliable, or the sluggish opinion of mankind so willing and anxious to follow the vision of truth as over the few years from 1919 to 1925.

Never had a democratic order seemed so altogether flexible, flourishing, or hopeful. . . . And wasn't Henry Mencken, who might claim to be a progenitor of the new epoch, altogether satisfied with his creation? Quite to the contrary, the success of his cause only stirred him into new outbursts. If his single rival, the merciless and bleak Jehovah of American puritanism, had ceased to deliver thunderbolts with the old éclat, it seemed that in the void new forces were forming, some of which gave H. L. Mencken cause for alarm. Since the old stock company of devils had been retired, he reported, and with it the old repertoire of private sins, the American masses appeared intent on clawing their way into heaven. 'Personal holiness has now been handed over to the Holy Rollers and other such survivors from a harsher day. It is sufficient now to hate the Jews, to hate the scientists, to hate all foreigners, to hate whatever the cities yield to.' This was, indeed, the essence of the 'New Protestantism'; these hatreds, with their attendant fears, were the basic religion of the American clodhopper today, and they were spread through the land by the 'rev. pastors, chiefly Baptists and Methodists.'

And maybe also by the rev. Menckens—for wasn't there a certain irony in the situation? Wasn't this a partial fulfillment of the Nietzschean ethics, a triumph over the Jewish-Christian 'slave-morality,' a crusade in which Henry Mencken himself had taken not a small part? Wasn't the new law of the talon merely filling the void left by the spirit of humility, which Mencken himself had hoped to eliminate? Perhaps Mencken's formula for the élite had merely penetrated down to the lumpish mind of the mass-man;* and wasn't his own view, in turn, the reflection of some deeper, subterranean shift in the foundations of contemporary society? —These were questions for a reflective spirit; but the outraged and denunciatory Henry could barely pause to reflect upon them.

Mencken himself could hardly plead guilty to the charge of idolatry with respect to the scientists, the foreigners, and whatever else the cities yielded to. At least not in an early piece like 'The Dismal Science,' where he had written off, with savage ridicule, whatever contributions Veblen had made to the social sciences; where he had also denied the contributions of psychologists like William James, and had sent our local philosopher, John Dewey, back to the dungeons of Columbia, there to lecture 'in imperfect Yiddish to classes of Grand Street Platos.' In the new age Mencken found himself in the position of defending some of these Grand Street Platos who happened to be active contributors to the American literary renascence. Through his own proudly affirmed heritage of 'mixed

* The American moron, Mencken also reported, now wanted to keep his Ford even at the cost of losing the Bill of Rights—but who had just lately exposed the 'fundamental nonsensicality' of the Bill of Rights?

blood,' and again through the dominant intellectual influences of his youth (between them, Nietzsche and Huneker accounted for at least five nationalities), he was in a position particularly to appreciate the value of the 'aliens' as against their native white Protestant critics.

Yet here too, the course of Mencken's argument was somewhat involved. There was no doubt, he asserted, that the Anglo-Saxon majority was decadent, and over this period his passages ring with such phrases: the wearing-out of the old Anglo-Saxon stock, the dying Anglo-Saxon strain, the declining Anglo-Saxon class which had gradually lost leadership and now must face the melancholy proof of its intrinsic inferiority. . . . For, he contended, the tendency of American literature to radiate 'an alien smell' was not an isolated phenomenon. But the phrasing of his defense was not altogether happy, while his view of the immigrants' was still somewhat uncertain. There was a line, not quite invisible, that wavered somewhere below the area of the pure Germanic stock; in the essay on 'The Woes of a 100% American' * these mixed feelings of Henry Mencken became almost luminous. He admitted there was unquestionably a difference between the Nordic Americans and those who were non-Nordic. There had undoubtedly been an assault on the cultural citadel (or should one say, chalice?) by men who were not Anglo-Saxons and 'whose Americanism was open to question.' These were undoubted facts, so Mencken declared, and if he were an Anglo-Saxon, they would fever him as much as they fevered his opponents. . . . Very good: that is, if you had to accept, as he (Mencken) seemed to accept,

* In the *Prejudices: Fifth Series* (1926). Doctor Wilbur Abbott, the subject, is here attacking 'the new barbarians,' while William Brownell, Brander Matthews, and even Stuart Sherman had performed roughly the same service for literature a little earlier. See also *Prejudices: Fourth Series,* in 1924.

such 'undoubted facts' and the whole nonsensical premise of a racial division. But then why, on the next page, did he turn and advise the true Anglo-Saxons to throw off their false-faces and come out with the 'bald, harsh doctrine' of their Nordic superiority? And call upon them further to set up an autocracy 'with high privileges eternally beyond the reach of the mongrel commonalty'? And assert that then they might get help 'from unexpected quarters,' though he was speaking, of course, for only one spear.*

It seemed that H. L. Mencken was tempted in other ways, too. While he viewed with alarm the provincial hatred of the city, his own comment on the metropolis smacked of the Innocent Abroad when it did not stem more directly from the prurient speculation of the hinterland: 'During many a single week, I daresay, more money is spent in New York upon useless and evil things than would suffice to run the kingdom of Denmark for a year'—

> All the colossal accumulated wealth of the United States, the greatest robber nation in history, tends to force itself at least once a year through the narrow neck of the Manhattan funnel. To that harsh island come all the thieves of the Republic with their loot—bankers from the fat lands of the Middle West, lumbermen from the Northwestern coasts, mine owners from the mountains, oil speculators from Texas and Oklahoma, cotton-mill sweaters from the South, steel magnates and manufacturers from the Black Country, blacklegs and exploiters without end —all laden with cash, all eager to spend it, all easy marks for the town rogues and panders . . . What town in

* Looking back, it is interesting to realize how sharply the racial issue was being drawn in literary affairs by the mid-twenties, as it had been, of course, in our political affairs by the eighteen-fifties. Mencken was against the contemporary Know-Nothings—the Klan—who seemed to be carrying out his suggestions here: but this will be taken up later.

> Christendom has ever supported so many houses of entertainment, so many mimes and mountebanks, so many sharpers and coney-catchers . . . so many miscellaneous servants to idleness and debauchery?

These were contrasted, presumably, with the civilized minority who subscribed to *The American Mercury.** But more, was Henry Mencken's view of the peasantry distinguishable in quality from their view of the urban centers? Certainly not, say, in his appreciation of William Allen White's literary endeavors. Nor in his Memoriam of William Jennings Bryan; the most sedulous flycatcher in American history, he claimed, and one whose quarry was not *Musca domestica,* but *Homo neandertalensis*—'Wherever the flambeaux of Chautauqua smoked and guttered, and the bilge of Idealism ran in the veins, and Baptist pastors dammed the brooks with the sanctified, and men gathered who were weary and heavy laden, and their wives who were full of Peruna and as fecund as the shad . . . there the indefatigable Jennings set up his traps and spread his bait.' And Mencken was not always so genial. What infuriated him here, as in the studies of White and Veblen, was not so much the socio-economic conditions of the farm states as any attempt to alter these conditions. Was there another interpretation of the simian gabble of the crossroads? When he viewed the latent tragedy of the agrarian reform movements, the degradation of rural hope which Bryan came to represent, Mencken saw only villains and horrors. Bryan, in his malice, had started something that it would not be easy to stop:

* The essay on Mencken by Louis Kronenberger which is in *After the Genteel Tradition* is particularly discerning about this phase of Mencken's work.

> He did his job competently. He had vast skill in such enterprises. Heave an egg out of a Pullman window, and you will hit a Fundamentalist almost everywhere in the United States today. They swarm in the country towns, inflamed by their *shamans,* and with a saint, now, to venerate. They are thick in the mean streets behind the gas works. They are everywhere where learning is too heavy a burden for mortal minds to carry . . . They march with the Klan, with the Christian Endeavor Society, with the Junior Order of United American Mechanics. . . . They have had a thrill, and they are ready for more.

The tone of this utterance was curious, perhaps, as was that central image of the solitary city-dweller, encased in his steel compartment, speeding across a corrupt and decaying hinterland—curious, I mean, for the prophet who was hot from announcing the birth of a new American literature and a golden age of American culture. . . . And a new epoch, not merely of the spirit, as you may recall, but of a remarkable material security, as the Jazz Age carried forward the development of an American technology. Even the city proletariat now heard the frou-frou of perfumed skirts, so Mencken said, while the advent of each new working-class baby was a miracle of scientific diligence. Furthermore, all this represented a control over our physical environment that, reaching its apex in the United States, had come about in barely two centuries of the Industrial Revolution. It had been a scant five generations since 'four-fifths of the people of the world, white and black alike, were slaves in reality, if not in name.'

Yet the book—*Notes on Democracy**—which opened

* Published in 1926, *Notes on Democracy* is the first of Mencken's more strictly philosophic studies since his *Nietzsche* in 1908. Just as it recalls his original interests after a lapse of almost two decades, it forms a sort of prologue to his later treatises on religion and on ethics.

with such a glowing and even revolutionary premise, led Mencken to a still more melancholy conclusion. Granted that we had now solved the main problems of our evolutionary progress, and had at last gained the technics for both material and spiritual freedom—what was the use? Mencken could see no possibility at all of abolishing sin or poverty or stupidity or other such 'immutable realities' which were still facing us. Worse, the central vice of the American democrat was that he believed these problems *could* be solved. And as for democracy itself, was it merely, like measles, a self-limiting disease?

> It is, perhaps, something more. It is self-devouring. One cannot observe it objectively without being impressed by its curious distrust of itself—its apparently ineradicable tendency to abandon its whole philosophy at the first sign of strain. Nor is this process confined to times of alarm and terror; it is going on day in and day out . . . I have rehearsed some of its operations against liberty, the very cornerstone of its political metaphysic. I offer the spectacle of Americans jailed for reading the Bill of Rights as perhaps the most gaudily humorous ever witnessed in the modern world. . . . But I am, it may be, a somewhat malicious man: my sympathies, when it comes to suckers, tend to be somewhat coy. What I can't make out is how any man can believe in democracy who feels for and with them, and is pained when they are debauched and made a show of. . . . How can any man be a democrat who is sincerely a democrat?

Remember this was Henry Mencken's sober and considered judgment—the peroration which summarized his *philosophical* study of the origins and meaning of the social arrangement in the United States of America. This was surely the reverse of that blind American optimism that had established itself in the latter half of the last century. Instead, it was close to the blank American negation which, from T. S. Eliot to Ring Lardner, was to prevail in the opening decades of our own century, and which, in the nineteen-thirties, brought forth Ernest Hemingway's supplication to the Omnipotent Nada.

Appearing as the book did in all the splendor of the nineteen-twenties, and presenting a long rehearsal of only the crimes and follies of man, a bleak, acrid chronicle of idiocy, a tedious monody of disgust, *Notes on Democracy* represents a low ebb of the democratic belief. Unrelieved by Mencken's usual eloquence and wit, it is at once his most sterile work and one of the gloomiest treatises on man's evolution to be penned by a supposedly evolutionary historian. And it is substantiated by a variety of similar testimonials from Mencken's other volumes over this period.

'The old rights of free Americans,' he had already said, 'are now worth nothing.' * If the decay of government in the Republic (which was at the core of these complaints) continued, and it showed no signs of stopping, it was certain that soon or late demagogues would come forward, and 'some of these demagogues will get themselves heard.' † Political organization in the United States was now so ignorant and incompetent that even a mob of serfs would be forced to protest against a government by orgy and orgasm. 'The danger is that the helpless voter, forever victimized by his false assumptions about politicians, may in the end gather such a ferocious indignation that he will abolish them teetotally and at one insane swoop, and so cause government by the people, for the people, and with the people to perish from this earth.' Furthermore, if

* 'Matters of State,' in *Prejudices: Third Series.*

† 'Justice under Democracy,' in *Prejudices: Fourth Series.*

Christian civilization was sick all over this pious land, there were those who seemed to be preparing for the wake:

> In all those parts of the Republic where Beelzebub is still as real as Babe Ruth or Dr. Coolidge, and men drink raw fusel oil hot from the still . . . the evangelical sects plunge into an abyss of malignant imbecility and declare a holy war upon every decency that civilized men cherish. First the Anti-Saloon League, and now the Ku Klux Klan and the various Fundamentalist organizations have converted them into vast machines for pursuing and butchering unbelievers. They have thrown the New Testament overboard. . . . Their one aim seems to be to break heads, to spread terror, to propagate hatred. Everywhere they have set up enmities that will not die out for generations.

Perhaps the storm would not last long as history goes, Mencken added, but it might be sufficient to break up the democratic illusion, already showing such signs of weakness. . . . And certainly the theme of democracy as a self-devouring force, in one diseased area after another, is the central theme of these volumes. In fact, it is the leit motif of the *Third* and *Fourth Prejudices,* just as the accent is half of fear and half almost of longing and desire.* How often, indeed, does the fantasy of destruction rise to the surface of Mencken's speculations about the Republic during these years! A destruction which was being brought about chiefly by decay in the body politic, aided and abetted by the tyrants in power or the tyrants who were seeking power, but which also might be hastened by external events. For the disturbing fact was not that dur-

* The change in fiber between the early and middle *Prejudices* is marked. Compare, for example, 'The National Letters' in the *First Series* with 'On Being an American' in the *Third Series*—the latter essay, one of the blackest and bitterest in our letters, almost approaching the satiric renunciation of, say, Swift's 'Modest Proposal.'

ing the First World War even the Socialists had begun whooping for 'Elihu Root, Otto Kahn, and Abraham Lincoln.' Nor that we had been drawn into the war through the sheer machinations of the English, who were now themselves under the control of 'upstarts from the lowest classes—shoddy Jews, sniffling Methodists.' * Nor that World War I had accelerated the collapse of whatever human rights or freedoms had been achieved in the Republic. —No, these facts were quite familiar to, and no longer much disturbed, H. L. Mencken. What did bother him was that the war had plainly indicated the weakness of the great conquering nation. Our own armies, rather than their outnumbered and weakened opponents, had constituted the real horde of cringing goose-steppers—and would men so degraded, so purged of human, not to mention martial, virtues: would such men offer the necessary resistance to a future public enemy who was equal or perhaps superior in force? 'It seems to me quite certain, indeed, that an American army fairly representing the American people, if it ever meets another army of anything remotely resembling like strength, will be defeated, and that defeat will be indistinguishable from rout.' †

Thus the sport of war itself, the only sport left that was, to Mencken's eyes, genuinely amusing, had been debauched by the democracies. And the First World War (which was, after all, a lesser war among our national wars, and lasted barely two years out of one hundred fifty years

* These lines may seem to anticipate the dicta of Herr Goebbels, but should serve to remind us that the Nazis were not so much inventors as exploiters of what had become common property in the civilized world by the nineteen-twenties. There are other elements of the diseased German mind that are not peculiarly Germanic, of course.

† The same general view of the war marks such works as Dos Passos's *Three Soldiers* or E. E. Cummings's *The Enormous Room.* In the last section of this essay, I take up the reasons why the post-war generation held such a view; and while the view is obviously absurd, the reasons are worth considering.

in the Republic's history) takes on the proportion of Armageddon in this blueprint for the decline of the American order. In all these omens of dissolution—whether it is the triumph of the politicians over democracy, or of the capitalists, or of the proletariat; or if these are not sufficient, of an outside military power—now England, now Germany, now Japan: in all these visions and fantasies of destruction, were there elements of the grotesque, almost elements of hysteria? Was there something of the fitful emotions of the mob-man, which Mencken had spent these years in attacking and condemning? 'The besetting intellectual sin of the United States,' he had said, 'is the vice of orgiastic and inflammatory thinking.' But the violence of a society was matched here by the violence of a prime critic of that society.

As his period grew increasingly gaudy, at any rate, H. L. Mencken grew more frantic. Now patriotism itself could only excite his loathing. 'The things that make countries safe, happy and prosperous,' he cried, 'are all intrinsically corrupting and disgusting.' * It was as impossible for a civilized man to love his country in good times as it would be for him to respect a congressman. And in time of stress, his native land might appeal to him only 'as any victim of misfortune appeals to him—say, a street-walker pursued by the police. . . .' And, having expressed his opinions in terms of what he felt to be an ever-constricted area of free speech, he served notice that he would not become a martyr for the sake of his opinions. 'In such matters I am broad-minded. What, after all, is one more lie?' Since, in the democracies, everything noble and of

* 'It seems to me that love has much to do with the fibre and quality of men as citizens of a country,' said Sherwood Anderson, who, with a very different point of view, was undergoing a like emotional experience at this time. 'But, can a man love a coal mine or a coal-mining town, a factory, a real-estate boomer . . . a movie or a movie actress, a modern daily newspaper or a freight car?'

good account tended to decay and smell bad, his own solution lay, instead, in 'no more false assumptions and no more false hopes.'

Such, then, were the sentiments of Henry Mencken in the mid-twenties, at the height of his career,* in the very midst of his own American renascence. Put it down, if you like, to the Menckenian manner, still stemming from the principle that violent denunciation was as effective in political as it was in literary commentary, and that, starting from this premise, the denunciation must become increasingly violent to be continuously effective. As I say, to some degree Mencken was the prisoner of his own aesthetic, and was led to the void by his own antics. But this *is* a void, or at least it is a step removed from the 'gaseous optimism' of the man who hopes absurdly.

And what of the man who is absurdly without hope? To return to Mencken's origins for a moment, and to his earlier and formative works, perhaps we can unravel some of these quirks in the Menckenian psychology circa 1925.

4. The Gemütlich Superman

MAYBE THE INFERIOR MAN had been lurking in the muggier recesses of some of the Founding Fathers, but it was probably not until 1908 that his presence on the western shore was announced with such panoplies and banners.

Here, in Mencken's *Philosophy of Friedrich Nietzsche,* it was clearly stated that the American ethic was the residue of a dead or dying system of ideas—of what was, to begin with, a not too prepossessing Christian slave-morality—

* The *Prejudices* ran as high as seven printings and were also published in England and Germany. By 1924, also, Mencken was editor of *The American Mercury,* almost the most enviable editorial post in the field.

and that our progress had been made, not as a result of our moral code, but as a result of dodging 'its inevitable blight.' However, could you really call it progress?

If all life was embraced in the survival of the fittest, then the *bête blonde,* innocent of good and evil alike, took precedence over the average citizen; and it merely remained for the élite to seize control over what had been, in poor Whitman's vision, the Race of Races. Without doubt, happiness consisted in the 'unrestrained yielding to the will to power.' It was only the under-dog, said this Nietzsche-Mencken, that believed in equality. And there was no mistaking the tone, not only of exposition but of partisanship. Mencken's *Nietzsche* was as much an expression of a native seeking a philosophy as of the Polish exile who had found one, and there were other curious insights in H. L. Mencken's first major work.*

Was the human intellect, for example, a symptom of the urge to dominate—almost a nervous reflex, if not a vestigial organ? Our philosopher 'knows nothing of mind except as a function of the body. . . . Reject empiricism and you reject at one stroke the whole sum of human knowledge'—provided, as Mencken didn't always provide, there *was* any sizable sum of human knowledge. In short, he was a monistic materialist, and to him the most intricate emotions were simple matters. Didn't the offering of sympathy from one human being to another—rather like a leak in a hydraulic valve system—weaken the mechanism of the one who offered it? Compassion, respect, insight, all the other human feelings, became a series of similar biological fluids to be watched over and cautiously measured out. Thus, maternity was viewed as a purely quantitative

* Mencken's *George Bernard Shaw,* in 1905, a guidebook to Shaw's plays, is interesting in so far as it leads into the ideational background of the *Nietzsche.* Very shortly, for reasons that we shall see, Mencken turned against Shaw's Fabian meliorism.

—or should I say spatial?—process which, at most, makes a woman 'utterly helpless for no longer than three months.' So, too, with sexual desire, another of the empirical fluids, and actually more limited than had been supposed. 'There are moments when it is overpowering, but there are hours, days, weeks and months when it is dormant.' But not at all so with certain other human impulses—those, for example, which were concerned with racial aggression. The South, parading under the show of a communistic-democracy, but ready, as the young Mencken felt, for a bust-up, lay directly before his view. The history of the 'hopelessly futile and fatuous effort' to improve the status of the Negroes had made it quite apparent that they must remain, as a race, in a condition of subservience so long as they retained 'racial differentiation.' True enough, the Southern Bourbons (who represented, though in a melancholy fashion, the Nietzschean First Caste) had found it easy to deprive the black masses of their elementary rights. But this was hardly sufficient. In fact, the white race as a whole, in order to preserve itself from the onslaughts of this inferior tribe, must now 'pronounce upon the black race and set out to execute . . . a sentence of extermination.'

You see how the new interpreter was not only translating Nietzsche into the American language, but also adapting the beyond-ethics to the local scene. Maybe the logic of his argument was a little involved—since an inferior race was not always altogether inferior, it seemed, and could be kept inferior only by the process of its extermination. Still, it is easy to understand the appeal, to a self-taught native materialist, of the Darwinian code which Nietzsche and Schopenhauer, among others, converted to their own uses, and it is easy, perhaps, to forget the impact of this new philosophy on American thought. If Darwinism evolved out of a nineteenth-century European scene, and was in good part the mythos of a raw industrial system, how much better was it suited to the twentieth-century United States! * It was natural, just as the European heirs of Darwin simplified the evolutionary thesis—since Darwin, as well as the earlier evolutionary thinkers, stressed the part of mutual aid in the struggle for survival, and even wolves hunt in packs—that the contemporary American should simplify the Europeans. A knowledge of our animal origins explains much about the bases of our existence. The Fallen Angel is more convincing—and more hopeful—as the Monkey-Man. To this early Mencken, however, it explains all: and the Monkey-Man emerges as a Baboon. . . . Even the anguished conflicts of Nietzsche himself, the poetic ravings of the mad Pole, the feverish embracing of pain as the antidote for pain, the almost hysterical Yes! of the wounded blond beast to all of life's tortures:† these, too, are missing here. Mencken's Nietzsche has more of the icon-smasher and less of the perverse poet; the disordered seer has become a 'realist.'

Thus has Mencken 'straightened-out' and polished down his European sources, and in other respects also *Friedrich Nietzsche* is an interesting example of the American man in search of a philosophy. It was from this area, and from the group of other illustrious Europeans—from Huxley to Ibsen—who clustered around the Darwinian nimbus, that Mencken drew the ideational background of his next, and

* Crane, Norris, London, Dreiser, and the American school of Naturalism, were among the literary effects, but the total impact of Darwinism on an American cultural framework that was peculiarly suited for it—that was a set-up for it—probably has not been sufficiently realized.

† Nietzsche's almost frantic exploitation of the survival principle is a tacit admission of the destructive elements in his own temperament. Those who do not doubt their power have no need to glorify it, and the recent cultural idolizations of survival and power mark a similar sense of disintegration.

more specifically 'American,' books. But as early as the sketches and satires of *Europe After 8:15* and *A Book of Burlesques,* written over the period from 1912 to 1916—already, in the more notable of these sketches, such as 'The Artist' or 'Death,' * the tone is not so much that of the evolutionary as of the sophisticate. 'I am by nature a vulgar fellow. I prefer *Tom Jones* to *The Rosary,* Rabelais to the Elsie books. . . . I delight in beef stews, limericks, burlesque shows. . . . When the mercury is above ninety-five I dine in my shirt sleeves and write poetry naked.'—This was certainly not so much post-Darwinian as it was pre-Babbitt. And in probably the best-known of these early pieces, 'Heliogabalus,' the Christian sklav-moral appears in what amounts to a neo-puritan bawdyhouse.

However, this is the effect of a new collaboration; the earlier Nietzsche-Mencken has become the more celebrated Nathan-Mencken, and the Blond Beast has joined the Smart Set. I have already mentioned the merit of the partnership; and the fact that the gold spoon was in part the lance of these contemporary cavaliers out for a tilt with the Bourgeoisie. My purpose at the moment is to locate another element in Mencken's earlier work, as witness the pith of *A Little Book in C Major* (1916) and *Damn! A Book of Calumny* (1918):

'A great nation is any mob of people which produces at least one honest man a century. . . . A husband is a 16 neck in a 15¾ collar. . . . The agents of human happiness are, in the order of their potency: a good bank account, a negative Wassermann, a clear conscience. . . . A courtroom is a place where Jesus Christ and Judas Iscariot would be equals, with the odds in favor of Judas.

* 'The Artist' is a take-off on the popular reaction to classical music. 'Death' is a take-off on popular behavior at a funeral, and one of the first such critiques (cf. Hemingway in *Death in the Afternoon)* to stress the inadequacy of American civilization in the face of biological realities.

. . . Love is the delusion that one woman differs from another.' —Perhaps the gilt has worn off some of these sparkling aphorisms; the contemporary La Rochefoucauld now seems a little tinny. But these were the bon mots and *pensées* which, adorning the pages of *The Smart Set* as well as these volumes of Mencken's collected maxims, vied with the gallantries of James Branch Cabell in drawing all the young men after them and setting a tone for the early twenties. And this was the tone—a satirical self-love, a practiced hedonism—of Mencken's next major work.

Ostensibly *In Defense of Women,* in 1918, is another evolutionary study of an animal more deadly than the male. This view of woman as the natural enemy of man, and of the wily, calculating, perpetually active maternal instinct which seeks, like the black widow spider, to use and then devour the sexual mate—this modern view of sex as the war of the sexes is a familiar thesis by now. In a clinch, Mencken remarks, men will bite, while women not only bite in the clinches, 'they bite even in open fighting; they have a dental reach, so to speak, of amazing length.' But that women also know the human body, except for a brief time in infancy, 'is not a beautiful thing, but a hideous thing.' That 'their own bodies give them no delight,' and that they never expose themselves aesthetically, 'but only as an act of the grossest sexual provocation.' And that even this is bound to fail, since the human body is too weak a sexual weapon and the average woman is too crudely articulated even for a woman—are these really, for all their obvious Shavian undertones, a series of evolutionary insights? Is it sound Darwinian lore to proclaim the fact that 'men of the first class' are selected out and don't marry, and therefore 'their superiority dies with them'? What has happened here to the naked power urges of the survival struggle,* not to mention the appeal of straight sensuous satisfaction, and not even to think of any sort of solid human relationship, which, as Mencken adds, can hardly survive the use of the same hot-water bottle and 'a joint concern about butter-and-egg bills'?

No, for all the obvious comedy, this view is closer to that which Whitman described as the view of 'shaved persons, supplejacks, ecclesiastics, men not fond of women, women not fond of men.' You may be puzzled, moreover, by the curious coldness in these amatory preachings, the lack of even a salacious pleasure in his subject on the part of this devotee of pure pleasure, the sense of fixed and rather narrow restraints in the advocate of the utmost self-gratification. It is just as though the whole complex of sexual emotion had been reduced to the anatomical studies of a student.

To be sure, there are certain national if not evolutionary traits to be noticed here: the pragmatic, mechanistic, and commercial aspects of this 'defense' of women. The reaction against the Victorian—and perhaps in Mencken's case, the Southern—idealization of the lady, taking the form of an almost brutal sexual frankness, is carried forward in contemporary literature, and finds its most intense emphasis in William Faulkner's work. This is surely the poetic reversal of that earlier nineteenth-century notion of a feminine sexual frigidity which just panders sufficiently to the gross male appetite. Here the sensual appetite is assigned purely to the female—when it exists at all, since in Mencken the post-Victorian sexual reaction amounts to a sexual revulsion. There is no mistaking, underneath the smart tone, the elements of the modern misogyny

* The course of love in modern literature, incidentally, is interesting. Though the nineteenth-century novelists after Stendhal accepted the pseudo-Darwinian interpretation of love as a purely aggressive act, a thinly disguised symptom of the power urges, *they* still admired and 'loved' women.

which Mencken both reflects and initiates in these early volumes. And beneath these 'philosophical' reflections we may notice other curious personal undertones and discords in the earlier work of H. L. Mencken—undertones of the nursery at times, or of a practically perennial and not altogether happy puberty.

It may be worth remembering, in this connection, the strong sense of domestic convention that is implicit in the youth of the Gemütlich Superman. 'Who but a German goes into woolen undershirts at forty-five, and makes his will, and begins to call his wife "Mama"?' Also the sense of sheer physical comfort that finds its customary expression in rather elementary modes—in the constant stress on oral sensations and on the gustatory tract, not to mention the alimentary canal—and that is often reflected in Mencken's early style, so rich, guttural, and succulent as to be almost a meal in itself. There is, again, the parallel sense of spiritual comfort, at once naïve and calculating, that marks the writing of this incipient gourmet and connoisseur: 'No healthy male ever really thinks or talks of anything save himself . . . he cannot imagine himself save as superior, dominating the center of situations.' Can't he? And is it the same healthy male* who penned, in 'The Divine Afflatus,' an almost classical portrait of the agonized and solitary neurotic who writhes in the torments of 'creating' at the awful moment when—

> the brain, as it were, stands to one side and watches itself pitching and tossing, full of agony but essentially helpless. Here the man of creative imagination pays a ghastly price for all his superiorities and immunities. . . . Sitting

* Mencken's constant stress on health is interesting, too. 'In exceptional cases a great mind may inhabit a diseased body, but it is obvious that this is not the rule.' Was it obvious to Nietzsche, for example, with his migraines, or to the early Mencken himself—a chronically ailing youth whose physical constitution at one point gave out almost entirely?

> there in his lonely room gnawing the handle of his pen, racked by his infernal quest, horribly bedevilled by incessant flashes of itching, toothache, eye-strain and evil conscience—thus tormented he makes atonement for his crime of being intelligent.

At any rate, this Alter Ego, pale, helpless, full of doubts and patent medicine, is a constant companion in the earlier work of Henry Mencken: a wavering shadow of the blustering adolescent, the hard-bitten crime reporter, the bawdy and robust journalist, the man of action, the philosopher of racial virility.

It was typical of Mencken to reduce this whole ambiguous emotional pattern—an emotional pattern that has ramifications in all of Mencken's future work—it was typical of him to reduce all this, including the Freudian complexes, 'themselves lurking in impenetrable shadows,' to a question of the blood stream, the liver, and flatulence. . . . Just so, all the complexities of human choice are resolved down to a flat determinism: 'The more the matter is examined, the more the residuum of free-will shrinks. . . . I can scarcely remember performing a wholly voluntary act.' Similarly, the earlier moments of anxiety are subordinated to an all-embracing skepticism. The Doubter's Reward, Mencken claimed, was a total immunity which is worth 'all the dubious assurances ever foisted upon man'—which is 'pragmatically impregnable.' But, one might ask, an immunity against what? Against, maybe, all the usual relapses, jitters, and hoo-ha's* that are

* 'When you're alone in the middle of the night and you
wake in a sweat and a hell of a fright,
When you're alone in the middle of the bed and you
wake like someone hit you on the head,
You've had a cream of a nightmare dream and you've
got the hoo-ha's coming to you.'

T. S. Eliot, 'Fragment of an Agon.' From: *Collected Poems of T. S.*

the mark and almost the core of a tottering humanity? And is the doubter's final reward the easy cynicism of Mencken's early verse,* the rise of that super-smart-set sophistication that marks the middle Mencken, and the increasingly thin and cold view of human emotions and relationships that is evident in his work over this period?

For the male egoism which is at the center of Mencken's values, and which is, to begin with, rather less appealing than the tortured impulses of the Nietzschean soul—this egoism has been operating in an increasingly circumscribed area. Springing, as Mencken did, from a highly conventional background, and with his convictions firmly rooted in what seemed to be a sanctuary of bourgeois bliss, the Baltimore sage has nevertheless come to scorn all the virtues of ordinary existence. Was beauty an attribute of Venus at the domestic hearth? The satisfaction of a man with an attractive wife, said Mencken, is chiefly that of parading her before other men. 'He likes to show her off, as he likes to show his expensive automobile or his big doorknob factory. . . . Her beauty sets up the assumption that she was sought eagerly by other men, some of them wealthy, and that it thus took a lot of money or a lot of skill to obtain the monopoly of her.'

Marriage, therefore, is chiefly an economic matter, and along with it the other activities of married life and the family were all run, presumably, on a strictly cost-plus basis. The purpose of divorce was now only to protect the children—but to employ such a clumsy device for this

Eliot. Copyright, 1930, by T. S. Eliot; copyright 1934, 1936, by Harcourt, Brace and Co., Inc.

* 'And the end of it all is a hole in the ground
And a scratch on a crumbling stone.'

H. L. Mencken, *Ventures into Verse.*

purpose seemed like cutting off a leg in order to cure what was probably, after all, merely a barked shin. And: 'Suppose there *are* no children? Suppose the marriage is entered upon with the clear understanding that there *shall* be no children?' Was it still believed, Mencken added, at least by the great majority of human beings, that there was something mysteriously laudable about achieving offspring? He could find no logical ground for this notion. To have a child was no more creditable or discreditable than to have rheumatism. 'Ethically, it is absolutely meaningless. And practically, it is mainly a matter of chance.' The earlier Mencken, it is true, had stressed sexual fertility about as much as he had human sympathy. But by the time of *Prejudices: Fourth Series,* in 1924, he was actively excoriating what he had hitherto dismissed. Could anybody show him, he cried, one hundred head of ordinary children who were worth one *Heart of Darkness* —and as for Conrad's *Lord Jim*—'I would not swap it for all the children born in Trenton, N.J., since the Spanish War.'

The by-products of sex were rated pretty low, then, and sex itself, as we know, had never been a first-rate matter to Henry Mencken. Certainly, too, if one relegates a primary source of sensuous enjoyment to the status of a diversion at the cool of evening—then the scope of hedonism is narrowed considerably. Even romantic love, which had been at least a battle of wits in the earlier Menckenian cosmos, turns into a fracas with a rat-trap; what had been a matter at least of a certain cunning or charm becomes one of braggadocio and snickering; amorous *Realpolitiker,* too, is the diversion of slaves, and, in short, love moves from the parlor to the smoking-room.

All love affairs, Mencken declared at this point, are farcical—

> When one hears that some old friend has succumbed to the blandishments of a sweet one, however virtuous and beautiful she may be, one does not gasp and roll one's eyes; one simply laughs. When one hears, a year or two later, that they are quarreling, one laughs again. When one hears that the bride is seeking consolation from the curate of the parish, one laughs a third time. When one hears that the bridegroom, in revenge, is sneaking his stenographer to dinner at an Italian restaurant, one laughs a fourth time. And so on.

And so on. . . . Earlier, the Menckenian view had fused a Rotarian sexuality with a curious sort of fastidiousness. As we have noticed, the human body hardly gave him a sense of wonder or mystery, while the female body in particular offered no particular delight. The plain fact was, he had stated in his 'Appendix on a Tender Theme,' that the majority of women a man meets 'offend him, repel him, disgust him.' And because human contacts are chiefly superficial, most of the disgusts we are conscious of are physical. It is difficult, he said, to conceive a romantic passion for a woman who suffers from acne, or who wears soiled underwear. Or whose ears stick out. Or whose mouth reminds us of our aunt's. Or who suggests that she may carry a bodily odor. . . . But then whom can a man love? 'Simply the *first* girl to sneak over what may be called the threshold of his disgusts, simply the *first* to disgust him so little, at first glance, that the loud, insistent promptings of the divine Schädchen have a chance to be heard.'

While the spell lasted, concluded Mencken, the lady could shave her head or smear her hair with bear's grease. However, the spell did not last long, for Henry Mencken at least, and by the time of *Prejudices: Fourth Series,* the threshold of his distaste had been elevated to a point where it was practically impassable. Here, in fact, these earlier accents take on an almost Swiftian hypersensitivity; there is an aversion to the normal habits of the body (witness Mencken's descriptions of the 'labial infamy') when there is not an actual revulsion against them. And here Mencken does approach the tone of Nietzsche, 'whom the touch of the crowd disgusted.' Nor is the converse of this emotional proposition lacking: the habitual use of a violence in both theme and expression which suggests something of the repressed intensity of these conflicts, and which, indeed, leads directly to the persistent Menckenian interest in arson, and homicide, and more—to the fires, the lynchings, the hangings which regularly punctuate the essays of his middle period;* and more: to the visions of national and even racial disaster which supplement the fancies of personal disaster.

But here, of course, through another sequence of events, which are more closely related to temperamental or biographical factors; through these interior lines of communication, so to speak, we have again reached the earlier intimations of disease and destruction: those grim fancies of dissolution which, in relation to the outward and larger forms of his American society, have also run through Mencken's work in the mid-twenties.

In the action and reaction of the temperamental and environmental forces which helped to produce H. L. Mencken's work, however, there is one more factor to be considered.

I think it is a central factor.

* 'The gallows and the firing-squad seem to haunt his thoughts,' says Isaac Goldberg in a perceptive aside in *The Man Mencken.* See also Mencken's preface to *By the Neck: a Book of Hangings,* by Augustus Mencken.

5. *Coda à la Capitalism*

For there was no doubt that Henry Mencken realized what had been happening to his society.

Hadn't he conceded, as early as his portrait of Roosevelt I in *Prejudices: Second Series,* that 'we are moving toward an inevitable internal centralization and external federation'? And that Teddy Roosevelt himself marked an apogee of the old-line American individualism? (Thus the 'Big Stick'—the stress on national virility—was not merely another foible of the Trust-Buster, but a direct and conscious attempt to alter the processes of an ascendant financial ethos.) * As early as *A Book of Prefaces* in 1917, at the outset of his popular career, Mencken had examined the Anti-Saloon League in almost classical terms, remarking that the whole support of the League 'devolved upon a dozen men, all of them rich,' while his analysis of the Comstock organizations could hardly be distinguished from that of the most ruthless critic of finance-capitalism.

Fifteen years earlier, moreover, the young Mencken had opened his entire literary career with an invocation to the 'Bard of our Grim Machines' who had made us kneel to a God of Steel and dream of a God of Steam.† And from 1903 to 1920 Mencken's work is studded with telltale phrases: 'the capitalization of Puritan effort,' 'the incorporated Church,' 'the powers which control the press.'

* But it was probably the first time in our history that an alleged lack of national virility had become a national question, and that such a notion as Teddy's could have been raised, even momentarily, to the status of a philosophy.

† *Ventures into Verse.* But the stress on the Joyless Town of industrialism in these early poems is balanced by a curious emphasis on the Charms of Cash.

Was this just a habit of phraseology, or of borrowing convenient phrases like John Fiske's 'disposition to domineer'? Mencken saw nothing against reason in C. E. Joad's reflections on the evils of a machine civilization in America. In a review of *The Goose Step,* he refused to accept the martyr's chemise worn by Upton Sinclair, but he did accept the martyr's conclusions on American education. 'The search for truth has had to be subordinated to the safeguarding of railway bonds and electric-light shares'—and 'the screws were tightening every year.' In fact, the collapse of the old public influence of the scholar in America was a salient characteristic of the new age, perhaps matched only by the collapse of the older American free press. Was there now really such a thing as an honest newspaper in the United States? Almost every journal, said Mencken, stood in awe of higher powers, 'some financial, some religious, some political.' And while the scholar's rôle had dwindled, the kept press was playing an increasingly active part in modern society.

By the mid-twenties, Mencken permitted himself the extension of an argument which he had often restricted to certain aspects of a dominant industrialism. The capitalists ran the country, Mencken conceded, as they ran all democracies, as they had emerged in Germany after the ruins of the late war, like Anadyomene from the sea. 'They organize and control the minorities that struggle eternally for power, and so get a gradually firmer grip upon the government.' Thus the *Boobus Americanus*—apparently uncontrolled and unrestrained—was actually led and watched over by 'the little group of sagaciously willful men which exercises genuine sovereignty over the country,' a zealous group, and highly skilled at training Boobus in the way he should think and act. And thus, when 'a gang of real estate agents (i.e., rent sweaters), bond salesmen and automobile dealers gets together to sob for Service, it takes no Freudian to surmise that someone is about to be swindled'—

> The Cult of Service, indeed, is half a sop to conscience and half a bait to catch conies. Its cultivation in the United States runs parallel with the most gorgeous development of imposture as a fine art that Christendom has ever seen. I speak of a fine art in the literal sense; in the form of advertising it enlists such talents as, under less pious civilizations, would be devoted to the confection of cathedrals and even, perhaps, masses. A sixth of the Americano's income is rooked out of him by rogues who have at him officially, and in the name of the government; half the remainder goes to sharpers who prefer the greater risks and greater profits of private enterprise.*

In the United States, indeed, the art of trafficking was king; no other human activity brought such rewards, none was more lavishly honored and never had the great trading nations of the past, from Carthage to England, gone so far in the sheer pursuit of profit. 'The United States, I believe, is the first great empire in the history of the world to ground its whole national philosophy upon business.' What was the ultimate purpose of this extraordinary Cult of Service—this Holy Crusade of Commerce which, under the heraldic sign of the Dollar and the war cry of *Midas Vult,* first glimpsed the New Jerusalem in the reign of Harding and Coolidge? It apparently existed, said the Mencken of *Prejudices: Fifth Series,* for the personal delight of United States Steel and its chairman, Judge Elbert Henry Gary. 'A vast nation of 110,000,000 human beings, all of them alike, seems to be organized to the one end of making him happy.'

* *Notes on Democracy.*

And when one such human being fiddles, others must burn, it was safe to say also. The aim of our jurisprudence, along with our education and almost all our central activities and social festivities, had become that of safeguarding business. 'If the rights of the citizen get in the way, then the rights of the citizen must be sacrificed.' Henry Mencken had already caught the undertones of irony in contemporary titles like 'mortician' and 'receptionist'—resounding titles which expressed ludicrous or pathetic aspirations. He felt the plight of other poor fellows in the great trading Republic of the West: the lower sort of clerks, workmen, wagon-drivers, farm-laborers, petty officials, grabbers of odd jobs, who were 'doomed their life long to dull, stupid and tedious crafts,' who must be downright idiots to get any satisfaction out of their work, and to whom the city was a complex and elaborate device 'for taking the slave's mind off his desolateness of spirit.' And how many of the puzzling political, religious, and economic phenomena of life in America could be almost fully accounted for on this basis?

> The hoop-la Methodist revival with its psychopathical basis; the violent bitterness of rural politics; the prosperity of the Ku Klux Klan and all the other clownish fraternal orders; the persistent popularity of lynching, tarring and feathering, barbarities of a dozen other varieties—all these things are no more than manifestations of the poor hind's pathetic effort to raise himself out of his wallow, to justify and dignify his existence, to escape from the sordid realities that daily confront him.

Now, indeed, the familiar diseases of the Menckenian hinterland are complicated by an appalling variety of industrial diseases, as the factories penetrate to the rural regions, and as the Cow State John the Baptists become the production-line Johnnies.*

Finally, just as the American Twenties represented the peak of this industrial penetration and consolidation, Mencken placed the origins of the new economic order with a reasonable historical accuracy when he noted (in his preface to Cooper's *American Democrat*) that it was the Civil War which 'finally blew the old Republic to pieces, and brought in that hegemony of the ignorant and ignoble which yet afflicts us.' Was William Jennings Bryan a favorite butt of the Menckenian invective? There was good reason. For Bryan was also symptomatic of the 'swinish materialism' that marked the United States after 1870—at once a figurehead of the abortive revolt against this materialism and a victim of its processes; while, pitted against this new force, the believers in Populist Reform may indeed have seemed like 'mere disordered enthusiasts—believers in anything and everything . . . incurable hopers and snifflers.' Bryan, in fact, like Teddy Roosevelt, marked the last and sometimes grotesque extremes of an older social arrangement going down in hopeless defeat.† 'The chances are that history will put the peak of democracy in America in his time; it has been on the downward curve among us since the campaign of 1896. . . . He will be remembered, per-

* In a brash moment Mencken even admitted the economic bases of romance in the U.S.A. 'For one shoe clerk who succumbs to the houris of the Broadway pave, there are 500 who succumb to the lack of means. . . .'

† The sense of this change marks and perhaps conditions the bulk of our writing in the nineteenth century: its advent is foreshadowed in the sometimes remote and sometimes overstimulated individualism of the Transcendental writers, its arrival is recorded in the dark Mark Twain and the gloomy Whitman. And there was behind these writers a century of confidence. . . .

haps, as its supreme impostor, the *reductio ad absurdum* of its pretension.'

So a new American cultural framework emerges in the writings of H. L. Mencken. Though Mencken himself often considers these events as separate or isolated phenomena, and you must put together the separate sections of the Menckenian critique which deal with them, here is surely a native instance of the rise of that modern industrialism 'which has borne so harshly upon the race in general.'

And what was his answer to the problem?

We have already noticed his emphasis on a select minority, an élite, which, as Nietzsche bows to George Jean Nathan, becomes increasingly absorbed in the arts and in 'culture.' But in back of the Cultivated Superman there stalks the Frontier Rebel: notice also Mencken's stress on the absolute liberty of the individual. 'I believe that any invasion of it is immensely dangerous to the common weal —especially when that invasion is alleged to have a moral purpose. No conceivable moral purpose is higher than the right of the citizen to think whatever he pleases to think, and to carry on his private life without interference by others.' Yet, just as Mencken defends the sanctity of the domestic hearth, without, however, stressing the human relationships or family life or, in short, the domesticity that goes along with the domestic hearth, so his notion of liberty lacks the usual attributes of human liberty.

Very often it approaches the liberty of that solitary urban citizen whom we saw speeding through a diseased American hinterland in his steel-encased Pullman. Or it is the liberty of this writer, fully cognizant, as we have seen, of the condition of the less-privileged citizens in the Republic, and of the pathological social impulses which spring out of and flourish in this condition: it is his liberty to suggest, as he did, the establishment of 'brass bands and bull fights' as a solution. It is the liberty of this total individualist to express himself to the utmost in order to 'compel the attention and respect of his equals, to lord it over his inferiors.' It is a liberty, nourished on the precepts of pure self-survival, that often yearns for authority and even dictatorial authority in the case of these inferiors; a liberty that, while it has steadily increased the limits of its own demands, has just as steadily delimited the areas of its general social applicability. . . . It is interesting to notice the change in Mencken's own attitude here. While earlier he had described the great emancipators of the human mind as 'gay fellows who heaved dead cats into sanctuaries and then went roistering down the highways of the world,' his later definition was less jolly:

> The free man is one who has won a small and precarious territory from the great mob of his inferiors, and is prepared and ready to defend it and make it support him. All around him are enemies, and where he stands there is no friend. He can hope for little help from other men of his own kind, for they have battles of their own to fight. He has made of himself a sort of god in his little world, and he must face the responsibilities of a god, and the dreadful loneliness.

It was true, as Mencken added, that Jefferson himself had said that blood was the natural manure of liberty—but would Jefferson have recognized this new concept of liberty, at once so bloody and so bloodless? For this is a sense of human freedom which is so precarious as to seem almost paranoiac, and so absolute as to be icy.

In a similar manner the corollary of the Menckenian quest for absolute freedom—the search for an absolute truth—leads the contemporary philosopher into some strange détour. Here, too, is a writer who realizes the change in American life since the Civil War period, and accepts as a historical truism the scramble for power of the new industrial barons upon the foundations of the older republic, and acknowledges the dominant materialism of his own century: an economic penetration that colors the last remnants of the Puritan conscience and extends to the last reaches of the rural hinterland. Yet his earlier indignation has centered on the Puritans, and his later bile is concentrated—in the face of an increasing and almost total industrialization—on a 'benighted peasantry.' Here is a writer who records all the elements of a steadily sharpening economic conflict. And he resorts (in a nation which represents the blending of racial stocks to a point where an attempt at racial distinction becomes almost ludicrous) to an almost mythological racial conflict: to a struggle between the non-existent Anglo-Saxons and the imaginary Aliens.

To such a pass, then, has his quest for liberty and truth brought H. L. Mencken: to an almost absolute inversion of liberty and truth. This is the net result of the newest New Freedom, the end of the road for the curious new American of the nineteen-twenties: this pure Menckenian individualist whose right to think whatever he pleases leads him only to think about what is pleasing to himself. Here the 'western spaciousness' of Mark Twain, an early idol, and one with whom, in the variety of humor and the instinct for language, Mencken had much in common, has shriveled down. It approaches, instead, the eastern speciousness of a Cal Tinney: the hard sense of the frontier has become rigid. There are echoes in Mencken of still earlier American figures. There is the Emersonian stress on self-reliance, on the courage to stand apart, to question, to dissent—these older national traits that are particularly valuable in the increasingly standardized American context which Mencken himself has recorded. Yet the transcendental strain has changed in Mencken's work: the self-reliance has turned into isolation, the caustic doubt into bitter negation, the delicate bond between the individual and his society into a barricade. The American preacher, who in the eighteen-thirties saved his own soul from the Calvinist fire, now, in the nineteen-twenties, condemns his brother's soul to the bottomless pools of finance-capitalism.

So, again, the Menckenian accents of wrath and rebuke are familiar. In these tones spoke the great preachers of the past to their flocks: thus spoke Zarathustra II, however demented. But to whom, for whom, does the Shepherd of the Smart Set speak? Here is a very special case of moral indignation without a morality: a Jonathan Edwards of Nihilism. And what a panorama of misdirected moral energies is spread before us! What spectacular forays on Home Cooking and on Prohibition,* on Comstockery and on the Mann Act, or at best, and with some equivocation, on the Klan—on all the offshoots, if not the odds and ends, of a disturbed society! What passionate defenses of bootleggers or beauticians! What eloquence, again, is expended on the welfare of the arts, and what a minimum of concern is manifested for the true welfare of the people that produce these arts! Never directed against its true object, the writer's indignation bubbles over everywhere, and, lacking a central focus, the whole perspective of his American critique is distorted until it becomes a child's view of history. If Mencken's is a last voice from an American age of innocence (an innocence

* It was in the culinary area that Mencken unleashed his most bitter condemnation of the increasing standardization of American life ('Victualry as a Fine Art'), and at times his purest aspiration was the repeal of the Volstead Act.

that was never quite so guileless as it seemed), it is now an innocence that is both tortured and devious.

For Mencken's account of the prevailing social arrangement in the United States was not projected by a radical critic of it, but, on the contrary, by a staunch believer in it, and the more clearly he saw its effects, the more blindly he seemed to cling to it. In this framework we can evaluate the otherwise peculiar Menckenian sociology from his earliest conviction in the *Nietzsche* or in *Men Versus the Man** that 'socialism undermines the workingman's healthy instincts' to his final and unalterable bias against Veblen and the 'Dismal Science.' It is interesting to notice here, at Mencken's most direct point of contact with Economics, how the 'Professor' is caught up in the whole Menckenian complex of the Masses and the Aliens—a complex that includes such other adjacent professors as William James or the John Dewey who was lecturing to his classes of Grand Street Platos in imperfect Yiddish. And indeed it was a Dismal Science which constantly, through its chief modern authorities, stressed all the cultural factors which Henry Mencken drew away from and all the economic facts which he had tried to put behind him. . . . Very shortly the Dismal Science becomes the Quack-Science, the Professors become the Charlatans, the Mob turns more menacing, the area of the individual's liberty grows ever more limited and sterile, the search for truth more perverse, as, in the increasing tension of Mencken's work over the middle twenties, the extremes of this emotional

* *Men Versus the Man,* published in 1910, is an exchange of views between Robert La Monte and Mencken, in which La Monte, a Socialist, presents the then prevailing criticisms of American capitalism, and Mencken, as an 'individualist' (or as a Nietzschean superman), defends capitalism. Neither of the young philosophers was very intelligent, perhaps, but what is curious is the bitterness with which, some years later, Mencken looked back upon the whole discussion.

pattern become more evident, and all its fantastic elements are steadily accentuated.

Was William Jennings Bryan a nightmarish figure in the earlier Menckenian cosmos? He was nothing as compared with Woodrow Wilson: the eloquent Professor, the Doctor Dulcifluous, with his 'glittering, lascivious phrases' and his repudiation of 'his most solemn engagements'—the most eminent President Wilson: 'the perfect model of the Christian cad.' From the Wilson of *The American Credo,* in 1920, to the Wilson of *Notes on Democracy* in 1926, the Menckenian virus, far from wearing itself out, flourishes and multiplies. From a misguided Presbyterian schoolmaster, Woodrow Wilson changes in turn to an intriguer, a schemer, a demented Machiavelli, a ghoulish designer upon, and then the obscene gravedigger of, American democracy. He is, at any rate, the ghoul, the incubus, of Mencken's thinking; seldom has a cultivated intelligence hunted down an already stricken enemy with such a relentless and consuming passion: this is a modern version of the Furies pursuing, so to say, a purely sociological Orestes through all the provinces of a distorted mind. . . . Well: was the issue really whether or not, against his pledge, Wilson had led us into the First World War? As an *Uebermensch,* Mencken had professed his pleasure in war. But in point of fact the First World War had completed the consolidation of the new industrialism in American life. It marked the triumph of the cartels, the end of free capitalism. And its extraordinary and disproportionate effect on the writing of a whole generation, now indeed lost, but on whom the horrors of the war itself had a relatively minimal impact, can be explained only in the light of this underlying cultural process.*

* The most typical of the post-war figures, F. Scott Fitzgerald, never saw action abroad, and composed *This Side of Paradise* during his week-

Thus, in Mencken's work, World War I not only seemed to be—it *was* a sort of Armageddon, and in this light a Woodrow Wilson was certainly another incubus. . . . And those industrialists and capitalists who actually run the country now, as they run all the democracies, have they also H. L. Mencken's devout blessing—in fact, his belief that they will extend their power over the American masses until the result of the struggle becomes crystal clear?—

> What I see is a vast horde of inferior men, broken, after a hopeless, fruitless fight, to the hard, uninspiring labor of the world—a race of slaves superbly regimented, and kept steadily in order by great brigades of propagandists, official optimists, scare-mongers, Great Thinkers and rev. clergy. And over them a minority of capitalist overlords, well-fed, well-protected, highly respected, politely envied, and lavishly supplied with endless stores of picture postcards, gasoline, silk underwear, mayonnaise, Pontet Canet, toilet soap, and phonograph records.

This was 'Bugaboo' in *Prejudices: Fourth Series,* and where else could one have found, in 1924, a better glimpse of the *quality* of an American Fascism? Was it, furthermore, H. L. Mencken's firm conviction that wheat produced by slave labor would be just as delicious and ten times more economical than wheat produced by free men?

ends in the service. Mencken himself, in some respects the worst war casualty of them all, was not in the army. Similarly, the real center of John Dos Passos's first war novel, *One Man's Initiation,* is a Gothic abbey near a hospital post in France, while it is interesting to compare E. E. Cummings's French concentration camp, in *The Enormous Room,* with Arthur Koestler's later one in *Scum of the Earth.* A comparison of these last two books alone will indicate the very remote impact of the First World War itself upon our typical post-war rebels. . . . That is to say, the war was probably the immediate cause, but the *effect* of the war upon the patterns of American life was the true cause of their discontent.

—Then it was hardly worth mentioning, as he had in *The American Credo,* that the average American of today 'probably enjoys less personal freedom than any other man in Christendom.' Or that the gradual decay of our freedom went almost without challenge. Or that there was 'no other such rigidly regimented man in the world,' while our whole social structure was based upon fear and abasement, as the hog-murderer's wife picked her way into an aristocracy of the abattoir, and the former whiskey drummer insinuated himself into the Elks, and the rising retailer won the imprimatur of the wholesalers, and the petty attorney became a legislator and statesman, while 'all of us Yankees creep up, up, up.' Are these accents of bitterness tinged with a certain acrid enjoyment now? Here, indeed, democracy seemed about to turn upon and devour itself; it was already too late for the doctors at its bedside to 'dose it out of a black bottle and make sinister signals to the coroner.' And here also, in the 'Totentanz' of *Prejudices: Fourth Series,* the impregnable isle of Manhattan itself, the last refuge of the superior and isolated city man who has cut himself off from the hills and valleys and bayous of the Republic just as he has from the great masses of the inhabitants of the Republic: here, finally, the proud, free City-State itself totters on the brink of catastrophe. As Manhattan goes, so goes the U.S.A.; and the essayist who opens with an idyll of the nation's center, closes with the vision of the nation's obliteration.

—An odd vision, no doubt, to be projected by such an unflinching American industrialist. But here, of course, we reach the crux of the matter. For the more blindly Mencken clung to the existing order, the more vividly he seemed to realize its true nature. The sense of disease in his work is matched only by his fear of change—and the fear of change is matched only by his sense of disaster. It would be difficult, on any other grounds, to explain the arrant superstitions, the absurd complexes, the gloomy phobias which mark the output of this cultivated talent. Was it actually Henry Mencken's confident opinion and dearest hope that the corporations would extend their power over the American man until they made him the slave in actuality that he was already in the writer's fancy? These, however, are hardly the symptoms of confidence and hope; they are the familiar and almost stereotyped symptoms of a sensitive historical mind within a steadily constricting social arrangement, from the visions of a Tiberius in Rome to those of a Proust in the Paris of Pétain. This is a view of life which moves, at a steadily accentuated pace, from a majority to a minority, to an élite, to a solitary individual, and then to a denial of even the individual: in short, to a denial of life itself. The steel towns of Westmoreland County, Mencken tells us in 'The Libido for the Ugly,' were familiar ground. 'Boy and man, I had been through it often enough. But somehow I had never quite sensed its appalling desolation–'

> Here was the very heart of industrial America, the center of its most lucrative and characteristic activity, the boast and pride of the richest and grandest nation ever seen on earth—and here was a scene so dreadfully hideous, so intolerably bleak and forlorn that it reduced the whole aspiration of man to a macabre and depressing joke. Here was wealth beyond computation, almost beyond imagination—and here were human habitations so abominable that they would have disgraced a race of alley cats.

Yet Henry Mencken had sensed this desolation throughout his career, almost from the very start: this evolutionary philosopher, as we have seen, who rejects all the potentials of evolution in order to seize upon its jitters, whose fear of the future is balanced by his narrow view of the past, and in whose work the 'natural laws' spawn only ghouls and ogres while the logic of the universe has become the logic of a nightmare.

6. *Our Theirns and Woulda Hads*

So THE LATER H. L. Mencken also set the tone for his generation, not now because he was such an eloquent Anti-Christ, but because he expressed with such eloquence the real historical moment, and because the blight on his work would extend to a variety of rich talents which succeeded his.*

Like his generation he equated the forms of cartel capitalism with those of a democratic order, or, more accurately, perhaps, he underestimated the residual resources of democracy in America, in his own time at least. For, just as Mencken had seen so clearly all the dangers of the triumphant and fantastic native economy in the mid-twenties, he saw, by the time of *Prejudices: Sixth Series,* in 1928, the first intimations of its crack-up: auto-intoxicated, as it was, and forcing, by all the miracles of its own technology, the seeds of its own destruction at a prodigious rate—gone hay-wire with a speed beyond the speed of light.

Nor is it a coincidence, I think, that *Prejudices: Sixth Series,* less well known than the earlier volumes and published at a point in Mencken's career when his popularity

* What such commentators as J. Donald Adams, in *The Shape of Books to Come,* and such historians as Bernard DeVoto, in *The Literary Fallacy,* do *not* tell us, when they tell us of our writers' 'despair and defeatism' in the nineteen-twenties, is simply the nature of the historical period. As a student of the 'arts,' Mr. Adams can probably be forgiven for this, but it is difficult to understand just what sort of historian Mr. DeVoto is.

had already declined, when the Superman of the Twenties was about to become the Forgotten Man of the Thirties—that this is one of the most notable volumes in the series, marked by great flexibility of thought and by a warmth and depth of feeling that have been missing in Mencken's work since his earliest essays.

For here Mencken admitted that even in the paradise of Babbitt, Babbitt was 'vaguely uneasy and unhappy.' He admitted that, while he remained no partisan of the Founding Fathers, there had been something exhilarating in their desire 'to augment and safeguard the dignity of man through the Bill of Rights, *Selig!*' In a piece on eugenics he refuted his own theory of racial superiority. 'The fact is that the difference between the better sort of human beings and the lesser sort, biologically speaking, is very slight.' In a brilliant study of Valentino, 'Appendix from Moronia,' he turned on his own dictum of power as the single end of life and egoism as the means of life.

> Here, after all, is the chiefest joke of the gods: that man must remain alone and lonely in this world, even with crowds surging about him. Does he crave approbation, with a sort of furious, instinctive lust? Then it is only to discover, when it comes, that it is somehow disconcerting—that its springs and motives offer an affront to his dignity.

And what, after all, was Fame but 'the ill-natured admiration of an endless series of miserable and ridiculous bags of rapidly disintegrating amino acids?' More interesting yet, did he not chastise a new generation of poets and novelists who had tried 'to detach themselves from the ordinary flow of American ideas, and convert themselves into an intellectual aristocracy'! * Thus the *Uebermenschen* of the Arts join the *Wille zur Macht* among the relics of local history. And here Henry Mencken confessed that the Nietzschean Gospel remained unbearable for most human beings 'and will probably continue unbearable for centuries to come.'

Surely this was a mellow Mencken in whose eyes even a Methodist bishop could retain a glimmer of humanity, and a congressman might regret his lost honor, 'as women often do in the films.' The glimpses of this maturity, moreover, mark his three important scholarly works: the revised—fourth—edition of *The American Language*, the *Treatise on the Gods* and the *Treatise on Right and Wrong*.† In the last of these works, the reversal of the Menckenian inversions proceeds apace and, with the familiar Menckenian histrionics, is practically brought to an

* As early as 'The Fringes of Lovely Letters' in *Prejudices: Fifth Series*, Mencken had begun to react against Fugitive Intellectuals, pointing out to them the richness of native American material, and urging them to write about it not to the tune of superior sneers, but with 'irony and pity.' It was with a certain poetic justice that Ernest Hemingway, the leading figure among the expatriates, threw the phrase back at Mencken in a famous passage of *The Sun Also Rises*—a passage that has been widely quoted, incidentally, without reference to its proper context.

Still earlier, in *Prejudices: Third Series*, Mencken had revealed the almost irreconcilable split in his own view of American life when he had waved good-bye and godspeed to the expatriates, whose exodus he claimed to approve of and had so materially contributed to—while he himself remained on the dock, 'wrapped up in the flag.' Here, too, he had clearly demonstrated his position as a transitional figure between the generation of Sherwood Anderson and the generation of Hemingway.

† A full discussion of these later works lies outside of the scope of this essay, since they are primarily scholarly works and bear only indirectly on Mencken as a social historian. But *The American Language* is a major contribution to philological research. And while Mencken's treatise on religion is still rather limited (it is actually a study of religious institutions, and deals with priests rather than prophets), the companion treatise on ethics is marked by the wider range of insights that I mention above, and is a valuable and interesting work.

extreme. To wit, the former philosopher of unstinting force now hints that morality itself is bred by natural selection. The psychologist of an inferior man dominated by fear and envy notices the 'rich variety of human wills,' including the will to peace, as well as the instinct of 'natural sociability.' The Anglo-Saxon anthropologist of undiluted racial superiority praises the 'mixture of virile stocks' in ancient cultures. The late historian of an iron determinism in nature describes the existence of a 'free mind' in man—and even a trusting spirit in woman! Finally, and perhaps worse, the professional pessimist who had diagnosed optimism as the disease of democrats and yahoos, now himself discarding Spengler and other such 'alarmists,' affirms that 'there is, in fact, such a thing as progress,' and that out of it has flowed 'a great richness, an immense enhancement of the human spirit.'

It is almost too much, this sense of a continuing historical process 'whose end is not yet,' and this mature Mencken who now blandly accepts all that he had earlier blindly ignored, as though there had never been a Nietzsche, and there had always been a Kropotkin. More clearly than anything else, however, these sections of his later works complete the Menckenian pattern: these residual traits of a former American democrat that still persist in the Cassandra of the Cartels, surviving in the individual just as they had survived in his society.* For how often, in truth, do the intimations of a more generous scheme of living break through the harsh and rigid framework of even this nightmarish poet of finance-capitalism!

* During the depression years; that is, when these later works were written (their publication dates are from 1930 to 1935). While it would be extreme to stress the crack-up of 'the great machine' as the sole cause for the change in Mencken's outlook, it is interesting to notice how closely the shift in his values parallels that of the other exiles and expatriates, at home or abroad, during the same years.

The peroration, for example, in the first edition of *The American Language*—

> Given the poet, there may suddenly come a day when our *theirns* and *woulda hads* will take on the barbaric stateliness of the peasant locutions of old Maurya in *Riders to the Sea*. . . . In all human beings, if only understanding be brought to the business, dignity will be found, and that dignity cannot fail to reveal itself, soon or late, in the words and phrases with which they make known their high hopes and aspirations and cry out against the intolerable meaninglessness of life.

—was this peroration struck out in the later editions as an example of 'rhetoric'? It was not always rhetoric, not for those earlier Americans in the centuries of Franklin or of Thoreau. Nor for the earlier Mencken himself who had, among his first burlesques of modern times, still remembered 'pale druggists in remote towns of the hog and Christian Endeavor belts, endlessly wrapping up bottles of Peruna. . . . Women hidden away in the damp cockroachy kitchens of unpainted houses along the railroad tracks. . . . Lime and cement dealers being initiated into the Knights of Pythias, the Red Men, or the Woodmen of the World. . . . Watchmen at lonely railroad crossings in Iowa, hoping that they'll be able to get off to hear the United Brethren evangelist preach. . . . Decayed and hopeless men writing editorials at midnight for leading papers in Mississippi, Wyoming, and Vermont. . . . Secret Socialists in Georgia, furtively reading the *Appeal to Reason* with the blinds down.'

On a purely philological plane, where he could momentarily at least forget the pressures of his environment, Mencken *was* a poet who could reveal the barbaric stateliness of our *theirns* and *woulda hads*. On another level, the one of craft, he remained a remarkable stylist: although it became increasingly impossible to agree with him, it was quite impossible to be bored by him. His early trivia are often just as fresh as when the ink first spilled on the page over two decades ago. His best pieces, such as 'The Husbandman,' which constitutes in itself an entire Anti-Agrarian movement in literature and is set in solitary grandeur against a tradition that extends from the Bucolics to Louis Bromfield; or his 'Meditations in the Methodist Desert,' or his 'Essay in Constructive Criticism,' or again, say, his translation of the Declaration of Independence into the vulgate: such pieces rise above the exigencies of his time and his temperament. His is also a special comic fancy, this native humorist with his 'scientific investigation' of ghosts in Maryland, his 'discovery' of the origins of the bathtub, his 'proposal' to educate our delinquent public officials by direct physical action, because—

> A Congressman with his ears cut off, you may be sure, would not do it again. A judge, after two or three rocket flights through his court-room window, would be forced by an irresistible psychological process, to give heed thereafter to the Constitution, the statutes, and the common rights of man. Even a police captain or a United States Senator, once floored with a bung-starter or rolled in a barrel, would begin to think.

These pieces may remind us of what he might have done, who became instead a Tom Paine of the American Counter-Revolution or, to suggest a deeper source of reference, a local Jeremiah who hymned the praises of Detroit in somewhat rasping tones. For it is not impossible, after all, that Mencken's peculiar irascibility as to the Jews was related to an innate sense of his affinity with the Hebrew moralists—and a sense of a broken affinity. On a larger plane, at least, Mencken could understand the predicament, before and after all social arrangements, of man himself who was eternally in the position of 'a turtle born without a shell, a dog without hair, a fish without fins.'

But that Herr Professor Veblen of the Dismal Science had his innings too, for this is, in the end, the moral splendor of the idle literary classes and the conspicuous consumption of a rare talent. The 'Vers Libre' at the close of *A Book of Burlesques,* in 1916, became the 'Suite Américaine' in the *Prejudices* of the early twenties, and by 1926 Mencken dropped this, too, as the mute and dark American hinterland became the American circus, and H. L. Mencken took over the part of the ringmaster, the animal tamer. The actor, finally, was indistinguishable from the act, the Menckenian masks became the reality; when he discarded *them,* at last, it was almost with a sense of shock that one saw Mencken clear; it was with a certain uneasiness that Mencken allowed himself to be Mencken. . . . Even in the later works, it is interesting to notice the change in tone as the historian draws near to the eighteenth century, the Industrial Revolution, the 'democratic poison.'

His value, therefore, lies as much in his profound and unwilling reflection of a period as in his brilliant reporting of it. If he helped to mold the spirit of the post-war epoch, he also betrayed its underlying pressures. (Have they changed in character, lessened in their intensity?) And if he undervalued the resources of our democratic social arrangement—exaggerating in this as in so much else, he could hardly exaggerate the blind consuming power as well as the blind fertility of our industrial machine. For otherwise, knowing as well as we do by now the distorted sources of the Menckenian imagery whose goatish prancings grew into such a macabre dance of death—still, why do those recurrent omens and portents of disaster, those acrid visions of dissolution and the whole unlovely prophetic end of what had been in its day the world's last best hope: why does all this linger so uncomfortably in our minds? *Ich bin der Geist der stets verneint. . . .* Very likely this was H. L. Mencken's most intense and aesthetically his most perfectly realized aberration.

Meanwhile we will take up the second of these representative figures of the Middle Generation: a figure who comes directly under Mencken's influence for a while and plays a rôle similar to Mencken's in the development of the contemporary American novel.

As you'll see, though, it is impossible for Sinclair Lewis to play any rôle except the one which was destined for him by fate and the middle classes.

Chapter Two

Sinclair Lewis: THE COSMIC BOURJOYCE

◇

Chapter Two

Sinclair Lewis: THE COSMIC BOURJOYCE

1. *A Dodsworth by Birth*

SINCLAIR LEWIS has been called the Bad Boy of the national letters. In a way the celebrated critic of the national manners who established the new realism of the nineteen-twenties in the American mind and established the American mind in contemporary literature, whose literary career, lasting over a quarter of a century, has been marked by controversy, dispute, and perpetual ferment, deserves his title.

He was born February 7, 1885, at Sauk Center, Minnesota, 'to a New England father, and a mother of Canadian extraction who died five years later.' His father, his maternal grandfather, an uncle, and a brother were all physicians; and from *The Trail of the Hawk* to *Ann Vickers,* the only true hero of Lewis will be the scientist, and the practical even more than the pure scientist: those aviators and doctors who are, as the later Lewis said, 'the only solid people in an insane world.'

It is interesting to notice the recurrent pattern of childhood in the literary work of this avowed iconoclast and social rebel: the *gauche* and solemn young hero who has had very little home life, who 'has no friends,' and is set apart from the 'Gang,' which represents the highest form of good fellowship and gaiety in Lewis's work, very early drifts into his own form of fantasy life. As a matter of fact, the preoccupation with youth, and with that Younger Generation which will at first seem to Lewis the acme of grace and sophistication and then the acme of ignorance and corruption, is a delicate theme in his work.

Meanwhile the young Lewis himself had taken a distaste 'to the curriculum of the local schools,' had become a nonconformist who decided to go East, and had entered Yale in 1903. He joined Upton Sinclair's Socialist community at Helicon Hall for a while; he had already begun to earn his living by writing, editing, and translating; in the years after 1908, he became a magazine writer and editor, and then the editor and advertising manager of a publishing house. He had already made trips to England on the cattle boats which form such a vivid experience for his earliest literary hero. With the publication of his first novel, *Our Mr. Wrenn*, in 1914, Lewis set out on an independent literary career, and by the time of his sixth novel he was free to pursue it.

In fact, *Main Street* sold over a million copies and was translated into a dozen languages. During those big years of his own career and of that whole new literary revolt of the twenties which Lewis, along with Henry Mencken, seemed in many ways to represent most fully, there was little doubt as to both Lewis's value and his sparkle. His journalistic sorties against the 'classical' critics, who then as now represented for the most part the alliance of little minds and great books, were bold and entertaining. His rejection of the Pulitzer Prize was based on the ground that it was an attempt to make writers 'safe, polite, obedient, and sterile.' His later acceptance of the first Nobel Prize to be given to an American writer contained an admirable statement of the new literature's intentions and achievements. 'The American writer ought to perceive,' Lewis said, 'that he has . . . the most exciting country in the world; the greatest diversity of races, from Icelanders to Japanese and Negroes; the widest sweep of climate.' In practice, too, Lewis seemed to be fulfilling Henry Mencken's vision of a national literature, no longer imitative and timorous, that would present a firsthand examination of the native scene in wholly native terms. As early as 1922, in *Babbitt,* Lewis had not only added a new word to the American language, and in all probability a new figure to world fiction, but had staked out the whole area of his own contribution to the national letters.

For here we receive our first intimations of Lewis's western state of 'Winnemac': that standardized chain-store state which ranges geographically from Catawba, the little farming settlement, and Gopher Prairie, the 'in-between town,' to Zenith itself, the hustling, bustling metropolis of the new urban order. And just as Lewis was establishing his literary topography in the grand manner, he would establish his literary genealogy. The social classes and their interplay in Zenith will range from George F. Babbitt through Martin Arrowsmith, the truth-seeker, and Elmer Gantry, the false prophet of Winnemac, to Sam Dodsworth, the true aristocrat of the Middle-Class Empire, and even to that obscure Mrs. Cour of *Ann Vickers,* who was 'a Dodsworth by birth.' Moreover, from the raw western settlements which have barely come to exist on the prairie, and which are already so strongly marked by the imprint of the industrial process and the accumulation of wealth, to those Zenith skyscrapers whose unbroken vertical lines are as 'contemptuous of friendly human efforts as a forgotten tower on the Siberian steppes,' Lewis has not only staked out a new native state and its language, habits, ethics, and symbols, but a state that is in the process of that sweeping cultural change which *Babbitt,* in its whisperings of the inferno, first gives us. 'Guess better hustle . . . hustle . . . gotta hustle.'

These are the outlines of a new world and of a big literary work, and in some respects the early Lewis is closer to Balzac, say, than to Dickens; although, with that fixed reptilian stare, that ear so perfectly attuned to the nuances of a nationally advertised lingo, and those bold, sweeping strokes which marked, in his early work, the merciless portraiture of our latest social types, Lewis also represented a talent that was almost altogether unique on the native scene. . . . What we are about to study here, however, is the true nature of Lewis's literary cosmos: that American Middle-Class Empire whose ruling dynasty is the House of Babbitt and whose destiny forms a strange chapter in the national letters.

For the fact that Lewis's true world is essentially a middle-class fantasy of life in America—rather than any sort of realistic picture of middle-class life in America—has been obscured simply because his superficial world, and particularly his visual world, seem so concrete. Apparently one of the most immediate novelists of his period, Lewis is actually one of the most remote. You will notice, too, the curious intellectual framework of Lewis's work: its narrow limitations, its blind rigidity, its overtones of fear and almost willful ignorance. Probably the real fascination of Lewis's career lies just in the fact that this intrepid social rebel and fierce critic of the national manners is in the end so completely at one with his subject: and not, indeed, with America, but with his America—that middle-middle portion of it with which Lewis is so absolutely involved, and from the values, beliefs, and the final illusions of which he will hardly, for an instant, be able to deviate. Not often before, in the history of our letters, has an artist been able to see so much and see so little, or been so rigidly constrained to do the only thing he can do.

This has its own value, of course. Sinclair Lewis's novels, and the worst of them along with the best, form a remarkable diary of the middle-class mind in America.

It has many volumes; we'll start with its opening pages.

2. *Origins of a Dynasty*

THE HERO of *The Trail of the Hawk,* in 1915—in some respects the most ambitious of Lewis's early novels—comes from those prairie hamlets of the northern Middle West in the eighteen-nineties: 'the straggly rows of unpainted frame shanties, the stores with tin-corniced false fronts that pretended to be two stories high.'

But Carl Ericson, son of a Norwegian carpenter, brought up among the 'New Yankees' of Wisconsin, Minnesota, and the Dakotas, who were, as Lewis says, a human breed that could grow, with a thousand miles to grow in—also knows the exhilaration of the western prairies: the pastures of wild clover, the creeks with minnows and perch, the hazelnut bushes around the sloughs, the quivering cry of the gophers. Here, along with the arc lights of the tiny farming settlements at night, are those provincial philosophers who figure so largely in the Ohio tales of Sherwood Anderson—indeed the 'Bone' Stillman of *The Trail of the Hawk,* a familiar type of village atheist who 'read Robert G. Ingersoll and said what he thought,' is the dominant influence of Carl's earlier years.

'Son, son, for God's sake live in life,' Bone Stillman tells the boy. 'It's a thing I ain't big enough to follow up, but

I know it's there. . . . You want to know that there's something ahead that's bigger and more beautiful than anything you've ever seen, and never stop till—well, till you can't follow the road any more.' And during his years at Plato College in Minnesota, Carl does remember this precept. He reads Shelley, Keats, Ibsen, and Shaw; he becomes something of a rural intellectual, or—caught up by the earlier and touching vision of the brotherhood of man that marked our provincial thinking in the nineteen-hundreds—a sort of prairie radical. Rebelling against the academic conventions, he leaves college in protest and in disgrace, to become, as Lewis says, 'utterly tough and reckless'—a day laborer in Chicago, a circus roustabout, a provincial wanderer and discoverer. 'Out of this wholesome, democratic, and stuffy village life, Carl suddenly stepped into the great world.'

Yet the 'great world' of the early Lewis hero has a curious history—it starts out with Carl's equal passion for a horseless carriage and for the Gertrude Cowles of his childhood. The Cowleses themselves, with their brick mansion, their hired maids, and their library—'the only parlor in Joralemon that was called a library, and the only one with a fireplace or a polished hardwood floor'—the Cowleses represent an early vision of luxury in the machine age. 'Gertie,' who has gone East for her education, remains fixed in Carl's mind as an image of grace and refinement, not only during his early adventures as a vagabond, but also during his more celebrated exploits as a pioneer aviator and stunt flyer. Unfortunately, these exploits occupy the entire middle section of *The Trail of the Hawk,* the earlier account of the western countryside fades into the 'romantic and miraculous' story of aviation, while the account of Carl Ericson's own education and human development is subordinated to the glamorous adventures of 'the best monoplane pilots America will ever see.' *

Meanwhile, in 1914, Lewis had already written *Our Mr. Wrenn,* a different sort of novel with a different sort of hero—one who has had no childhood to speak of, whose entire horizon is contained in the disorganized files of the 'Souvenir Company,' and who would apparently regard a prairie hawk as he would a dodo. Unlike Carl Ericson, 'Wrenny' is no adventurer. He has never had a drink or a woman, he is full of fears rather than recklessness, while even his animal instincts have been sublimated into a sort of vague yearning and anxiety. He dreams of becoming a rabbit. His single standard is 'respectability'—respectability means his job with the Souvenir Company—and, adds Lewis, 'his fear of losing the job was about equal to his desire to resign from the job.' His only escape is the 'Fairyland of Travel,' into which he slips nightly by means of a large collection of steamship advertising brochures.

Yet *Our Mr. Wrenn* also deals with the emotional education and even the spiritual emancipation of the early Lewis hero. Through receiving a small legacy, Mr. Wrenn is released from his economic servitude. Through his European trip he meets both Harry Morton, a Socialist vagabond, and Istra Nash, an alluring and exotic bohemian. And through Istra and her contact with a wider world of art and culture, Mr. Wrenn begins his own revolt against respectability. He gains sophistication and self-confidence; he learns not only how to discuss 'Yeats and the commutation of sex energy,' but also how to play. In fact, he now wants to shout to Istra across all the city: 'Let us

* In this connection it is interesting to notice that the first recorded work of Lewis's, a juvenile by 'Tom Graham,' in 1912, is called *Hike and the Aeroplane.*

be great lovers! Let us be mad! Let us stride over the hilltops!' Just as Harry Morton has given Mr. Wrenn a sense of that 'fine flame of shared hope' that was the common heritage of the workers of the world in the nineteen-hundreds, so Istra (with her red hair and her savoir-faire, her lack of corsets and her knowledge of all the really 'interesting' artistic people) seems to sum up, in Lewis's mind, a phase of the Aesthetic Revolt that followed hard on the heels of the Progressive Movement in America. Moreover, with *The Job,* in 1917—a less whimsical and more fully realized novel—Lewis carries forward this pattern of his early development.*

For his new heroine, Una Golden—the first full-length portrait in the series of Lewis's American women that will extend from the Carol Kennicott of 1920 to the Bethel Merriday of 1940—is a sort of fusion of Mr. Wrenn and Istra Nash. She is both the white-collar office worker and the emancipated woman; she has both more of a past and more of a future. She comes from those lower-middle-class folk who believe that Panama, Pennsylvania, 'is good enough for anybody'—and this village scene is viewed somewhat differently from that of Carl Ericson's western origins. 'To Una there was no romance in the sick mansion, no kindly democracy in the village street, no bare freedom in the hills beyond.'

So Una sets out on her own. 'She *would* go to New York, become a stenographer, a secretary to a corporation president, a rich woman, free, responsible.' New York,

* A sort of sub-realistic whimsicality also marks what is probably the worst novel of Lewis's first period, *The Innocents,* in 1917. The story concerns the adventures of an aged and rather pathetic lower middle-class couple. But the account of their exploits is so incredible, and their final 'success' (financial and social) is so unattractive, that the novel can justly be called 'a flagrant excursion,' as Lewis admits, and a tale 'for people who still read Dickens and clip out spring poetry and love old people and children.'

as Lewis says, which aspires to the heavens in her sky-scrapers, and dreams a garden dream of Georgian days in Gramercy Park, and 'bares her exquisite breast and wantons in beauty' on Riverside Drive. And the recurrent early dream of these Lewis characters—their belief in a rather hazy Utopian Socialism—blends into the vision of Scientific Business:

> For business, that one necessary field of activity to which the egotistic arts and sciences and theologies and military puerilities are but servants, that long-despised and always valiant effort to unify the labor of the world, is at last beginning to be something more than dirty smithing. No longer does the business man thank the better classes for permitting him to make and distribute bread and motor-cars and books. No longer does he crawl to the church to buy pardon for usury. Business is being recognized—and is recognizing itself—as ruler of the world. With this consciousness of power it is reforming its old, petty, half-hearted ways; its ideas of manufacture as a filthy sort of tinkering; of distribution as chance peddling and squalid shop-keeping; it is feverishly seeking efficiency. . . .

And, Lewis adds, this vision of a business efficiency so broad that it can be kindly and sure, this search for systems and charts and new markets and the scientific mind, is growing everywhere—'is discernible at once in the scientific businessman and the courageous labor-unionist.'

It is a vision of mercantile bliss, however, that isn't immediately discernible in the actual facts of Una Golden's life. New York is also the city of boxlike apartments and unvaried streets, of the 'loveless routine' of office jobs, of an unceasing round of unessentials against which Una bruises herself from hour to hour. It is the city of such 'organisms' as Bessie Kraker, who has been modified by the

Ghetto, Lewis says, to the life which still bewildered Una; of Walter Babson, the disillusioned poet who has turned into a cheap publicity man; of Phil Benson, the hall-room Lothario who would have been an excellent citizen 'had the city not preferred to train him . . . to a sharp unscrupulousness'; and of the unsuccessful salesman, Eddie Schwirtz, whose 'thwarted boyish soul' never can understand the reasons for his failure. Nor is Lewis's 'Bewildered New Muse' of Scientific Business any more apparent in the high-pressure efficiency of that Pemberton's Cosmetic Supply Company, to which Una graduates and which operates on the principle 'of giving the largest possible number of people the largest possible amount of nervous discomfort, to the end of producing the largest possible quantity of totally useless articles.' In fact, as Lewis traces the course of Una Golden's business career—the succession of tedious and exhausting jobs, the series of unfulfilled and uneasy men whom she meets through these jobs, and then her own attempt to escape from the impending disaster of middle age through an even more disastrous marriage—this entire lower-middle-class office world of 'respectability' and 'success' is dissected and laid open.

In these sections of the novel, *The Job* is the best and solidest example of Lewis's early realism. Yet in some respects it is an odd realism. Is the Lewis heroine still haunted by that dim view of a better society? Does there still come, into her workaday mind, a low light from that fire that was just then kindling the world—'the dual belief that life is too sacred to be taken in war and filthy industries and dull education; and that most forms and organizations and inherited castes are not sacred at all'? But it is actually through her friendship with Miss Beatrice Joline, the aristocratic type of successful business woman—the

New York 'thoroughbred'—that Una Golden finds the chance to salvage her ruined life. And it is through her own successful operation of the 'White Line Hotels' that she meets and marries the now successful Walter Babson, and simultaneously conquers Job and Home. 'We can both work, keep our jobs, and have a real housekeeper—a crackajack maid at forty a month—to mind the cat.'

It is interesting to remember that the earlier Mr. Wrenn follows a similar course of salvation. Was Istra Nash the epitome of Modern Sophistication—the Bohemian Revolt incarnate? Her sense of freedom is hardly matched by her sense of achievement—toward the close of *Our Mr. Wrenn,* indeed, the Sophisticate is more miserable than the Businessman. 'For when a person is Free, you know,' Lewis points out, 'he is never free to be anything but Free.' And just as Mr. Wrenn's European trip leads him to a new discovery of America, his experience with Istra's larger world of art and intellect brings him to a new recognition of the business world itself: to a determination to reform its manners if he can, but to advance his own status at all events. Even his earlier sense of isolation in the economic pattern is resolved through his success, as a more widely cultivated person, both in captivating his 'business friends' and in developing the theme of 'Friendship' as an advertising motif.

Similarly, the boldest and most rebellious of these early Lewis figures—the Carl Ericson of *The Trail of the Hawk*—becomes the most financially secure. In the midst of his exploits as an aviator—as one of Lewis's new heroes of the machine age—Carl dreams of becoming rich 'as soon as he could,' and Wrenn, in his wildest fantasies, cannot touch the twenty-five thousand dollars a year which Carl finally achieves through his masterpiece, the 'Touri-Car.' Indeed, if Carl conquers and then leaves the Gertie Cowles who was the tormenting symbol of eastern sophistication during the years of his midwestern youth, it is because he has found, in the later Ruth Winslow of *The Trail of the Hawk,* a more authentic representative of that sparkling and aristocratic New York society: of 'the inside view, the sophisticated understanding of everything.' And if Lewis opens his work with an evocation of that equalitarian frontier society which flourished with the arc light and the hired girl, one sees that he is really describing the impact of the machine and of wealth on this society—and the establishment, along with 'servants,' of rather rigid social classes. The human breed that could grow, and that had a thousand miles of prairie to grow in, is now chiefly concerned with getting ahead in society.

Perhaps this explains the curious emotional pattern of these early Lewis figures: their fear of expressing, or having, deeper feelings or strong convictions, and their retreat into whimsicality as a refuge from both emotion and ideas; their great desire to be young and have 'fun' and their equal uncertainty as to what 'fun' really is; their hurried excursions into a realm of defiance and revolt, and their swift return to the familiar security of their own economic and social routine—their 'own folks.'

And while they seem really to believe that a change of environment is equal to a change of personality, their uneasy view of their own geographical origins is matched only by their very definite sense of their economic destination. The closing pages of *The Trail of the Hawk,* at any rate, are devoted to an almost interminable discussion of this issue between Lewis's Ruth Winslow and the 'Hawk' himself—'he remembering the fact that she was a result of city life; she the fact that he wasn't a product of city life.' The real fact was, Lewis says, that Carl Ericson had come in a few years from Oscar Ericson's back yard to

Ruth Winslow's library—'he had made the step naturally, as only an American could, but it was a step.' It isn't definitely established, however, that Ruth Winslow uses her library, and meanwhile there is another interesting element in the early work of this novelist who is to become the outstanding satirist of the social patterns of the new American money society.

For the dominant characteristic of all these early Lewis novels is that they are not essentially satires at all, but 'romances.' * Just as the middle section of *The Trail of the Hawk* is devoted to the 'romance of the machine,' the main emphasis of *Our Mr. Wrenn* is on the 'romance of culture,' and the main emphasis of *The Job* is on the 'romance of business,' while the realistic elements of these novels—the earlier agrarian society of Carl Ericson or the white-collar office world of Mr. Wrenn and Una Golden—are in turn subordinated to the demands of the romance. Moreover, in the last of Lewis's early novels, *Free Air,* in 1919, the element of fantasy is almost completely released.

The story deals with an improbable automobile trip through the western states that is undertaken by a young society girl from Brooklyn Heights, and her father, a New York financier. In a sense the machine is still the central figure of Lewis's imagination. The title of the novel—the 'Free Air' that Claire Boltwood first meets in the West—is taken from a sign in a local garage, while the novel is filled with observations on the erratic behavior of Claire's seventy-horsepower Gomez-Dep roadster, as against that of Milt Daggett's proletarian 'Bug.' For, just as Claire is again the aristocratic eastern heroine, Milt,

* 'One of the things interesting to the author,' Lewis himself says, in the introduction to his *Selected Short Stories,* in 1935, 'is the discovery that he, who has been labeled a "satirist" and a "realist," is actually a romantic medievalist of the most incurable sort.' But this new description of himself, as we shall see, is not altogether accurate either.

who saves her at once from the foibles of the machine and the perils of the frontier, is also the western democratic hero. In fact, the basic theme of Lewis's literary apprenticeship emerges most clearly in the streamlined narrative of *Free Air*. The western countryside—the background of Gopher Prairie and of Zenith—is cruder now, with its dirty and littered farmyards, its ugly and run-down 'hotels,' its crossroads settlements like Schoenstrom, Minnesota, whose entire business district consists of

> Heinie Rauskukle's general store, which is brick; the Leipzig House, which is frame; the Old Home Poolroom and Restaurant, which is of old logs concealed by a frame sheathing; the farm-machinery agency, which is galvanized iron, its roof like an enlarged washboard; the church; the three saloons; and the signs . . . The Agency for Teal Car Best at the Test, Stonewall Tire Service Station, Sewing Machines and Binders Repaired. Dr. Hostrum the Veterinarian every Thursday, Gas Today 27c.

And, correspondingly, the eastern city life of Claire Boltwood, with its gracious talk and smart clothes and elaborate social distinctions, is, for the young Milt Daggett, even more rarefied.

The machine is transforming the western provinces also, to be sure. The 'missionaries of business,' who are instructing the rural merchants in how to build up trade and trim windows and 'treat customers like human beings,' are binding East and West together. 'They,' says Lewis, 'as much as the local ministers and doctors and teachers and newspapermen, were the agents of spreading knowledge and justice. It was they . . . who encouraged villagers to rise from scandal and gossip to a perception of the Great World, of politics and sports, and some measure of art and science.' And it is through these businessmen and drummers that Milt Daggett gets his first glimpse of the correct clothes and manners that go along with financial success, just as it is through his assiduous cultivation of the arts and sciences, as well as tennis, dancing, and bridge, that he finally becomes acceptable to the belle of Brooklyn Heights.

In the raw frontier towns of the early Sinclair Lewis, then, social position is even more desirable than it is in the drawing rooms of the eastern metropolis. How fervently, how studiously, in any case, these young Lewis heroes, reared on the immense empty western plains, seek to emulate an eastern sophistication: a sophistication which implies social poise, to be sure—and the effort 'to be gracious and aphoristic and repartistic and everything,' as Lewis's heroine admits—and also limousines and marble bathrooms and pâté de foie gras. How devoutly they aim to be, because of their native western heritage, better Easterners than the Easterners! Sometimes both the eastern girls and western boys of Lewis's first period appear to be so fundamentally similar in their approach to life that it is questionable whether their large sacrifices for the sake of each other are justified.

As a matter of fact, always proclaiming their desire for adventure and excitement and 'New Horizons,' these early Lewis figures as a group are probably the least well suited of all the restless young Americans in our letters to enjoy new horizons—or to recognize them. From Will Kennicott to Sam Dodsworth, too, this set of emotional responses is to remain dominant, fixed, and almost rigid in the work of Lewis's maturity. . . . Yet, for all that, there are ambiguous undertones in the novels of Lewis's age of innocence, while the conflict of cultural values that has been embodied in his 'East' and his 'West' will remain a persistent and disturbing theme in the next and most celebrated period of Lewis's work.

One might say that these cultural extremes are the true poles of Lewis's modern American world: that Middle-Class Empire and its House of Babbitt which we now approach.

3. The Middle-Class Empire

MAIN STREET (1920), says Lewis, is the story of Carol Kennicott: 'a girl on a hilltop; credulous, plastic, young, drinking the air as she longed to drink life'—a rebellious girl who is the spirit 'of that bewildered empire called the American Middlewest.'

In a certain sense this is true; at least it is a story that is difficult at first glance to relate to the author of *Our Mr. Wrenn* or *Free Air*. In the delicate and shifting marital relationship of Carol and Will Kennicott, Lewis has brought domestic drama almost to the point of classical tragedy; and in the beautifully controlled balance between Carol's view of Gopher Prairie and Gopher Prairie's view of Carol—an equilibrium of opposing human impulses in which nobody is to blame and everybody suffers —he seems for the first time to have the makings of a major realist.

For if *Main Street* has usually been considered, along with *Winesburg, Ohio,* as a landmark in the 'Revolt from the Village,' we shall see how inaccurate that view is with respect to Sherwood Anderson's country tales, and so, too, here, the whole dramatic force of Lewis's novel depends upon the fact that the village society and the critic of that society are so evenly paired off. In another sense this is the story of Gopher Prairie's revolt against Carol Kennicott. But it is actually closer to a description of that familiar condition of our existence in which two equally imperfect forces are locked together in an irreconcilable conflict. If anything, *Main Street* is a landmark in the 'Revolt Against Life.'

One realizes how the quality of life has changed for the author whose earlier characters had moved so largely along the lines of a clever plot, a journalistic 'idea,' a happy ending. Carol's first revulsion against the Scandinavian immigrants of the Northwest—the unbathed farmers and workers whom she meets on the Minnesota way train—is linked with her first sexual revulsion against the sober and honest Will Kennicott. 'She could not believe that she had ever slept in his arms. That was one of the dreams which you had but did not officially admit.' And her first impression of Gopher Prairie itself is rather like one of those dreams which you have and are forced to admit: this 'frontier camp' of oil tanks and stockyards, muddy and trampled and stinking; this 'junk-heap' of the Minniemashie House and Dyer's Drug Store, of the Rosebud Movie Palace, Olsen's Meat Market, and the Ford Garage, which is imprinted on Carol's mind through a vista of soiled tablecloths, a film called *Fatty in Love,* a reek of blood, and the rattling of a truck that is shaking itself to pieces; and which leaves her weeping in terror in her new home—'her body a pale arc as she knelt beside a cumbrous black-walnut bed, beside a puffy mattress covered with a red quilt, in a shuttered and airless room.' Very shortly, too, the earlier motif of isolation and loneliness in Carol's life—the attempt to make friends and to create a little gaiety for herself—takes on a more somber aspect. 'Oozing out from every drab wall, she felt a forbidding spirit which she could never conquer.' And her brief attempt to 'reform' the town subsides into the long-drawn-out and sometimes quite desperate attempt to protect herself from the town.

To a certain degree, of course, Carol deserves the 'hidden derision' that she feels everywhere about her in Gopher Prairie. Her values are as naïve as her methods are blundering. Her dreams of Culture on the Prairie are both conventional and artificial. ('Stately and aloof among vainglorious tiring-maids, a queen in robes that murmured on the marble floor,' she treads the galleries of Dunsany's Irish palaces in her fantasy of theatrical fame.) And the surrender of her dreams is hasty and complete. What is interesting, too, is that the other social rebels of Gopher Prairie—and it is equally interesting that in this traditionally disturbed area of the American hinterland, there are so few of them—are hardly less ineffectual than Carol herself. Miles Bjornstam, the 'Red Swede,' is a radical in the town's mind rather than in his own. Erik Valborg, the second of these provincial iconoclasts, is even more adolescent, and is just as incapable of human passion as he is of social protest—the amatory verbs he uses most frequently are 'implore' and 'beseech.' The aesthete of Gopher Prairie, Mr. Raymond P. Wutherspoon, is a pathetic homosexual; the 'philosopher,' Guy Pollack, is by his own confession a 'tiny leashed hawk'; and the young schoolteacher, Fern Mullins, collapses at the first indication of academic pressure. In the whole of Gopher Prairie, in short, there hardly seems to exist not so much a radical as a dissenter, and not so much a dissenter as an individualist who is strong enough to face up to public opinion—and these discontented rural figures of Lewis not only lack the courage of their convictions: they also lack convictions.

There are other ambiguous elements in the social framework of *Main Street*. Would its story be the same in 'Ohio, or Montana, or in the Carolina Hills,' as Lewis says? The 'common American past' may not be quite so common as Lewis implies, while the frontier past that is actually described here seems to be a little more bleak and desolate than it probably was.* But certainly there is that common American future of washing machines and suburban real-estate developments: for the imprint of an industrial money society is already fixed on the declining mores of a hunting and trapping community. Carol's first appalling vista of Gopher Prairie is also the vista of 'ten thousand towns from Albany to San Diego.' Was Will Kennicott's old family house full of the 'shadows of dead thoughts and haunting repressions'? Their new place would be 'smooth, standardized, fixed.' The novel is filled with references such as this, and descriptions of the 'universal similarity' of these new American towns: 'the same lumber yard, the same railroad station, the same Ford garage, the same creamery, the same boxlike houses and two-story shops . . . the same standardized, nationally advertised wares.' This historical change in the character of American life is at the heart of *Main Street*, and here, for the first time, Lewis seems to be evaluating it in its entirety. Doubtless all provincial towns, Lewis's heroine admits, tend to be dull and mean—

> But a village in a country which is taking pains to become altogether standardized and pure, which aspires to succeed Victorian England as the chief mediocrity of the world, is no longer merely provincial, no longer downy and restful in its leaf-shadowed ignorance. It is a force

* Lewis also stresses, to be sure, the 'heroic past' of the Northern Middle West, but the whole evocation of the frontier—of Willa Cather's 'Wild Land'—is curiously thin—typed—and 'gotten up.' 'It was a buoyant life,' Lewis says, but one that apparently can't sustain his own interest in it.

> seeking to dominate the earth, to drain the hills and sea of color, to set Dante at boosting Gopher Prairie, and to dress the high gods in Klassy Kollege Klothes.

'The dollar sign,' Miles Bjornstam adds, 'has chased the crucifix clean off the map.' And in fact, during the course of the novel, Gopher Prairie, which starts out as another Schoenstrom, Minnesota, ends up as a sort of amateur Zenith.

Babbitt carries forward the chronology of *Main Street,* of course. Zenith, in turn, is Gopher Prairie come of age. The crossroads hamlet has become the replica of the eastern metropolis, if in miniature, and here the democratic revolution is embodied in what is practically an orgy of Tocqueville's 'virtuous materialism.' The opening pages of the novel are ripe with the promise of sleek, noiseless limousines, concrete bridges, dictaphones, gleaming railway tracks, immense new factories, and 'the song of labor in a city built—it seemed—for giants.' Babbitt's house is trim, glossy, laudable, and endowed with outlets for all types of electrical devices. The mattresses in Babbitt's bedroom are 'triumphant modern mattresses' while the radiators have just the proper area for scientific radiation. This is a masterpiece among bedrooms, right out of Modern Houses for Medium Incomes, and every second house in Floral Heights has a bedroom precisely like it.

Such is George F. Babbitt's inviolable castle in Zenith, U.S.A., the new capital of the rising Middle-Class Empire. 'In fact there was but one thing wrong with the Babbitt house: it was not a home.' There is probably only one thing wrong, too, with Babbitt's wife: the loyal, industrious Myra who has passed from a feeble disgust for their closer marital relations to a bored acquiescence. Then there are Babbitt's two children, male and female, of course, who are respectively motor-mad and movie-mad, who are always escaping from their home directly after dinner, and whom Babbitt is no more conscious of than he is 'of the buttons on his coatsleeves'. As the novel moves outward from Babbitt's private to his public world, one realizes how admirably also Lewis has caught other salient characteristics of a whole middle portion of our society. And as Babbitt himself, the Equalitarian Emperor, flourishes and expands in the novel, one sees the increasingly narrow and rigid character of this society: the spiritual restrictions that accompany all this accumulating material grandeur.

For material possessions are the symbol of power to Babbitt. 'In the city of Zenith, in the barbarous twentieth century, a family's motor indicated its social rank as precisely as the grades of the peerage determined the rank of an English family—indeed, more precisely, considering the opinion of old country families upon newly created brewery barons and woolen-mill viscounts.' These possessions mark the difference between a real-estate salesman and a realtor—between the Athletic Club and the Union Club—between the state university and the eastern colleges—between Babbitt's less successful friends, the Overbrooks, whom he snubs, and the socially prominent McKelveys, who snub him. For the sake of these possessions Babbitt sacrifices both his physical vigor ("Ought to take more exercise; keep in shape . . .') and his peace of mind ('Like to go off some place and be able to hear myself think . . .'). In the course of acquiring possessions he is forced to alienate himself from the human beings who work with him. And, having acquired them, he is forced to mold his own personality into the pattern of the social institutions which dispense or safeguard these possessions—

> Just as he was an Elk, a Booster, and a member of the Chamber of Commerce, just as the priests of the Presbyterian Church determined his every religious belief and the senators who controlled the Republican Party decided in little smoky rooms in Washington what he should think about disarmament, tariff, and Germany, so did the large national advertisers fix the surface of his life, fix what he believed to be his individuality. These standard advertised wares—toothpastes, socks, tires, cameras, instantaneous hot-water-heaters—were his symbols and proofs of excellence; at first the signs, then the substitutes, for joy and passion and wisdom.

And yet, just as the eight thousand dollars that Babbitt finally works up to is a princely sum as compared with the twenty-five hundred a year that marked the economic royalty of Gopher Prairie, so, too, the increasing social pressure to own and display his possessions destroys whatever financial security Babbitt gains—and from Babbitt himself, the first portrait of this new economic citizen, to the Gideon Planish who will represent, in 1943, the last citizen of the boom period, it is difficult to think of a Lewis figure who is not frantically seeking a larger income in order to keep abreast of his debts.

Uneasy lies the head that wears the middle-class crown. Babbitt's greatest act of self-expression is the 'gorgeous abandon' of tearing up a frayed collar. Similarly, his happiest memory is of his youthful relationship with 'Paulibus'—Paul Riesling, the 'bohemian' of Zenith—while his deepest spiritual fulfillment is centered around the Fairy Child of his dreams—

> He was somewhere among unknown people who laughed at him. He slipped away, ran down the paths of a midnight garden, and at the gate the fairy child was waiting.

> . . . He was gallant and wise and well-beloved; warm ivory were her arms; and beyond perilous moors the brave sea glittered.

It is interesting to notice, though, that even in these subliminal meditations Babbitt's sexual urges are sublimated. And what is remarkable about the novel's whole view of life is the 'muted tone,' as it were, to which everything in the novel must conform: there can be no full release, or the promise of release, for the characters' aspirations as well as their inhibitions. Thus 'Chum' Frink, the High Poet of Zenith, out on a drunken spree, expresses his own sense of failure: 'Know what I could've been? I could've been a Gene Field or a James Whitcomb Riley.' And when Paulibus himself, the outcast of this society who is quite as imperfect as the society itself, does finally shoot his wife in desperation, the bullet lands in her shoulder. No wonder—uneasy as Babbitt is in his own domain, restricted on the one hand by these rigid emotional taboos, surrounded on the other hand by these mysterious Economic Presences whose whims actually determine his every move: no wonder that the prevailing mood of this new Middle-Class Mogul should be one of increasing irritation.

—If not of actual fear, or dread. Over the last half of *Babbitt,* indeed, as these psychological and economic pressures are more fully exerted on the novel's hero, there is an increasingly curious tone to Lewis's celebrated realistic study of the average American man, a tone that is suggested by the architecture of the Zenith Athletic Club itself—

> The entrance lobby of the Athletic Club was Gothic, the washroom Roman Imperial, the lounge Spanish Mission, and the reading-room in Chinese Chippendale, but the

> gem of the club was the dining-room, the masterpiece of Ferdinand Reitman, Zenith's busiest architect. It was lofty and half-timbered, with Tudor leaded casements, an oriel, a somewhat musicianless musicians'-gallery, and tapestries believed to illustrate the granting of Magna Charta. The open beams had been hand-adzed at Jake Offutt's car-body works, the hinges were of hand-wrought iron, the wainscot studded with hand-made wooden pegs, and at one end of the room was a heraldic and hooded stone fireplace which the club's advertising-pamphlet asserted to be not only larger than any of the fireplaces in European castles but of a draught incomparably more scientific. It was also much cleaner, as no fire had ever been built in it.

This is certainly the rape of the ages to house the dupes of the great American fortunes—or even, in the realm of the Middle-Class Empire, a sort of gatehouse to the regions of the damned.* And so it is.

For aren't the furnishings of the Zenith A.C. more than matched by its activities? Within these walls Vergil Gunch, president of the Boosters, Professor Pumphrey of the Riteway Business College, and T. Cholmondeley—'Chum'—Frink himself, these august personages and their associates, form the new Apostles of Commerce whom 'They' have especially commissioned to preach the Gospel of Profits and to preserve only the financially fit. 'They,' of course, are represented in turn by the Chamber of Commerce, the State Association of Real Estate Boards (the SAREB), the Good Citizens' League, and the other organizations whose conferences and conventions fill the pages of *Babbitt* with that series of incredible and ghastly scenes of good fellowship and good business. Such an

* T. K. Whipple, in a discerning essay in *Spokesmen,* has caught this undertone in Lewis's work, and Robert Cantwell has amplified it in his excellent study of Lewis that appears in *After the Genteel Tradition.*

episode as that where Chum Frink pleads for the cause of Music in Zenith— 'Some of you may feel that it's out of place here to talk on a strictly highbrow and artistic subject, but I want to come out flat-footed and ask you boys to O.K. the proposition of a Symphony Orchestra for Zenith. . . . Now, I want to confess that, though I'm a literary guy by profession, I don't care a rap for all this long-haired music. I'd rather listen to a good jazz band any time than to some piece by Beethoven that hasn't any more tune to it than a bunch of fighting cats, and you couldn't whistle it to save your life! But that isn't the point. Culture has become as necessary an adornment and advertisement for a city today as pavements and bank-clearances. . . . The thing to do, then, as a live bunch of go-getters, is to *capitalize Culture;* to go right out and grab it.' —Or where the various delegations from Zenith, the Zip City; Shelby County, the Garden Spot of God's Own Country, Monarch, the Mighty Motor Mart; Hamburg, the Big Little City with the Logical Location; or Galop de Vache, the Town for Homey Folks—present their credentials to the State Association of Real Estate Boards.* —Or where 'Mike Monday,' who has turned the minds of workmen 'from wages and hours to higher things, and thus averted strikes' in every city he appears in, opens his spiritual exhortations. ('There's a lot of smart college professors and tea-guzzling slobs in this burg that say I'm a roughneck and a never-wuzzer and my knowledge of history is not-yet. Oh, there's a gang of woolly-whiskered book-lice that think they know more than Almighty God,

* It is interesting, incidentally, to compare the main emphasis of Willa Cather or of Sherwood Anderson on the western countryside—the land itself—with Lewis's emphasis on real-estate developments. Miss Cather's heroes, for example, are those who own the land 'for a little while,' as she says, because they love it—but Lewis's heroes would probably be in a bad spot if they were forced to own the land for more than a little while.

and prefer a lot of Hun science and smutty German criticism to the straight and simple Word of God. . . .') —Or where Babbitt himself, as he approaches his office, the core of his life, the central source of all that material power and splendor that is spreading and flourishing as Zenith itself spreads and flourishes, finds himself walking faster and faster and muttering, 'Guess better hustle,' since—

> All about him the city was hustling, for hustling's sake. Men in motors were hustling to pass one another in the hustling traffic. Men were hustling to catch trolleys, with another trolley a minute behind, and to leap from the trolleys, to gallop across the sidewalk, to hurl themselves into buildings, into hustling express elevators. Men in dairy lunches were hustling to gulp down the food which cooks had hustled to fry. Men in barber shops were snapping, 'Jus' shave me once over. Gotta hustle.' Men were feverishly getting rid of visitors in offices adorned with the signs, 'This Is My Busy Day' and 'The Lord Created the World in Six Days—You Can Spiel All You Got to Say in Six Minutes.' Men who had made five thousand, year before last, and ten thousand last year, were urging on nerve-yelping bodies and parched brains so that they might make twenty thousand this year; and the men who had broken down immediately after their twenty thousand dollars were hustling to catch trains, to hustle through the vacations which the hustling doctors had ordered.

—Such episodes as these—steadily accumulating in the course of the novel, growing more and more macabre in tone and more and more dense and oppressive in their atmospheric pressure, as it were, until they are finally almost overwhelming in their effect—form the milieu of Babbitt's public life. Notice, too, the series of nightmarish impressions he begins to have about his private life: the 'incessant hiss of whispering' that he hears as he walks the streets in his moments of rebellion or of dissipation; the fits of primitive terror that he endures at night as he lies awake shivering at the prospect of 'anything so unknown and so embarrassing as freedom'; the relapse into the 'close hot tomb' of his Pullman berth after another jovial business session. Even the Fairy Child of Babbitt's dreams who has come to life in the Tanis Judique, who is his mistress, takes on, in a curious turn of the narrative, a dreamlike quality that is not altogether pleasant. And Myra Babbitt herself, as Babbitt sees her lying on the operating table, becomes in turn 'a swathed thing . . . a mound of white in the midst of which was a square of sallow flesh with a gash a little bloody at the edges; protruding from the gash a cluster of forceps like clinging parasites. . . .'

But Lewis has set his stage very early in one of the most violent and effective episodes in the novel—the first big 'party' on Floral Heights at which Babbitt, the glad host, is practically overcome by the food and drink, the gossip, the boasting, the 'jokes.' 'Everything about him was dim except his stomach, and that was a bright scarlet disturbance. He felt as though he had been stuffed with clay; his body was bursting . . . his brain was hot mud; and only with agony did he continue to smile and shout as became a host on Floral Heights.' It is in this state that there appears before him the apparition of 'the Wop poet' who has been called from the shadows by Zenith's amateur spiritualists.

'O, Laughing Eyes, emerge forth into the, uh, ultimates,' cries Chum Frink. 'You forgot to give um the address,' chuckles Vergil Gunch—'1658 Brimstone Avenue, Fiery Heights, Hell.' And Fiery Heights is absolutely the proper address, and the mangled specter of Dante is the true presiding genius of Zenith. . . . The central scenes of *Babbitt* can hardly be explained by the ordinary categories of 'satire'—and this almost classical example of photographic American 'realism' is realistic only in terms of its introductory setting—and there, also, only to a degree. In the central concept of the novel, in its final and dominant mood, and in the craft technics which first suggest and then fully project its true theme, *Babbitt* is, on the contrary, an imaginative work of a high order. It is, if anything, close to poetry. Or at least, from its inception in Babbitt's bedroom, 'as neat and as negative as a block of artificial ice,' to the conclusion of its latest and biggest real-estate deal, it is almost a perfectly conceived poetic vision of a perfectly standardized money society; it is our native *Inferno* of the mechanized hinterland. Even the 'Great Strike' that grips Zenith toward the close of the novel is a middle-class nightmare of a workers' revolt in which the workers are as vague as they are ominous.

In this connection the familiar objection to the novel—the fact that even George F. Babbitt himself could never possibly be so *complete* a Babbitt—becomes, of course, the novel's main virtue; while the familiar criticism of the novelist's 'ear' must also be set aside, temporarily anyhow. The language of Lewis's people is certainly not the language of the small-town and city people who have hitherto existed in the United States, nor even that of our present-day Rotarians. It is not Mencken's and Lardner's language of the American people, either. But it can serve very well—tricky, synthetic, and prefabricated as it is—as the medium for some future Utopia of Rotary. It is the verbiage of a super-public-relations counsel in an absolute hysteria of brotherhood; it is the vocabulary of International Big Business designed and tooled for a race of synthetic and prefabricated common men; it is the new global lingo of the machine and the cartel.

The third of Lewis's major novels, however, *Arrowsmith,* in 1925, does return to the more realistic elements of Lewis's work. The opening sections of the novel—the dingy and drowsy country doctor's office in the village of Elk Mills, 'Winnemac,' * in the late eighteen-nineties, the early episodes of Martin's youth in Mohalis—are more carefully and warmly done than has been the case in Lewis's previous descriptions of that older rural scene which marked our national life 'before the invention of sex and the era of the petting parties.' Like the young Carl Ericson of *The Trail of the Hawk,* Martin Arrowsmith himself is intended to be one of Lewis's few full-fledged heroes, and here, too, we get something just about as rare in Lewis's work: Martin's early pleasure as a manual worker in a telephone-wire crew, and the beauty of the western countryside itself. 'As though he had just awakened, he saw that the prairie was vast, that the sun was kindly on rough pasture and ripening wheat, on the old horses, the easy, broad-beamed friendly horses, and on his red-faced jocose companions; he saw that the meadow larks were jubilant, and the blackbirds were shining by little pools, and with the living sun all life was living.'

This is almost a note of lyricism for Lewis, after the smoky and darkened interiors, the pushing and shouting

* This is apparently the first direct mention of the composite imaginary middle-western state that is the geographical center of Lewis's midwestern world. The Schoenstrom and Gopher Prairie of *Free Air* and *Main Street* are located in Minnesota; the Zenith of Babbitt seems to exist anywhere and everywhere—it is really its own state. But here we are told that the town of Mohalis, in Winnemac, is fifteen miles from Zenith, and so, by inference, the Zip City becomes the metropolis of the Zip State. The pre-industrial and provincial 'up-state' town of Catawba, incidentally, from which Babbitt hails—though, like most of Lewis's 'city' people, he isn't anxious to mention it—also figures as the home of the Reverend Andrew Pengilly, the wholesome country minister of *Elmer Gantry.*

personages of *Babbitt.* Similarly, the Leora Tozer of *Arrowsmith,* coming out of Martin's own people, vulgar, jocular, unreticent as she is, but also gallant, full of laughter, and capable of a loyalty 'too casual and natural to seem heroic,' is Lewis's full-fledged western heroine, while in Max Gottlieb himself—the research scientist who consistently opposes the commercial exploitation of medicine—Lewis has also drawn one of the most sympathetic portraits in the whole range of his work, and one which exemplifies the pervading faith of the novel. 'God give me unclouded eyes and freedom from haste,' the Lewis hero says—

> 'God give me a quiet and relentless anger at pretense and all pretentious work and all work left slack and unfinished, God give me a restlessness whereby I may neither sleep nor accept praise till my observed results equal my calculated results or in pious glee I discover and assault my error. God give me strength not to trust in God!'

—and the story of Martin's medical career is full of the elaborations and accompaniments of this vision of 'scientific truth.'

Yet is it true, as Gottlieb also claims, that in this vale of tears 'there is nothing certain but the Quantitative method'? Such a belief, or at least such a statement of it, is probably not quite adequate for the research scientist himself; it is certainly a narrow code for a novelist whose precise business is with the uncertain elements in this 'vale of tears'—with the *qualitative* method of evaluating life. And this is a singularly typical statement for Lewis himself to make: a rarefication of his earlier enchantment with applied science, a reflection, not too distant, of that latest American credo of efficiency and machinery, of that new faith in charts, diagrams, and statistics which underlies the novels of Lewis's first period, and which, in *Arrowsmith* itself, sets up a new cycle of contradictions in Lewis's work even while it fails, in the end, to resolve the earlier ones.

For if *Arrowsmith* represents Lewis's fullest attempt to discover those qualities of western character and human relationships that will offset the divided view of the contemporary town that he has presented in *Main Street* and the almost completely despairing vision of the city of the future in *Babbitt,* it is also true that the 'Wheatsylvania,' Dakota, which Martin Arrowsmith reaches at the conclusion of his troubled voyage West is just about as crude and synthetic as its name. 'Dakota. Real Man's country. Frontier. Opportunity. America!' says Martin, and Lewis's picture of his subsequent life there hardly varies from this initial mode of description.

> He came to know all of Leora's background. Her bedridden grand-aunt in Zenith, who was her excuse for coming so far to take hospital training. The hamlet of Wheatsylvania . . . one street of shanties with the red grain elevators at the end. Her father, Andrew Jackson Tozer, sometimes known as Jackass Tozer; owner of the bank, of the creamery, and an elevator, therefore the chief person in town; pious at every Wednesday evening prayer-meeting, fussing over every penny he gave to Leora or her mother. Bert Tozer, her brother; squirrel teeth, a gold eye-glass chain over his ear, cashier and all the rest of the staff in the one-room bank owned by his father. The chicken salad and coffee suppers at the United Brethren Church; German Lutheran farmers . . . the Hollanders, the Bohemians and Poles.

Where is the girl of the Golden West now? As a matter of fact the Tozers are among the pettiest and most provincial of Lewis's large family of petty provincials; while

Leora herself soon begins to show the defects of her western virtues.* The first of Lewis's heroines to admit sensuous passion as a factor in her temperament, she is confined merely to passion. What's more, along with the deterioration of the central characters and human relationships of *Arrowsmith,* there is a corresponding deterioration of the novel's own central belief—the vision of scientific truth itself.

Lewis's main purpose is, of course, to satirize the exploitation of medical research by the vested interests. Yet, in a curious shift of the novel's focus, his animus is directed not so much against medical or commercial institutions as against the chief victims of these institutions. Martin's bungling attempt to reform the public health system in Nautilus, Winnemac—an attempt that is very similar to Carol Kennicott's Campaign for Culture in Gopher Prairie—leads, not, as one might suppose, to any sort of self-examination on the part of Lewis's hero, or to a further examination of the human elements in the situation, but to a sort of contempt for public service and the public welfare itself. Quite similarly the First World War is in Martin's eyes 'chiefly another interruption of his work.' Although the scientific spirit allows him only a very hazy notion of what is going on, it is bound to be 'something idealistic and nasty.' (It is interesting, incidentally, that so vigorous a chronicler of the national manners as Lewis should be satisfied with such meager and stereotyped references to the war.) Furthermore, 'Does truth itself

* The fundamental uncertainty of Lewis's view of his own origins is often betrayed by a phrase as well as by a character. Thus, while Leora's appeal is directly attributed to the fact that she is an unspoiled product of the western land, the voice of Madeline Fox, the Easterner, is described as 'shrill and cornfieldish.' It is interesting, too, in the novel which represents Lewis's search for a western ideal, that the most sympathetic character—Gottlieb himself, with his memories of Munich and references to 'Father Nietzsche'—should be a cultivated European.

matter?' Martin finally asks himself—'Clean, cold unfriendly truth . . . ? Does anything matter except making love and sleeping and eating and being flattered?' And it is actually this tone of fashionable cynicism rather than of scientific skepticism that marks both the concluding sections of *Arrowsmith* and the last two novels of this period of Lewis's work.*

The first of these is also the most notorious of Lewis's novels, and probably with some cause. Just as *Arrowsmith* represents the upper range of human aspiration in the world of Lewis's fiction, and its positive pole, *Elmer Gantry,* in 1927, represents the lowest range, and the negative pole, of the Middle-Class Empire. Certainly, too, the whole area of the lunatic fringe in American religious activity, from the orgiastic sects of the hinterland to the spiritualistic cults of Park Avenue and Hollywood, including the various versions of moral rearmament, vegetarianism, and religious 'science,' the demagogic sociology of radio 'priests,' and that whole superstructure of commercial and publicized religion—this is a legitimate and natural area for an American satirist. Moreover, if Martin Arrowsmith is meant to illustrate the purest type of Lewis's truth-seeker, so Elmer Gantry, in person, is the archetype of the opportunist and false prophet, the epitome of bourgeois villainy and vice—of sin in Winnemac.

And *Elmer Gantry* also marks a sort of increasing vital-

* *Mantrap,* in 1926, the story of a New York lawyer's rest-cure in the North Woods, is a curious throwback to Lewis's earliest 'romances.' Although the nature scenes of the novel are hardly as convincing as they are, apparently, therapeutic, the novel's heroine, an ex-manicurist and one of the few lower-class figures in Lewis's work, is an interesting and rather vivid character. But, she too, recalling the Fairy Child of Babbitt's dreams, and reminding us somewhat of John Steinbeck's compassionate harlot in *Of Mice and Men,* becomes in the end merely a stock figure of middle-class American romanticism—a heroine of our suburban sexual fantasies, as it were, who might be almost classified as the Whore-Virgin.

ity in Lewis's realism as the 'Hell Cat' emerges from the twilight zones of the Mizpah Theological Seminary and the Kayooska River Baptist Association in all the glory of a physical and sexual prowess—and from Mr. Wrenn to Babbitt the bodies of the Lewis heroes have never been the secret of their charm—that is unhampered by a religious or even a moral sense. 'My God, Gantry, what a perfect specimen you are!' In the direct and raw quality of his lust for Sharon Falconer, too, Gantry almost lives up to this description, while Sharon herself—this self-made enchantress and messianic evangelist—is even more brazen, unscrupulous, and direct. 'I hate the little vices—smoking, swearing, scandal, drinking just enough to be silly. I love the big ones—murder, lust, cruelty, ambition!' Very clearly here, and this time through the medium of evil, Lewis is attempting to transcend that dominant 'respectability' which has conditioned the whole range of his middle-class American characters—and is responding to that earlier yearning for 'fun,' for 'adventure,' for 'new horizons,' for life in all its manifestations.

The central scene of the love affair, which takes place on Sharon's Virginia estate, and in which, surrounded by her heathen idols and naked Venuses and by all the other trappings of primitive and orgiastic ceremonials, Sharon herself takes on the rôle of an ancient fertility goddess ('for the service of the altar'), points all this up. 'She was fantastic in a robe of deep crimson adorned with golden stars and crescents, swastikas and tau crosses; her feet were in silver sandals, and round her hair was a tiara of silver moons set with steel points that flickered in the candlelight. A mist of incense floated about her, seemed to rise from her, and as she slowly raised her arms he felt . . . that she was veritably a priestess.' Sharon is certainly a symbol of the primitive human impulses that survive in even the most respectable of all respectable worlds. This is almost a touch of Hitlerism in Old Virginia. . . . Yet Sharon's aristocratic background is a complete farce, of course, and very shortly the whole exotic love affair itself slips into the more familiar pattern of passion as it has existed in Lewis's literary world.

In the midst of this pagan revival, indeed, these two neo-primitives indulge in a bit of whimsical athletics. 'You *can* run!' cries Sharon. 'You bet I can!' responds Elmer. 'And I'm a grand footballer, a bearcat at tackling, my young friend,' while Sharon 'grudgingly admires' his strength. . . . If Elmer views Sharon as a priestess, moreover, he does so in 'schoolboyish awe.' He is still 'the small boy seeking the praise of his mother'—a small boy who, however, in the wildest flights of this dissolute passion, hardly forgets that Sharon is a shrewd and successful woman as well as an attractive one. 'Before long she would probably make fifty thousand.' It is only at the moment of the fire which destroys Sharon's New Jersey temple, and during the course of which Elmer yields Sharon herself to the flames in order to save his own skin, that the whole syndrome of Lewis's pseudo-pagan instincts actually does seem to operate—and there, of course, in the single area of self-preservation. (Similarly, in the area of social motivation, the one full release of the middle-class emotions which *Elmer Gantry* depicts is through the persecution of heretics and disbelievers.) In short, if Sharon Falconer is intended to represent the instinctual drives in Lewis's work, the violence and shadow of this middle-class world, she is still mainly a figment of Babbitt's unconscious. And if Elmer Gantry himself is unmistakably a bounder, he is still a middle-class bounder: he is the Anti-Christ of *Zenith*. . . . And the fact that such a view of his leading figures stems quite as much from Lewis's own view of reality as from the satiric presentation of his material is clear from the whole intellectual framework of *Elmer Gantry*.

For there are sections of the novel which remind us of the best things in *Babbitt*. The later account of Elmer's rise to power as a religious 'crusader' and a pillar of organized morality does take on a kind of extra-realistic and extra-satirical quality. The descriptions of the New Thought in Zenith, of Elmer's famous Lively Sunday Evenings, his Committee on Public Morals, and his Salesmanship of Salvation ('Wake Up, Mr. Devil!'), make *Elmer Gantry* close to another excursion into the inferno: an inferno that is composed of the blind religious paroxysms of a society which has lost all sense of religion.

But this is also a vision of corruption in which the novelist's own view of life is separate from, but hardly superior to, the life he is describing, and in which even the novelist's craft has been affected by the taint in his subject matter. If the larger scene of *Elmer Gantry* presents a cross-section of religious activity in the United States, and if there are some witty descriptions of this activity, there is also remarkably little insight into the more fundamental aspects of religious motivation—either personal or cultural—or into that commercial exploitation of religion which is the ostensible theme of the novel. The religious reformer of the novel, Frank Shallard, is cast in the familiar mold of Lewis's ineffectual rural rebels; the religious scholar of the novel, Doctor Bruno Zechlin, is a weak repetition of Lewis's Gottlieb; and the 'good minister' of Lewis's older provincial order, the Reverend Andrew Pengilly of Catawba, is hardly more than a shadow in the novel. Furthermore, while Lewis does have an occasional glimpse of the 'diffident tenderness' and the 'unlettered fervor' of his provincial preachers and prophets—

the true-believers of the hinterland—it is also true that he now sees the American hinterland itself mainly in terms of bottle-pool and the farmer's daughter, of loafers and yokels, of 'dead eyes,' 'sagging jaws,' and 'sudden guffawing.' Perhaps the whole cheapened and coarsened quality of Lewis's satire is implicit in his early reference to the 'Gritzmacher Springs' of *Elmer Gantry*—the springs which have dried up, and the Gritzmachers who have gone on to Los Angeles 'to sell bungalows and delicatessen.' At any rate, the tone of fashionable cynicism which first appears in *Arrowsmith*—that uneasy tone of urban superiority and of a hurried sophistication—here again, in *Elmer Gantry*, takes the place of those deeper values and roots for which Lewis has been searching. Here also, in the microcosm of Lewis's style, the 'folks' have become the 'mob,' while the 'Gang' and the 'Bunch' are almost a Zenith chapter of the Smart Set.* Even more clearly, these literary abstractions and clichés which Lewis has substituted for artistic insight and conviction form the intellectual framework of *The Man Who Knew Coolidge,* in 1928.

Within a very sharp focus indeed, Lewis's last novel of this period presents Lowell Schmaltz, the typical citizen of the Boom: his domestic life and private affairs, his sports, vices, and pleasures, as well as his public utterances, political opinions, moral sentiments, and practical workings. As a case history of an epoch, a guidebook to the industrial folkways of 1929, and an illuminating appendix to *Babbitt* itself—*The Man Who Knew Coolidge* probably deserves wider recognition than it has received. You may see very easily here what has been happening both to

* Or merely notice the exclamations of Lewis's young people in the 'Mizpah Theological Seminary': 'Golly. . . . Well, I'll be switched. . . . Gee, honest. . . . You bet your life. . . . Whew!' These college scenes also constitute a fantasy world of adolescent behavior, of course—of youthful vim and enthusiasm—but a popularized and trite world.

American life and to Lewis over this decade of Lewis's work.

For a whole range of earlier Lewis characters have been confused about the 'great world,' but Lowell Schmaltz is absolutely incoherent; political events are quite as esoteric to him as artistic events were for Will Kennicott and George Babbitt. Yet, if Babbitt was naïve and complacent, Schmaltz is arrogant and assertive; his abysmal ignorance is matched only by his conviction of his own influence. Babbitt had his little moments of revolt against Rotary, however futile; his more generous affection for his 'Paulibus,' however ludicrous; and even a certain confused generosity about life in general. Schmaltz is all narrowness and meanness; the epitome of complacency and conformity, of self-righteousness and moral virtue under the heavens and under the Boom Market, while, according to the financial imperatives, God himself, the Mysterious Stranger of Zenith, has become a Junior Partner of the Board. But why continue? Babbitt, in short, was a second-class citizen; the hero of *The Man Who Knew Coolidge* is a second-class Babbitt. By comparison, Lewis's earlier figure is a rarely gifted and unique personage—a Leonardo of the Realtors—and one who marked the flowering of an individualistic society.

The Economic Inferno first fully glimpsed in *Babbitt* becomes a reality here—and a blueprint. The children of this latest Lewis hero (although there are still two of them) are even vaguer, and not without the suggestion of corruption. Myra Babbitt may have been an all-too-solid symbol of the domestic flesh, but Lowell Schmaltz's wife, more emancipated and worldly, is altogether useless. 'I might as well not have a wife at all'—and, in truth, their common possessions are their only common interest. Similarly, in Lowell's amorous escapades, even the Fairy

Child of the Rotarian has become standardized, cheaper, at once more patently sexual and more mechanical. . . . And why not? Isn't she now primarily a vehicle of sexual satisfaction—another product of the increasingly standardized social arrangement of the nineteen-twenties which has spread, in Lewis's own picture of the decade as well as in the decade itself, from the business activities of his heroes to their domestic affairs and even to their secret fantasies—from their office files to their most intimate moments of pleasure?

Thus the scenes which describe the drunken hero of *The Man Who Knew Coolidge*—and the release of his inhibitions—merely represent an infinitesimal extension of the sober Lowell Schmaltz: the realm of the Freudian *Id* has also become a sort of mercantile unconscious which is sensitive only to the stimuli of a money society. Thus the latest Lewis hero's affirmation of his own personality runs through the novel with the insistence of a paid advertisement, a spot recording, a transcription. 'Yes sir, it's a wonderful thing . . . how American civilization . . . has encouraged the . . . free play of individualism.'

Yet *The Man Who Knew Coolidge* is a blueprint, rather than a novel. Its hero, hardly so much an individual as the product of a standardized cultural mold of 'individualism'—of the mass-production temperament and the Woolworth personality—is presented simply *as* another standard brand on display. There is no longer an attempt on Lewis's part to face the socio-economic factors or the underlying cultural pattern of Lowell Schmaltz's cosmos; very much like his own businessmen, the writer is interested only in *results,* which are all taken for granted, which are even, in a way, enjoyed. The cultivated aesthetic superiority of the American twenties, the ironical indifference of the speakeasy set, the *Weltanschauung* of the expatriates, from Chicago and St. Louis and Sauk Center itself, are triumphant here—are reflected in the 'historical' footnotes to the novel as well as in the name of the novel's hero, while the artist himself, after illustrating the farthest vistas of the Middle-Class Empire, has withdrawn to the Olympian, or, say, the neo-Menckenian heights of exposé and mockery.*

In some respects this is an odd climax to the first big period of this native satirist—a period which opens with his famous studies of the American hinterland. But actually, according to the inner logic of Lewis's work in this period, it is an almost inevitable conclusion. We have noticed the divided view of the contemporary scene in *Main Street*—a deeply ambivalent and sharply divided view—and also the almost completely destructive vision of the common American future in *Babbitt*. Yet nowhere after these novels has Lewis been able to come to grips with the real elements of his own literary projections, or, indeed, of the native scene itself. On the contrary, what has become increasingly clear in both the truth-seekers of *Arrowsmith* and the false prophets of *Elmer Gantry* is the curiously limited nature of Lewis's own view of reality. Just as there is really no sense of vice in Lewis's literary world, there is no true sense of virtue. Just as there is practically no sense of human love in the whole range of Lewis's psychological values, and no sense of real hatred—there is no genuine sense of human freedom.

So the familiar traits of Lewis's literary figures: their lack of inner security or of outward grace, of integrity and

* Mencken's influence is much more directly noticeable here, as is also Ring Lardner's. But remember that Mencken's merit was in the deeper cultural insights that inferentially or almost inadvertently accompanied his social comedy. Similarly the Lardnerian bitterness, the sense of a deep human protest, is missing in the smooth satire of *The Man Who Knew Coolidge*.

manners alike, of any conscious style in life and, apparently, of any unconscious ties with it;* all these small, cheap, and acutely embarrassing human traits which Lewis describes so brilliantly and which have taken over the exclusive possession of the human soul in his literary cosmos at the expense of all larger human feeling—almost as if they were the *only* human traits, as though Lewis's people, by some secret and binding agreement with their Creator, their Maker, their Source of Spiritual Supply, had set a fixed limit on both the upper and lower ranges of ordinary human emotions and had established a sort of Spiritual Cartel which operates in restraint of any natural human exuberance: all these familiar and humiliating traits of Lewis's people which almost appear to be the direct reflection of an increasingly standardized economic order and which are regulated on every side by the middle-class aspirations of genteel respectability—are still confined to the single achievement of getting ahead in the world.

Now the truth about human nature, of course, is that it is always changing. It does adjust to its environment with incredible speed; it is almost infinitely malleable. Given enough time, probably nothing seems unnatural to it. Yet it can hardly have lost *all* the basic human instincts in a century of American industrialism and barely a half-century of the middle-class ethos. It is easy to recognize all the ignoble aspects of human behavior that appear in Lewis's work: in a sense his virtue is that he

* Lewis's people *do* have nervous breakdowns, as in *Arrowsmith* and *Mantrap*—breakdowns which are described alternately in terms of 'ancient bloodless horrors' or of 'agoraphobia, claustrophobia, pyrophobia,' and which are cured by a trip to the woods, a brief rest, or merely by the exercise of one's will power. But as to the unconscious, either racial or individual, as a living force in one's life, there is little evidence in Lewis's work. Or, to put this more accurately, the individual unconscious seems to have disappeared in Lewis's work, while the racial unconscious, as in *The Man Who Knew Coolidge,* has been thoroughly modernized.

continually reminds us of these, and only these. He hardly so much tries to destroy us in one stroke as to make us continuously uncomfortable. Similarly, in terms of Lewis's portraits of love itself, we may very well appreciate his recurrent scene: a scene in which the chief actors continually display all the ridiculous by-products of human desire, but never the desire itself—in which they are never really up to their rôle and never understand that they are not up to their rôle.

Yet, perpetually frustrated and distorted as the human passions are, they are nevertheless passions. They do exist in fact, whereas they never possibly can exist in Lewis's notion of the facts. So, too, continuously describing a literary society where life and death are equally unlived and, as it were, undied, he has nowhere been able to persuade us that life—even middle-class life in America—is livable or that death must be died. And this is not his main artistic intention but his chief artistic limitation.

For what is obvious is that the inner existence of Lewis's figures follows just as sharply defined a pattern as their outward behavior. But what seems curious in the end is that Lewis's own set of values should follow the same pattern as that of his people. It is almost as though the writer who has been describing over and over again one way of life, one type of personality structure, one set of instincts—or rather, one set of cultural reflexes, since, as we have now seen, the essential fact about the natural instincts in Lewis's work is that they hardly exist: it is just as though this writer, always following the same circumscribed line of human behavior, had mistaken it for the perfect circle of human experience. . . . In the cultural area, also, if Lewis has followed up Carol Kennicott's directive that 'institutions, not individuals, are the enemies,' and that the only defense against them is 'unembittered laughter,' it is clear that his own laughter has become a substitute for, rather than an accompaniment of, a deeper insight or a bolder conviction. In both areas the surface of things, sharply and often brilliantly illuminated as it is in Lewis's work, has taken the place of the thing itself, and Lewis has turned from morals to manners, as they used to say.

Yet the strength of a true satirist of manners lies in the fact that they, too, are a not altogether distant reflection of morals. During the next decade of Lewis's writing—a decade that is marked by a severe shock to and a sharp change at the very base of that middle-middle section of American society whose fictional history Lewis is recording: during the economic turmoil and social flux of the nineteen-thirties, in brief, the pattern of Lewis's literary values is still more sharply defined.

Perhaps you should keep in mind that first and almost completely realized poetic vision of a cultural damnation which Lewis himself has almost completely put aside by now. Like the spirits of ancient days who could not rest until they were properly interred, the ghost of George F. Babbitt will wander through the land of Lewis's cosmic bourjoyce.

4. The Cosmic Bourjoyce

THE YEAR NINETEEN-TWENTY-NINE was a sort of preliminary showing for a new decade of domestic jitters. In the national letters the Aesthetic Individualist of the twenties gave way to the Economic Man of the thirties and the Smart Set to the WPA, and it is interesting that Lewis's next three novels should mark a return to the 'middle realism' of *Main Street:* to a further study of the actual facts of American life, that is, as against the Babbittry of the Myth.

The first of these novels, the *Dodsworth* of 1929, can be regarded as probably the best example of Lewis's realism. The portrait of Sam Dodsworth is certainly that of a more complex and more interesting middle-class American businessman—the Babbitt, as it were, of reality. As an independent automobile manufacturer, Sam is both a worker and a craftsman in his own sphere; along with his talent he has, which is rare for Lewis's people, a sense of achievement in his own work.

Is it necessary to have, as Sam Dodsworth has, a sizable fortune in order to get pleasure from one's life? In his temperament, and in his language,* at any rate, Sam represents the best product of the new provincial-urban pattern of American life. Perhaps, as Lewis says, he 'would never love passionately, lose tragically, nor sit in contented idleness before tropic shores.' Yet, with his solid backlog of all the leisure-class luxuries and decencies—Sam is the aristocrat of Winnemac. An actual ruler of the Middle-Class Empire instead of a self-deluded one, an apotheosis of the small industrialist, he is the Zenith Titan and Lewis's Last Tycoon.

Along with his flat declaration for this type of American man, Lewis almost resolves another central issue of his work, one that seems at once cultural and curiously personal. Just as the Leora Tozer of *Arrowsmith* was the first full portrait of the frank and sensuous western heroine, so the Fran Voelker of *Dodsworth* is the sharpest study of that longing for eastern sophistication and 'culture'

* Sam is the first Lewis hero to 'drawl' instead of 'bark' his commands, and to use relatively proper English—or American. One notices also the frequent use of Latin or French phrases in Lewis's narrative style here; a general heightening of the narrative tone, that is, to fit a more elevated subject matter.

which has marked a whole line of Lewis's ladies. This note is struck with the earliest mention of Fran—at the time 'she was East, in finishing school'—and with the first statement of her lifelong ambition. 'I want the whole world, not just Zenith! I don't want to be a good wife and mother and play cribbage pettily. I want splendor! Great horizons! Can we look for them together?' From the days of his youth and the start of his business career, Sam struggles to live up to this ideal of feminine sensibility—'Ah, if she desired Europe, he would master it, and give it to her on a platter of polished gold'—and is as much in awe of Fran's cultural aspirations as he is of her physical attraction. 'Fran, you've got to marry me!' 'The great Yale athlete speaks! The automobile magnate!' 'No, just a scared lump of meat that's telling you he worships you!'

There is a flaw, however, in all the grace and polish of this midwestern brewer's daughter. If Fran is an angel, as Lewis remarks very early in the story, she is 'an angel made of ice'; and the central story of *Dodsworth* deals with Sam's increasing realization of her true nature; her rigid limitations and smallness of spirit; her final incapacity to receive even that glittering eastern and European experience which has been her lifelong desire. . . . Yet the imperfect relationship of the Dodsworths is not altogether one-sided; through the process which leads to his own rejection of Fran, Sam also comes to learn something about himself, and about love and human relationship in America. Is Fran's sexual frigidity ('But don't you think it's a little icky, this sudden passion for embracing when you're, well, exhilarated') part of her entire contempt for Sam's world and his way of life? While Fran wants all that Sam can get her—and a little more—she has very little use for the way he gets it. One must be in business in order to make money. But the purpose of money is to enable one to forget about business. And similarly, one must have a husband in order to provide the means to escape the fact that one has a husband.

In turn, though, isn't it Sam's own way of life—his concern with machines and with property; his own indifference to human relationships and his actual fear of emotional entanglements: isn't it all this, as Sam comes to ask himself, that has contributed to Fran's disdain for him and that leaves him so empty and powerless in the midst of his economic triumphs? Should he really condemn the woman to whom life was a fashion show or the man who had thought carburetors more fascinating than 'the souls and bodies of women?'

Thus, while *Dodsworth* marks the final rejection of the 'eastern' heroine who has figured so largely in Lewis's work from the exotic Istra Nash to Carol Kennicott herself, it also indicates a changing view of Lewis's western hero. Here the shifting scenes of domestic life—the 'zigzag incalculability' of Fran's feminine moods, the 'surprising, uncharted emotions' of Sam when he discovers his wife is being unfaithful to him; this whole tragi-comic area of marital manners which Lewis handles so well—are supplemented by a series of acute observations on the fundamental nature of human relationships in an economic society;* and on the nature of that economic society itself. In fact, as Sam's auto factory is finally taken over by the Unit Automotive Company, the U.A.C., which, through its mass-production methods, will cheapen Sam's

* With what astonishment do some recent literary heroes of our 'individualistic' society discover that they are, or can be, people: their delight in this realization can be compared only to that of the Molière figure who discovered he was talking in prose. 'He was Somebody!' Sam Dodsworth thinks in his own moment of insight. . . . 'Not just the president of the Revelation, but in himself, in whatever surroundings.' His social personality has been, of course, that of Fran Dodsworth's husband.

pride, the 'Revelation,' and turn his 'Thunderbolt' into a sort of standardized cigar-lighter, the true outlines of the Middle-Class Empire are revealed in *Dodsworth* as they have never been revealed in Lewis's previous novels. For George F. Babbitt was never more than the unconscious dupe of the Zenith Traction Corporation. But now Sam Dodsworth himself, an industrial artist and economic ruler in his own right, feels as rootless and placeless amidst the automotive corporations and cartels as any unemployed mechanic. 'He had no longer the dignity of a craftsman. He made nothing; he meant nothing; he was no longer Samuel Dodsworth, but merely part of a crowd vigorously pushing one another toward nowhere.' Now, indeed, the shaft of the Plymouth National Bank Building, its unbroken vertical lines aspiring upwards like a cathedral, is 'as lone and contemptuous of friendly human efforts as a forgotten tower on the Siberian steppes.' How was it, Sam thinks, that his America, which had once been so surely and comfortably in his hand, had slipped away? He was not happy, Lewis adds, when he let himself think about it abstractly—'But he was extremely well trained from his first days in Zenith High School, in not letting himself do anything so destructive as abstract thinking.' In the moment of his final isolation and suffering—that is, when his wife, his home and his work are 'lost forever' as he now realizes—Lewis's American man is deprived of the one immemorial recourse of suffering: the capacity to understand what one can't control.

In the illumination that *Dodsworth* throws on its central figure, then, it is one of the most thoughtful and mature of Lewis's realistic novels.* In his next novel, too, the *Ann*

* The sometimes inadequate treatment of American literature by even the best of our cultural historians is displayed by the Beards' characterization of *Dodsworth* (in their *America in Midpassage*) as a 'mild lampoon.'

Vickers of 1933, Lewis sets up a new heroine who is apparently intended to be the counterpart of his most fully realized western man.

At any rate, Ann Vickers herself, independent, capable, and decent, is a very different person from the ambitious Fran Dodsworth or the scatter-brained Carol Kennicott. It is interesting, also, while Ann belongs to Lewis's 'rackety and adventurous people,' as opposed to the steady folk with their 'fear of living,' that she is actually the first Lewis figure who is not only not ashamed of her provincial origins but who has profited by them. After childhood, to be sure, she too, as Lewis says—'like most Americans who go from Main Street to Fifth Avenue or Michigan Avenue or Market Street'—has little interest in her home town of Waubanakee, Illinois:

> Yet that small town and its ways, and all her father's principles of living, entered into everything she was to do in life. Sobriety, honest work, paying his debts, loyalty to his mate and to his friends, disdain of unearned rewards . . . and a pride that would let him neither cringe nor bully, these were her father's code, and in a New York where spongers and sycophants and gayly lying people, pretty little people, little playing people, were not unknown even among social workers and scientists, that code haunted her, and she was not sorry or Freudian about it.

In New York, in other words, Ann, who has also indulged in the 'terrible travail' of abstract thinking and is one of the first Lewis heroines to read with any seriousness of purpose, or maybe even to read at all—in New York Ann attempts to pick up a little more than the mannerisms and clichés of the artistic life. As well as being a study of her intellectual emancipation, *Ann Vickers* is certainly intended to portray the emotional emancipation of the new

Lewis woman. Having transcended the usual moral boundaries of the Middle-Class Empire, Ann has an illegitimate baby in addition to several illicit love affairs—indeed, if, very early also, Ann has decided that she wants the essence of love and not its husk, she comes to realize that 'the flesh is not the foe, but the interpreter of love.' And the novel is full of curiously frank discussions of the flesh and such deviations of the flesh as the nymphomaniacs and lesbians, with their 'glossy, warm scent' and their 'sickening tenderness,' whom Ann encounters in her search for social justice.

But it is the search that is at the center of *Ann Vickers.* And here, too, in the outward career of his heroine: her early lessons from a Socialist shoemaker, her first contact with the working classes who teach her 'how much less the gentlewomanly caste know than French Canuck mill-hands about love, birth, weariness, hunger, job-hunting'; her activities with the Suffragettes and in the field of prison reform—in all of this Lewis approaches social and economic issues more directly and bluntly than he has at any time up to this point. As a matter of fact, Ann, becoming conversant with the life of that portion of the American population which is not putting over real-estate deals or manufacturing automobiles and which is living on considerably less than ten thousand dollars a year, almost becomes a radical. And this is the prelude to Lewis's most celebrated novel of social revolution.

It Can't Happen Here, in 1935, is the first novel of the new decade to allow Lewis the full play of his satirical imagination. (As a fully developed fantasy of a Fascist Dictatorship, *It Can't Happen Here* is in the direct line of *Babbitt* and *The Man Who Knew Coolidge.*) And how good—how brilliant—that imagination can be, now that Lewis has a proper target for his indignation and, dropping off the fashionable cynicism and speakeasy sophistication of the late twenties, lets himself go. From the opening scene of the novel, in which Mrs. Adelaide Tarr Grimmitch, the Unkies' Girl and renowned lyric poet of the nursery—

> All of the Roundies are resting in rows
> With roundies-roundies around their toes—

and a raging member of the D.A.R., addresses the Vermont Rotary on the subject of Discipline—Will Power—Character—and War:

> 'You've been telling us about how to secure peace, but come on, now, General—just among us Rotarians and Rotary Anns—'fess up! With your great experience, don't you honest, cross-your-heart, think that perhaps—just maybe—when a country has gone money-mad, like all our labor unions and workmen, with their propaganda to hoist income taxes, so that the thrifty and industrious have to pay for the shiftless ne'er-do-wells, then maybe, to save their lazy souls and get some iron into them, a war might be a good thing?'—

to the account of 'Bishop Paul Peter Prang's' weekly radio talk which,

> coming from an airless closet, smelling of sacerdotal woolen union suits, in Persepolis, Indiana . . . leapt to the farthest stars . . . circled the world at 186,000 miles a second—a million miles while you stopped to scratch—

or to the description of Buzz Windrip's presidential campaign, *It Can't Happen Here* is among the most eloquent and savage of Lewis's novels.

And among the best-informed. If Sam Dodsworth's America had slipped out of his hands some years before he had realized it, this is certainly a new America, a new scene in Lewis's work, and practically a new country. Has the Horatio Alger tradition, from rags to Rockefellers, gone clean out of the society it had dominated, as Lewis's Doremus Jessup concludes? At any rate, this is now a society that has 'maybe twenty-eight million on relief, and beginning to get ugly.' No American whose fathers have lived in the country for over two generations, Doremus also believes, 'is so utterly different from any other American.' Yet this is also a country that is ridden by group antagonisms and racial prejudices; that almost seems to be constituted of Kikes, Wops, Niggers, Hunkies, and Chinks; of dirty foreigners, labor racketeers, corrupt politicians, and a tiny minority of pure Economic Nordics who, like the Louis Rotenstern of the novel, are not only 100 per cent American but 'exact 40 per cent of chauvinistic interest on top of the principal.' Here the rigid class distinctions of Lewis's earlier work have become the actual lines of class warfare; the industrial ruling class, faced with an industrial crisis, have decided what they want; and a society that has been nourished on the radio and the comics is ripe for the earthy humor, the calculated sadism, and the unflinching capitalism of its own Buzz Windrip.

Nor is Lewis content with establishing this diagram of the economic structure and cultural conflicts of a corporate United States. In Doremus Jessup, the old-fashioned Vermont editor whom Lewis places in opposition to Buzz Windrip, there is an apparent resurgence of Lewis's democratic beliefs, and a much more explicit statement of the values and convictions that have determined his own work.

Yet, as admirable as *It Can't Happen Here* is in these respects, the novel becomes progressively more disappointing; while Doremus himself is a curious sort of auctorial spokesman. Does he accept the fact that the eternal enemy is the 'conservative manipulators of privilege,' while the persecution of any minority, such as the Jews, is always 'the scientific measure of the cruelty and silliness of the régime under which they live'? Doremus comes to admit his own moral responsibility in allowing such persecution—and the consequent necessity of overthrowing the Fascist Dictatorship. Yet, is any form of violence, or any revolution, including the American Revolution, really worth the cost? Was there any great historical preacher, prophet, or reformer, except possibly Brigham Young, 'who not only turned the Utah desert into an Eden but made it pay,' who was not in the end merely a rabble-rouser?

> 'Was it just possible, indeed [says Doremus], that the most vigorous and boldest idealists have been the worst enemies of human progress instead of its greatest creators? Possible that plain men with the humble trait of minding their own business will rank higher in the heavenly hierarchy than all the plumed souls who have shoved their way in among the masses and insisted on saving them?'

Perhaps it is no wonder that Doremus, afflicted with these sentiments and unable to become an active revolutionary because he has a family to support and only twenty thousand dollars of capital to live on, spends most of his time in a concentration camp. Nor are the 'masses' of *It Can't Happen Here,* during the last half of the novel, very grateful to the plumed souls who take a more active part in saving them. In fact, Shad Ledue, the hired man whom Doremus has been trying to educate, turns into a provincial fuehrer; while the Socialist worker, John Pollikop, conducts an endless and futile dialectical dispute with the Communist worker, Karl Pascal; and it is actually the urban proletariat—the horde of 'Manhattan peasants' whom Doremus considers to be 'most facile material for any rabble-rouser'—who become the backbone of Buzz Windrip's fascism. So, too, the anti-fascist movement of Walt Trowbridge, the solid, practical midwestern politician who, in Lewis's version of history, finally rescues the country from its peril, almost automatically excludes any members of the lower classes, as well as any radicals or political thinkers. Just as *It Can't Happen Here* clearly sets out to express the fundamental values of Lewis, so it finally reveals the limited nature of those values; intellectual and spiritual, as well as purely sociological.

What *It Can't Happen Here* actually demonstrates—after having outlined a fundamental social maladjustment of its time, and a consequent perversion of the life forces of the time—is Lewis's inability to deal with this situation, or to appreciate its implications in terms of his own country. If the novel's virtue is in its Americanization of the European patterns of social crisis, its final and almost appalling limitation is the degree to which it is 'American': in the sense of Lewis's America, I mean, always within the strait limits of the Middle-Class Empire. For here, finally, the native equivalent of the Nazi Terror, with all its barbaric reversions, becomes a sort of bad joke. And here the democratic faith itself, as Lewis views it, becomes a kind of dubious game. The note of genuine social protest, or merely of human dignity in the face of social tragedy, is hardly to be found in the later pages of *It Can't Happen Here*.*

* It is probably not necessary to compare Lewis's narrative with the tradition of modern revolutionary novels, from the works of Malraux, Silone, or Koestler to those of Dos Passos and Hemingway, to make this point clear.

What *is* here, though, is a continuous and remarkable sympathy for all the reasons and emotional inhibitions which allow respectable people to accept outrageous social conditions which they do not understand, and which they do not want to understand. Doremus Jessup, musing about his 'rugged individuals,' never measures up to their stature—or to that of any old-fashioned countryman in the pages of, say, Willa Cather or Sherwood Anderson. But Doremus is merely another variation on the whole line of Lewis's ineffectual social dissenters; and very similarly, if, as Lewis says, the central theme of *It Can't Happen Here* is 'Revolution in terms of Rotary,' the novel's solution appears to be Counter-Revolution in terms of Rotary.

You may notice that while Lewis has finally taken a more rigorous view of the socio-economic patterns of his own society—the society of the middle nineteen-thirties which was just then in the throes of economic unrest and social change—he has taken this view in a curiously modulated way. Through his portrait of a partly imaginary American scene, he can ignore the actual American scene; and through the presentation of a more remote social crisis he can avoid the exigencies of an immediate social crisis. At any rate, there is barely a mention here of the forces of social reform that were actually present and operating in the United States during these years—they are, indeed, dismissed with something close to ridicule—and if *Babbitt* was a literary fantasy that pointed to a more immediate sort of reality, *It Can't Happen Here* is a fantasy that leads only into the realms of whimsy. . . . It is essential to appreciate these factors, in order to follow the otherwise curious, if not extraordinary, direction which Lewis's career takes in his last novel of the nineteen-thirties—*The Prodigal Parents,* in 1938.

Meanwhile, in 1934, Lewis had written *Work of Art,* an

almost equally strange document. For, in the very midst of the depression years, when the work of practically every other first-rank American writer, including the aesthetes and expatriates, was beginning to reflect the pressures of the new age, Lewis has concocted a perfect Success Story of the nineteen-twenties.* At least the story of Myron and Ora Teagle is intended to be a parable of business and the arts in the United States. Myron's consuming ambition is to manage a Perfect Hotel, while Ora's is to write a Perfect Novel; and from the start of the novel Ora is the 'villain,' while Myron is again one of Lewis's 'good' heroes. . . . The main stress of *Work of Art* is on Myron's 'Vision': his long and assiduous struggle in the hotel business ("Cut the costs, my boy, cut the costs, cut the horrid costs") and his final triumph in the Black Thread Inn in Connecticut.

One must add that Lewis is very imaginative about the technics of hotel management. Within the perfectly sound-proofed, insulated, and air-conditioned chambers of the Perfect Hotel—this Triumph of Gadgetry, this Nirvana of Indirect Lighting, for the wayfarers and the wanderers of a medium-priced civilization—there are few echoes, not merely of the disturbed world of the nineteen-thirties, but of the real world of the nineteen-twenties.

Yet it is strange that Lewis hardly allows his native hero to enjoy the fruits of his industry. Rather like Moses, Myron Teagle has only a glimpse of the promised land of materialism. At the exact climax of his career, the Black Thread Inn is destroyed by a scandal and Myron is pushed out by those forces of Big Business whose bold philosopher, whose scientific entrepreneur, and whose humble

* It is interesting that a year later, in 1935, Lewis put out his *Selected Short Stories*—stories, selected from his obviously commercial work, which reflect the prevailing values of the nineteen-twenties in their most extreme and vulgar form.

servant he has been. Moreover, it is Ora Teagle, the second-rate artist, the irresponsible dilettante and bohemian whom Myron has been forced to support throughout most of his life and who is apparently Lewis's own figurehead of the Creative Life in America—it is Ora Teagle who becomes a great financial success by stepping from one fraud to another. . . . If there is something perverse in Lewis's return to the materialistic dream of the nineteen-twenties in the middle of the decade which turned that dream into a nightmare, there is also a curiously ambiguous quality in the nature of the return.

For *Work of Art is* a Horatio Alger tale which appeared just at the historical point when the tradition of rags to Rockefellers had vanished, as Lewis says—or had become more like a tradition of Rockefellers to rags. But this is an uneasy, a disturbed, an almost schizophrenic Horatio Alger tale, as though its author were setting up and then destroying his own framework of values through a divided emotional compulsion. In the later history of Myron Teagle's career, too—the nervous collapse of Lewis's hero after the failure of his hotel and the steadily descending course of his life into the mercantile oblivion of the provinces—there is certainly an element of retribution and purification through suffering. . . . But the author's doubts and conflicts which are at the base of both *It Can't Happen Here* and *Work of Art,* which are represented, that is, both in Lewis's boldest attempt to meet the new age of the nineteen-thirties and in his almost desperate attempt to return to the old age of the nineteen-twenties: all these familiar literary symptoms of a divided point of view, a moral confusion, a blind thrashing about, will disappear in the perfect tranquillity, the aesthetic peace and oblivion of *The Prodigal Parents* itself.

Frederick William Cornplow, to be sure, opens the

novel as another typical Lewis figure. 'Like most Americans, he was perfectly democratic, except, perhaps, as regards social standing, wealth, political power, and club membership.' And like most Americans—or anyhow like most of Sinclair Lewis's Americans—Frederick William lives in a home which is distasteful to him, has children whom he ignores except when he is nagging at them, a wife who is more or less of a domestic mediocrity, and a business life selling autos in Sachem Falls, New York, that is marked by almost continuous moods of anxiety or moments of actual revulsion. 'It had been with the tension of a crusade that he had engaged himself in loving like a brother anybody who had $1100 for a car. He was suddenly and inexplicably weary.' * So he has also Babbitt's dream of Escape, Adventure, New Horizons—a dream of retiring and really enjoying himself with 'a few crazy things' like horses and music and travel, although meanwhile his new car is his only legitimate source of pleasure and driving at seventy miles an hour his only emotional outlet. As a lineal descendant of the House of Babbitt, Frederick William Cornplow hardly ever *talks* to anybody. Instead he 'wails' and 'snaps' and 'howls' and 'implores.' Indeed, just as he is the last Lewis hero of the nineteen-thirties, so he is the epitome of all those wailing, snapping, howling, and beseeching citizens—those babbling, chattering, pushing, and panting citizens—of the Middle-Class Empire in the great trading Republic of the West.

But this Lewis hero is now living in a world 'where the

* 'Inexplicably,' that is to say, to Fred Cornplow himself; and we realize again the brilliance of Lewis's best cultural insights in a reference like this one. . . . For the lack of any genuine warmth or affection that is so noticeable in the middle-middle areas of American life may be directly related, of course, to the enforced and stylized affection of our commercial behavior.

commonplaces of jobs and rent and food'—the commonplaces which have represented the extreme aspirations and the farthest reaches of the Middle-Class Empire—have also become 'as difficult as winning an empire.' And just as *It Can't Happen Here* presented the imaginary social scene of the nineteen-thirties, so *The Prodigal Parents,* at last, at almost the end of the decade, but with a dreadful certainty, presents the actual scene. I mean the contemporary scene of actual unemployment, social unrest, and political reform: this entire troubled American scene which Lewis has consistently avoided throughout his writing of the decade—which he has retreated in back of and which he has moved ahead of. . . . And it is Frederick William Cornplow who discovers that his son has been taken over by the radicals, that his daughter is in the clutches of a Freudian doctor, that his country relatives, the Tilleys, have become shiftless members of a New Deal resettlement project ('Gov'ment owes everybody a living, don't it?'), and that almost every intellectual influence of the nineteen-thirties, as well as every form of political activity, has been designed to mislead and corrupt the younger generation and to destroy the foundations of his own older American world. It is Lewis's Cornplow who first realizes that the Communists are making the whole country into a WPA and who first fully appreciates the true nature of Eugene Silga, the young labor organizer:

> He was neat and quiet-voiced . . . and he was to the world of Frederick Cornplow—to the world of Franklin and Emerson and Mark Twain, of Willa Cather and William Allen White—as dangerous as a rattlesnake.

No wonder, then, in this moment of national peril, and in the face of an historical crisis that grows steadily more menacing in the novel, that Frederick William Cornplow becomes the only remaining source of human stability in a society that has gone haywire. (It is Cornplow who saves his daughter from the psychiatrist and rescues his son from alcoholism and radicalism simultaneously.) * No wonder that Cornplow steadily grows in stature until he takes on a mythical sort of grandeur. Just as he has been taken into the company of Franklin, Emerson, and Twain, among the immortals of local history, he is soon linked with the greatest achievements of all history:

> When Fred Cornplow was an Egyptian, it was he who planned the pyramids, conciliated the mad pharaohs. . . . In the days when he was called a Roman Citizen, he was a centurion and he conquered Syria. . . . As Frederick Abbott Cornplow, in the bright Dark Ages, he developed agriculture and the use of building stone; later, as a captain under Cromwell, he helped tame the political power of the ecclesiastics. The American Civil War was not fought between General Grant and General Lee, but between Private Fred Cornplow of Massachusetts and Private Ed Cornplow of Alabama; and a few years later it was they who created bribery and railroads and gave all their loot to science.
>
> From Fred Cornplow's family, between B.C. 1937 and A.D. 1937, there came, despite an occasional aristocratic Byron or an infrequent proletarian John Bunyan, nearly all the medical researchers, the discoverers of better varieties of wheat, the poets, the builders, the singers, the captains of great ships. . . .
>
> He is the eternal bourgeois, the bourjoyce, the burgher, the Middle Class whom the Bolsheviks hate and imitate, whom the English love and deprecate, and who is most of

* The alcoholic 'cure' which Lewis's hero uses here, incidentally, is almost identical with that which Mr. Wrenn employed in 1914, to save a drunken friend.

> the population worth considering in France and Germany and these United States.
>
> He is Fred Cornplow; and when he changes his mind, that crisis is weightier than Waterloo or Thermopylae.

— For who in the world, as Lewis adds, has ever been more important than Fred Cornplow? — 'the eternal doer, equally depended upon—and equally hated—by the savage mob and the insolent nobility.' What could be clearer than the fact that Lewis's familiar protagonist—the standardized middle-class man who has been cut off from both the abiding human impulses of the 'mob' and whatever human grace has been achieved by a 'nobility': that this latest victim of history's whirl has become history's only hero? And that all time and all space have become nothing but a middle-class moment in this bourjoyce fantasy of the universe, while mankind is defined as an Eternal Cornplow?

This is One World with a vengeance—from the origins of the universe to the creation of the Duplex Trailer. There is an element of truth here, of course. To paraphrase Mark Twain's remark, perhaps the worst that could be said of Lewis's middle-class man is that he also belongs to the human race. But surely the Middle-Class Empire is one of the most limited phases of the innumerable phases of history—and not only of world history but of American history—and not only with respect to its time span but also as to its cultural values and aspirations. . . . Furthermore, what has distinguished Lewis's own work as a whole has been the narrow view he has taken of even that narrow orbit of history: the fact that he has presented the worst possible examples of his own theme.

Yet the actual limitations of Lewis's literary world do much to explain the final apotheosis of that world: as a matter of fact, they make it almost inevitable. Even in *Dodsworth* and *Ann Vickers* the accent on wealth, on material possessions, and on those polished 'aristocrats' of Lewis's is the final as it was the initial note of Lewis's literary scene. (Just so, the James Buck Titus of *It Can't Happen Here,* equally rich and suave—'as near to a country squire as one may find in America'—is at once the only major figure in the novel who hasn't the slightest interest in the revolutionary struggle and the one whom Lewis views with the least qualms.) And Lewis's aristocrats differ merely in degree from his middle-class figures, and not in kind. They have more money, more social position, more culture. But their culture and their social position are simply used to proclaim the fact that they have money.

There are really no aristocrats in Lewis's work, nor is there, as in Dreiser, or Willa Cather, or Thomas Wolfe, any convincing middle-class aristocracy. Neither, on the opposite side of the social scale, does Lewis attempt to project a single working-class figure of any dimension; while in the entire body of work by this major critic of middle-class manners in the United States, from Carol Kennicott to Doremus Jessup, there is hardly an effective or even attractive social rebel. Actually, of course, this writer whose historical position is that of having established the 'classes' in American literature, deals only with the establishment of the middle class in American literature—with that 'bourgeois colony' which, up to 1917, as Lewis says in a curious historical inversion, 'was the only America,' or which, anyhow, after 1917, considered itself as the only America. It is interesting to notice the narrow social stratification of this purely middle-class cosmos of Lewis. There are no musicians, dancers, painters, poets, or sculptors of consequence in Lewis's work. The

Ora Teagle of *Work of Art,* who is the only full-length study of a writer, and who does at least write one honest novel—a novel which is 'financially unnecessary,' and which convinces Ora of the futility of serious writing—is indeed Lewis's prototype of the artist in America. Furthermore, from the Raymond P. Wutherspoon of *Main Street* to the Lycurgus Watts of *Dodsworth,* are there any 'intellectuals' in Lewis's work who are not also by inference dilettanti or actual perverts—that is, when they are not 'radicals' and dangerous as rattlesnakes?

No, early and late, as I say, the only true hero of Lewis is the scientist. But in *Arrowsmith,* too, we saw not merely the inadequate nature of Lewis's 'scientific truth,' but also his failure to project that view of a native life and character which he had linked with this ideal. Right there was the very epitome of that petty, nagging, backbiting, provincial existence which the western scene seems to be identified with in Lewis's mind when it isn't a stereotype of the frontier or a ghastly vision of suburban standardization. So, too, the town of 'Catawba' in Lewis's novels, the up-state town of Winnemac which is intended to represent the best features of an older rural and democratic society, is actually a ghost town. . . . In the whole range of Lewis's work, where is there a view of life which could sustain a novelist's belief in life, or even in his own work? Perhaps this helps to explain the increasingly curious view that Lewis has taken of the eastern metropolis itself: the accumulating references to the bohemians and anarchists, the 'intellectual parasites' and 'one hundred per cent mongrels' who have become the typical inhabitants of the metropolis. ('Russian Jews in London clothes,' as Lewis tells us in *Dodsworth,* 'going to Italian restaurants with Greek waiters and African music. . . .')

In these tones of superstition, as well as in his earlier

tones of naïve yearning, Lewis clearly shows his own lack of cultural roots or of any historical perspective. The country people and the city people of his tales are neither true country people nor true city people. Just as every extreme of Lewis's inner world has been eliminated, and the whole gamut of human feeling has been reduced to what you might call the medium-priced emotions, so, in his whole outward scene also, the true poles of his society have been removed—or, more accurately, perhaps, have never been established. As we have now seen, though, the central dramatic conflict of Lewis's work is precisely the conflict of these inadequate—or missing—extremes: of a specious aristocracy and an almost invisible working class; of a romantic socialism and a visionary capitalism; of Westerners who are trying above all to be Easterners and of Easterners who in spite of everything are exactly like Westerners. . . .

Yet, without these cultural roots or abiding human values—without a sense of either the flesh or of the mind—perpetually oscillating between such extremes, none of which are satisfactory, none of which are really imagined or felt, none of which are actually *there,* how can this writer do otherwise? Marked by a thin past and a narrow future, Lewis is indeed the Last Provincial of our letters: a provincial who wanders, homeless, between a barren and deteriorating hinterland and an increasingly appalling industrial order—a hinterland with which he feels no ties, an industrial order with which he cannot come to grips.

And it is interesting to realize just how little of the 'real' United States is in the work of a writer who is so full of its manners, habits, and idioms.

I mean, of course, the United States which is actually forming and determining Lewis's whole literary world: the U.S.A. of the Corporations and the Cartels, as well as of the factories, the mines, and the slums, which is the source and conditioning factor of Lewis's Middle-Class Empire and his Economic Man. If Lewis's work is in the literary tradition of Frank Norris, Theodore Dreiser, or Upton Sinclair, what a limited view it gives us, after all, of the North American continent, and with what a tender and tardy sort of 'realism'! The U.A.C. of *Dodsworth*—that Unit Automotive Corporation—is the true *Deus ex machina* of Lewis's world, but, showing as he did all its consequences at the dawn of the nineteen-twenties, it was only at the outset of the nineteen-thirties, at the point when the God of the Machine was Himself temporarily out of order, that Lewis allowed himself to take another look at it. Perhaps the most violent and brutal example of Lewis's social satire in the later twenties was directed, in *Elmer Gantry,* against rural life and evangelical religion. Just as Lewis has foreshortened the whole exterior scene of his people's activity, so he ignores the basic determinants of the life which surrounds them. The real institutions of finance-capitalism lie outside his world: a world of continuously worse results and no causes.

Thus the writer, who most clearly shows the effects of the new industrialism in the United States, least understands it, or has the least inclination to understand it.*

* In this connection it is interesting to notice the series of articles Lewis wrote on the textile strike in Marion, North Carolina, as early as 1929, and reprinted in the pamphlet called *Cheap and Contented Labor.* Here, certainly, in barely thirty-two pages, is a résumé of the whole industrial change in America from the descriptions of mill-workers' houses to the examples of industrial justice in the southern mill towns. 'In these towns, the mills control the banks, the banks control the loans to the small businessmen, the small businessmen are the best customers of the professional men—even when the latter are professional men of God—and so the mills can back up the whole human train down to the clerical caboose.'

Yet there is barely the slightest reflection of these articles in Lewis's subsequent novels, or anything to indicate that he considered that this, too, was part of the American scene.

But in the clear pattern of Lewis's values—a pattern that is finally almost a spiritual blueprint in itself, without deviations or ambiguous areas—things can hardly turn out very differently. This is a literary world where the conflicts of 'Society' take precedence over the intimations of social conflict, where it is more important to *be* a middle-class aristocrat than to understand the nature of the middle-class rulers of America.

All through Lewis's work we may trace a curious transformation of that earlier and more intricate conflict of 'East' and 'West' which has marked the national letters. Perhaps never before has the familiar and uneasy artistic search for the cultivated and aristocratic 'eastern' life been so swiftly and surely transposed into the search for financial security and the material consequences of wealth. But what Lewis has done is to *bourgeoisize* this whole cultural conflict too; to make it completely middle-class, to remove both the upper and lower limits of this search—to reduce it all again to another formula where the 'East' simply means a little more money and the 'West' a little less money: where the Easterners are the people who have got the money, and the Westerners are the people who are going to get the money.

So Zenith is Lewis's true home, after all; Zenith, which is in itself an in-between world, a by-product of the cartels, a psychological suburb of the new money society in America which lives on financial sufferance as well as on the nationally advertised brands—this middle world of derived goods and derived values which is actually the whole world of Lewis's literary achievement. Perhaps we can now appreciate the fascination of hotel life for Lewis, from the Una Golden of *The Job* who found her salvation in running the White Line Chain to the Myron Teagle of *Work of Art* whose lifelong aspiration is to manage the Perfect Inn. To Zenith's Child, at any rate, a good hotel is all that home should be. . . .

Nor is it as difficult as it might seem for Lewis to move from the Zenith of 1920 to the New Zenith of 1940. The fact that the picture of George F. Babbitt's town was a fantasy of horror, a vision of the mechanized inferno—that Lewis neglected or ignored the residual resources of a democratic society as well as the natural human resistance to having human life stamped, labeled, and packaged—makes it so much easier, indeed, for the picture of Frederick William Cornplow's cosmos to become a fantasy of bliss. . . . Doesn't the artistic secret of this complete bourjoyce lie precisely in the fact that, just *because* Lewis's sense of reality is so limited, his fantasy life can be so varied, so flexible and so irresponsible—can move so easily from a ghastly notion of the future to a childlike notion of the past?

In a rather gruesome way it is logical that *The Prodigal Parents* should have a warmth and vitality that have been largely missing from Lewis's work since the early twenties. Lewis cares about these people as, with the exception of Sam Dodsworth, he hasn't cared about anybody since George F. Babbitt. And why not? For, safely ensconced now in this blind, dark, close bourgeois womb of time, he can move about in perfect ease and comfort. And in the final moments of Frederick William Cornplow's apotheosis, at the point when the 'little round man at the desk' has become as fully the world's philosopher as the world's doer, Lewis's hero's 'Mind Your Own Business Association'—the equal partners of which are his own ignorance of, and his blind indifference to, the world outside of him—turns into a sort of rationale of the Higher Intelligence. 'I guess those are the real wars—men against women—

parents against children,' Cornplow says, 'and not all this monkey business in Europe.'

And with the docile and devoted Hazel Cornplow of *The Prodigal Parents,* Fred Cornplow's wife who has become in turn a kind of hinterland goddess of the hearth, a Myra Babbitt with a halo, even the Revolt of the Women in Lewis's novels—that abortive revolt of those witless women who have nevertheless been the most persistent source of irritation in Lewis's literary cosmos: even this last possible source of danger to the Middle-Class Empire seems to have been eliminated.

At last the Lewis hero may enjoy his European trip in perfect ease and comfort: a Europe in which a Spanish Civil War or a Nazi Dictatorship can be viewed as a passing 'incident'; and a trip which leaves far behind it the most remote intimations of trouble in America.

5. *The Land of Faery*

'UNTIL THE NINETEENTH CENTURY, actors were classed as Rogues and Vagrants,' says the inscription of Lewis's next novel. 'They were outside of respectable society—like Kings—and I am not sure but that this was better for their art and their happiness. . . .' It is interesting that the *Bethel Merriday* of 1940 should deal with the theatrical world. And although Lewis's rogues and vagrants still appear pre-eminently respectable, there is no doubt they are outside of their society.

As a matter of fact, Lewis consolidates his position here: he moves from an involuntary land of make-believe to a voluntary one:

> Five months after the six-year-old Bethel gave her imitation of the old lady, the Black Shirts marched bravely into the maws of the movie cameras in Rome, and five months after that, Hitler bounded out of a Munich beer garden. But perhaps it was as important that at this time John Barrymore was playing *Hamlet* and Pauline Lord *Anna Christie* and the Theatre Guild producing *Back to Methuselah.*

Now all the world's a stage, where everything is viewed, not only as illusion, but as an entertaining illusion, while that melancholy picture of 'human crimes and misfortunes'—history itself—may serve to while away an interval between the acts.

For *Bethel Merriday* actually marks a deliberate and sustained attempt to reduce everything outside of the theater to inferior play-acting. 'They were all serious children,' Lewis tells us about Bethel's troupe—'very childish, very serious, and apparently the only people still existent, in a world of Hitler and Buchmanism, who enjoyed life. At every mistake, at every dropped line, they laughed and laughed together.' Was a planet just then in tears? At least Lewis's laughter is truly 'unembittered,' while America has become a nation of one hundred and thirty million Neros. And in this final realization of the Free Life—'all magic and madness'—even the 'talk' which has been the bugaboo of Lewis's depictions of the Intellectual Life has become bearable. 'It dealt entirely with the theatre.'

Notice also the singularly remote quality of Lewis's theatrical world itself. The great achievement of Bethel's company—an achievement around which the novel is centered—is the production of *Romeo and Juliet.* The private lives of Lewis's figures are rigorously set, not only outside of the world of Hitler and Buchmanism, but almost outside of the whole modern age. 'In the house was electricity; Mr. Merriday was reading about the tear-gas bombing of strikers in the aeroplane industry. . . . But Bethel and Charley sat on a porch in New England and . . . no one could have told them from their grandparents.' In personal terms also the secret of Bethel's success as an actress isn't her knowledge of the world or her emotional experiences ('all those amateurs–they spend too much time working up an artificial sex stimulation'), but merely her infinite capacity to daydream:

> Like all artists—all painters, all musicians, all poets, even some of those plodding recorders, the novelists—actors are glorious children, with a child's unwearied delight in the same story over again, and the child's ability to make dragons grow in a suburban garden.

What is interesting is that a novel devoted with such an absolute and frightening simplicity to the 'stage' should in the end reveal so little about the stage.* Probably Bethel's deepest fear–that she will remain an eternal amateur, that she will only 'play at playing'–is based on her only genuine insight. But *Bethel Merriday* is by far the poorest of Lewis's late novels. Almost as though he were rebounding with a new vigor from this extreme of his fantasy life, Lewis's next two books are marked by a fresh and remarkable vitality.

In any case the Peony Jackson of *Gideon Planish,* in 1943, with her infantile morals, her adolescent values, and

* Compare Bethel, for example, with the Esther Jack of Thomas Wolfe's *The Web and the Rock,* or, in a closely related art, the Thea Kronborg of Willa Cather's *The Song of the Lark.* In view of Lewis's own lifelong interest in the stage, it is hard to understand how his Civil War play, *The Jayhawker,* written in collaboration with Lloyd Lewis in 1935, could be *quite* so poor—unless, that is, one also understands that even Lewis's feeling for the theater is in its own way a sort of fantasy of a fantasy world.

her mature body, is one of Lewis's most engaging if not altogether commendable heroines. What Peony wants out of life may not be very interesting, but the way she gets it is. As her wiles first entice and then trap poor, pompous Professor Planish, you may realize, almost for the first time in Lewis's work, the charms as well as the ironical tortures of the flesh. And as Peony starts her 'Gidjums' going, and Gideon leaves his academic position to become a rising social worker in Des Moines and Chicago, an executive of 'social reform' in New York, and a director of 'Dynamos of Democratic Action' in Washington, U.S.A.—you feel the full extent of Gideon Planish's passion for his Peony, and the destructive power of the flesh.

For the theme which emerges from all the fantastic nonsense of *Gideon Planish's* larger scene, cast as the novel is in the lunatic fringe of political action during the nineteen-thirties, is another variation on Lewis's familiar American Success Story. But for Lewis it is a very different variation.

The sensuous appeal of Peony is matched by her insatiable desire to 'get ahead,' and her ambition to glide in that 'metropolitan stream of elegance, excitement, and fame' is matched only by her extravagance and bad taste. (The descriptions of Peony's various and always more expensive apartments are among the best of Lewis's visual reports on the American scene.) When the Planishes make the grade and become the intimates of the lords of the economic creation, and as the Planishes' income steadily increases, and so do their expenses, and Peony sings more exuberantly and only her 'Gidjums' is bewildered, *Gideon Planish* also presents some of Lewis's best satiric portraits: among others, those of William T. Knife, the Okey-Dokey King, or Winifred Homeward, the Talking

Woman, or Colonel Charles B. Marduc's group of promising young publicity men:

> Each of them allowed himself daily exactly twenty-seven cigarettes—carried in a quiet silver case—with two highballs, two cocktails, three cups of coffee, one Bromo Seltzer, and fifteen minutes of sharp and detestable exercise. They averaged 1½ spirited minutes of love per week, one rather unsatisfactory adultery per year, and one wife—always from a Good Family, usually a dark pretty girl whom you could never quite remember.

And when Doctor Planish finally comes to recognize the meaning of 'the world of fame and philanthrobbery,' and his own status amongst these native demagogues and fortune-hunters; when Planish begins to understand 'how dead men feel,' and Peony, still exulting, still driving him on, begins to grow increasingly indifferent to what his feelings are—in all this, *Gideon Planish* doesn't omit the implication of the Planishes' moral, as well as sexual, corruption: that whole darker side of human nature which up to this point has never been adequately represented in Lewis's work.

However, the earlier cultural observations of *Gideon Planish*—the description of Maple Grove, which had leaped from crossroad hamlet to small city 'without ever having had the leisure to stop and be merely a pleasant village,' or of Ipswich, which was 'exactly like Chicago, except that it was only one two-hundred-and-fiftieth as large': these, also, show a deeper concern with what has been happening to the State of Winnemac. This is our introduction to the novel which marks the final return of Lewis to that midwestern scene which has been the real battleground of his work, the source of his divided emotions and the object of so much hidden as well as obvious conflict. And both the central figure and the milieu of *Cass Timberlane,* in 1945, represent Lewis's most sustained and mature attempt to record the virtues of a purely western way of life.

Judge Cass Timberlane himself surely typifies Lewis's highest order of native man in his background and descent as well as in his profession. In the security of inherited wealth and social position and in his larger indifference to wealth and social position, he is a cut above Sam Dodsworth; he is almost the *passive* as against the active middle-class aristocrat; and almost for the first time Lewis is able to visualize an aristocracy that is established rather than an aristocracy on the make.* There is little doubt as to the quality of Cass Timberlane's interest in his native city of Grand Republic: his 'ancestral and proprietary right' to it, and his paternal and loving hopes for it:

> 'It's just that I have some kind of an unformulated ideal that I want to be identified with Grand Republic—help in setting up a few stones in what may be a new Athens. It's this northern country—you know, stark and clean—and the brilliant lakes and the tremendous prairies to the westward—it may be a new kind of land for a new kind of people, and it's scarcely even started yet.'

And in the panoramic view of Grand Republic which forms the background of the novel, such portraits as that of Boone Havock, whose success as a steel baron is due 'less to his knowledge of how to handle steel than to his knowledge of how to battle with steel-workers'; or of those 'fine, big, bouncing hussars' who are known to the ribald as the Zebra Sisters; or of Lilian Drover to whom, by con-

* A genuine *haute bourgeoisie,* that is, as against Lewis's aggressive and pushing *petit bourgeoisie* who consider themselves *haute bourgeoisie.*

trast, the whole business of sex 'had become a horror related to dark bedrooms and loud breathing'; or of Don Pennloss who 'quarreled or made love or said the bacon was good or denounced the unions in exactly the same basso'; or of Rose Pennloss who wants to know just what is a woman to do

> who is still good-looking at thirty-six but not beautiful enough to make a career of it, clever enough to know she wouldn't be clever on any job, aware, through reading, of all the glamor and luxuries of life but with no money for them and no rich relatives to murder, active and yet contemptuous of amateur charities and artistic trifling and exhibitionistic sports, untrained in anything worth fifteen dollars a week on the labor market and not even, after years of marriage, a competent cook or nurse, no longer in love with her husband and bored by everything he does—and he always does it!—and yet unwilling to have the thrill of being vengeful toward him or of hurting him intentionally, liking other men but not lecherous nor fond of taking risks, possessing a successful daughter and too interested in her to desert her—just what is this typical upper-middle-middle-class American Wife to do?

—certainly, in such portraits as these, Lewis is at last expressing something of the variety and mystery of that ordinary middle-western life which has been so largely ignored in his work, and which, even in the *Main Street,* upon whose heroine Rose Pennloss is now in a sense delivering a final verdict, was viewed within such a narrow framework of values.

It is worth mentioning that Lewis has located the city of Grand Republic in Minnesota rather than in that appalling chain-state of Winnemac—that in *Cass Timberlane* he has completed the whole cycle of East and West which we have been tracing and has come back full-circle to his earliest origins. . . . And yet it is a curious cycle, as we have seen, and, for all of the novel's merits, a somewhat ambiguous return.

Although Cass does belong to that older western tradition which is 'informal but not rackety,' it is also a middle-western scene where, in Cass's set, which is largely above the seven-thousand-dollar line, it is 'as obligatory to dress for party dinners as in London.' Unlike London, however, Lewis's Midwest views the 'universal multiple revolution, just then, in the early nineteen-forties, from sulfa drugs and surrealism and semantics to Hitler' with complete and sublime indifference—an indifference that is marked, perhaps, when the fact of this revolution becomes inescapable, by just the slightest tinge of irritation. 'Oh, curse the luck,' says Cass when the news of Pearl Harbor bursts upon his honeymoon. It is a Midwest which shares Lewis's now firmly established conviction that love—married love—conquers all, and that the fate of Europe, as Cass decides, must be subordinated to the fate of his own marriage:

> If the world of the twentieth century, he vowed, cannot succeed in this one thing, married love, then it has committed suicide, all but the last moan, and whether Germany and France can live as neighbors is insignificant compared with whether Johan and Maria or Jean and Marie can live as lovers.

And finally this is a Midwest which has relegated all signs of its own troubles, as well as those foreign 'incidents,' to Lewis's new conception of a happy marriage as 'a blissfully shared community of ignorance.' It is true that Grand Republic has 'leaped from clumsy youth to senility without ever having had a dignified manhood,' and exists on western land that is almost exhausted, as Lewis says, from the uncouth robbery of forests and mines. Still wondering whether to become a ghost town or a living city, it is also marked by labor trouble, racial prejudice, and industrial unrest. Yet these elements are almost completely subordinated to the story of Cass, his 'half-tamed hawk of a girl,' and the hawk's little flights. And here it is difficult to understand just why the central love-story of the novel, developed as it is at the expense of every other theme in the novel, is so meretricious until one realizes that Lewis's Ginny Marsh is a postscript to his whole line of emancipated heroines: a last and more unpleasant figurehead of modern youth and of 'Young Revolution' who, through her disastrous extra-marital romance, is forced to receive her just deserts, and repents.

Thus, in the final accounting of *Cass Timberlane,* Lewis's world is probably not well lost for love. But it is undoubtedly well lost. 'Yep,' says the Governor Blizzard of *Gideon Planish,* 'I'm reverting to Main Street with some of the fastest reversion you ever saw.' And this is in fact a 'reversion' rather than a return to Lewis's western origins: a reversion that has partially sublimated, but hasn't altogether resolved, the familiar elements of Lewis's conflict: that is also directed against all thought and talk outside of Main Street, and that, dismissing the eastern metropolis quite as blindly as it had once embraced it,* has exalted the vices as well as the virtues of small-town life into the order of a completely detached, a wholly self-absorbed, an absolute cosmogony.

* New York is clearly described as 'a jungle spawning of people and buildings, fierce and purposeless,' while, as Lewis says, 'anything printed, a timetable or the rich prose of a tomato-catsup label, is more stimulating than any talk, even the screaming of six economists and an intellectual actress.' And particularly, one supposes, the screaming of the economists.

You may now realize the value of that recurrent image in these later Lewis novels: the vision of the northern Middle West as 'the fabulous Great Land of the year 2000 A.D.' For in a sense this land, with its brilliant lakes and tremendous prairies, its long bleak winters and rich hot bursting summers; this 'stark and clean' midwestern land which Lewis has just begun to appreciate *is,* in Lewis's mind, already in the year 2000 A.D. Or anyhow it is well beyond the reverberations of either the European conflict or of that disturbed American industrial order whose material products and moral values seem everywhere to have conditioned it. This is a land of prefabricated prairies that float in a synthetic infinitude: a 'new kind of land' indeed.

And 'a new kind of people.' There is an element of truth, again, in Lewis's almost complete reversion to the domestic affairs of his characters. Just because ordinary people insist on living ordinary lives in the midst of social catastrophes, they have managed to survive such catastrophes in the most incredible way. But were ever private lives *quite* so private as they are in Lewis's final philosophy —a philosophy that excludes not only the 'more' that is dreamed of on heaven and earth, but almost the notion of heaven and earth itself? If this is to be the price for the survival of the human race, it is at the cost of practically every feature that has made the race human. Moreover, just as *Gideon Planish* is the most vigorous and acute of Lewis's late novels in artistic terms, it is also the most explicit about his repudiation of all larger human values.*

* Lewis's most recent novel, *Kingsblood Royal,* which deals specifically with the Negro problem, seems to be an exception to this rule. In part, it is a return to his earlier vein of social satire. But notice that the most vivid passages in the novel deal with the almost nightmarish horror of an eminently respectable Northern white man who is confronted by the dreadful possibility of becoming a Negro. . . . Just as in the case of *It*

For Lewis's 'World of Philanthrobbery,' the world outside of Main Street, includes not only those odious radicals or revolutionaries, but the most discreet liberalism, not only the lunatic fringe of social reform, but all social change, and not only the racketeers of the humanitarian impulse, but the humanitarian impulse itself. Probably *Gideon Planish's* brightest satiric passage—

> So Gideon Planish firmly set his plump foot upon the upward path that would lead through the miasma of lecturing and the bleak wind of editing to the glory of cloud-cuckoo-land, yet, even unto the world of committees and conferences and organizations and leagues of implementing ideals and crystallizing public opinion and molding public opinion and producing informed public opinion and finding the greatest common denominator in all shades of opinion——
>
> Of grass roots and liberal thinking and blueprints for democracy and the system of free enterprise and far-flung armies and far-flung empires and far-flung money-raising campaigns, together with far-flung night-letter-telegrams about the imminence of the crisis and far-flung petitions to Congress about the state of politics in Chile or Iran, and ideologies and ideological warfare and in general the use of the word 'ideology' as meaning everything except Far-Flung and Coca-Cola, and the longing to serve and the need of discussion and constitutional measures and challenges and rallying-points and crises, lots of crises, practically daily crises, and basic appeals and spiritual ideals and the protection of the home, and the sickness in our civilization . . .

Can't Happen Here, the real elements of social conflict in *Kingsblood Royal* are subordinated to a childlike fantasy of social conflict, while the profoundly disturbing factor of mob violence in the United States today becomes, at the close of the novel, another sort of parlor game played with imaginary shotguns.

—such a passage most clearly illustrates the final nature of Lewis's Great World and his final reversion to 'the comic strips and to anarchy.'

In the age of Hitler and Expressionism, the bourgeois counter-revolution has run amok; this is the nightmare of a nihilist. . . . One cannot but admire the glitter of such passages as these; for eloquence and sheer vitality Lewis has probably done nothing better over a full quarter-century of his literary career, and notice that the structure and rhythms of Lewis's prose have become much more flexible and fluent. Similarly, in the larger range of Lewis's work as a whole, one may admire that stubborn persistence which results, for example, in this least 'feminine' of artists having established such a long line of feminine figureheads, or in this least sensuous of writers perpetually dealing with, and finally limiting himself almost purely to, the senses. Although Lewis's realism does not in the end compare with either Dreiser's or Dos Passos's, although his values are quite inadequate when compared with Willa Cather's or Sherwood Anderson's, there is a curious sort of solidity in his work, a fundamental sense of human decency, and a fundamental human perversity which is at the base of any mature individualism. It isn't, moreover, that Lewis is not always serious about the craft of a novelist. It is simply that he doesn't always know how serious the craft of a novelist can be.

Bethel Merriday, so the author tells us, had been reared 'to the solid American Protestant belief in the glory and efficacy of human will power'—

> If anyone wanted enough to do anything, he would unquestionably do it, and his resoluteness was somehow very beautiful, if his ambition was to devour the moon or become the Queen of Sheba.

And in a sense this description of Lewis's actress, which illustrates so beautifully the vulgarization of the frontier ethos within the subsequent framework of Horatio Alger and Hollywood, is the clearest description of both Lewis's own source of power and his tragic limitations.

So all this wit and eloquence and artistic vitality operates in a sort of intellectual vacuum in the end. You could say that the whole import of Lewis's work shows that he has learned nothing, answered nothing, solved nothing: that those Lewis characters who, in his first novels, left the West for an imaginary East are the same characters who leave the East for the imaginary West of his last novels; and that Lewis himself, like his most typical figures, is the Eternal Amateur of the national letters. Even the intellectual and emotional break-throughs of his last period: the final touching upon the perennial human impulses in the love-story of *Gideon Planish,* or the insight into cultural patterns which is contained in that brief note on the Beluca, Indiana ('pop. 277,000; site state aviation sch; Beluca, Univ., Littlefield Art Museum cont. a Fra Angelico, an El Greco; mfrs. plumbing supplies. . . .'), of *Bethel Merriday,* or merely the description of that Howard Pyle-ish courthouse in *Cass Timberlane*—

> It was of a rich red raspberry brick trimmed with limestone, and it displayed a round tower, an octagonal tower, a minaret, a massive entrance with a portcullis, two lofty flying balconies of iron, colored-glass windows with tablets or stone petals in the niches above them, a green and yellow mosaic roof with scarlet edging, and the breathless ornamental stairway from the street up to the main entrance without which no American public building would be altogether legal.

—perhaps such bright passages as these, more than anything else, only serve to light up the gap between what Lewis's work could have been and what it actually is.

Furthermore, the point isn't that Lewis lives so completely in illusion. This is one of the prime sources of an artist's power and one of the reasons why Lewis's work, for all its limitations, has its own appalling validity. The point is that the illusion which nourished Lewis was so inadequate, and in the last analysis so transient. . . . For the Happy End to Lewis's unhappy historical vision—the vision of Middle-Class Bliss which marks the entire last period of Lewis's work—came at almost the precise historical moment that marked the crack-up of the Middle-Class Empire in America; at least in its first natural exuberant form. And if Lewis sees clearly enough the failure of the Horatio Alger tradition in American life, it is just as true that the brand of economic individualism for which he yearns was, almost from the very start of his career, more of a vestigial than a vital force in his society: even then, in the dawning age of the cartels, a myth and a memory of the past.

Here, too, we can appreciate Lewis's curious relationship with the Younger Generation. In the last of the broken antitheses which form the real dialectic of Lewis's work, we have noticed how the writer who has sought after 'youth' most fervently hardly expresses it with the greatest conviction. How prematurely sober Lewis's typical young people are, and how perennially gauche and infantile his adults are: almost as though, never having had a true youth, they can never achieve a true maturity. You might almost say that the typical Lewis hero is an adolescent with a paunch. And in this respect, rather like those western settlements which have jumped from crude hamlets to ersatz cities, Lewis's people are reflecting the broken life-line of the Middle-Class Empire itself—that uneasy empire whose own youth in America was capped by a hurried and frantic maturity, and for whose brief flourishing Lewis has been forced, in *The Prodigal Parents,* to substitute a mythical and timeless splendor.

And doesn't George F. Babbitt himself, the Grand Mogul of the Middle-Class Empire, take on an added glory simply because he was allowed such a brief span on history's moving stage? The dupe of time as well as of the great American fortunes, Lewis's single big creation is a pathetic clown in truth. The clock goes faster in the United States, too fast for both Lewis's many-volumed diary of the economic man and for the diarist too. . . . And it is interesting that the cultural lag in Lewis's work should be so marked: that just as the real social forces of his time are placed for the most part quite outside of his literary scene, so the real social changes of his time are reflected so cursorily and so late. The ordinary mark of a first-rank author is that his writing is generally in some degree ahead of its time; the typical characteristic of Lewis's writing is that it is generally, to a marked degree, behind its time. Very likely this is the final key to Lewis's achievement—the key which opens the secret chamber in this otherwise absolutely uninspiring middle-class mansion.

For it would appear that Lewis's whole literary world, so extraordinarily prosaic for the most part, so lacking in subtleties and shadows; a world of perpetual daytime, on which night, with its enigmas and mysteries, never falls—that this whole uniquely commonplace literary universe of Lewis's *is* in the end haunted by the sense of its own destiny. This is also a middle class which is essentially without a home life, without children, without religion, and, finally, without an economic status to speak of: a middle class which is without all the historical props of a middle class, and which, hardly established in power, has every appearance of dissolving—including the escape into a dream world of the middle class. . . . At any rate, that is the impression that Sinclair Lewis's work leaves with us, as it turns from the barricades to the Land of Faery, while the true and final fascination of his own career, as we have noticed, is the degree to which he has become identified with the illusions of this class.

Is it the fascination of the victims, and not the creators of history?—'What was the use of keeping up the feud?' a symbolical spokesman of Willa Cather's will ask himself with respect to an old enemy—'It was a draw . . . they had both been beaten.' In Miss Cather herself, the third of these typical figures of the Middle Generation, you will find a very different approach to things. Her work will illuminate just those areas of human behavior—the cultivated sensibility of the individual, the untamed impulses of the race—that have been missing in our study of the pushing and shouting bourjoyces.

In her own terms, though, the lady in the wilderness will present another example of a 'draw' between the contemporary American novelist and contemporary society.

Chapter Three

Willa Cather: LADY IN THE WILDERNESS

◇

1. A Point of Ethics

2. The Wild Land

3. A World Above the World

4. My Chamber, My Terrestrial Paradise

5. The Tragic Necessity

Chapter Three

Willa Cather: LADY IN THE WILDERNESS

1. A Point of Ethics

IN APPROACHING OUR FIRST FEMININE WRITER among the dozen or so contemporary American novelists who deserve a full literary consideration, it is essential, of course, not to consider her as a 'feminine' writer.

Willa Sibert Cather made this clear herself in those early reflections on the discipline and austerity which mark the career of Thea Kronborg in *The Song of the Lark.* There are also her reflections on the character of Flaubert, who almost becomes the later Cather's model of personal behavior as well as of aesthetic excellence: the meticulous and disdainful French artist, that is, in whose case, as we are told, it was a point of ethics 'to encourage no familiarity at any time.' In *Shadows on the Rock,* you may remember Father Hector's little sermon to the apothecary Auclair—

> Listen, my friend. No man can give himself heart and soul to one thing while in the back of his mind he cherishes a desire, a secret hope for something very different. You as a student, must know that even in worldly affairs nothing worth while is accomplished except by that last sacrifice, the giving of oneself altogether and finally.

In these brief, lucent lines you may get a sense of the lifelong dedication, the complete moral consecration which is at the base of Willa Cather's work: that final giving, as Henry James also pointed out in a memorable but more abstruse manner, which is at the root of all serious work.

The outlines of her life are simple enough. Born in Virginia, on a farm near Winchester, December 7, 1876, she came from 'an established Virginia family' of English, Irish, and Alsatian extraction. At eight or nine she was taken to Nebraska and spent the years of her growth among the Bohemians, Scandinavians, Germans, and French-Canadians of a pioneer environment. Yet there may be traces of her original background in, say, that Jim Burden of *My Ántonia,* who is always comparing immigrant vitality with native refinement, but who still can never quite cross a social line he sees so clearly and detests so strongly. These earliest Virginia origins of Willa Cather, obscure and almost hidden as they are, are to form an important element in her work.

Meanwhile, she spent her days on the Nebraska plains—her open western prairie scene, with its ridges and draws and blowing sea of red grass, its badgers, 'possums, cranes, earth-owls, and rattlesnakes. She learned reading and writing at home, studied Latin with a neighbor, read the English classics in the evenings. In 1891 she graduated from the state university, and took up journalism and teaching in Pittsburgh. This is also the period of her 'especial delight in the work of Henry James,' while her impressions of Pittsburgh—'that smoke-palled city,' as she tells us in one of her earliest short stories, 'enamoured of figures and grimy toil'—are not quite so pleasant.

The virtuoso publisher, S. S. McClure, whose later autobiography, edited by Willa Cather, contains an illuminating account of a frontier childhood, noticed Miss Cather's early stories and invited her to join the staff of his magazine; two years later she was made managing editor. Her relations with that nest of young radicals, muckrakers, and embryonic political reformers who developed *McClure's Magazine* remain somewhat intangible, however—she spent a great deal of her time in travel to Europe, the southwestern states, and 'the New York world of art, literature, and music.' In 1912 she published her first novel, and, a year later, *O Pioneers!* marked the start of the series of frontier tales which established her reputation as one of the most gifted novelists of her period.

Yet there are very ambiguous elements in these luminous chronicles of 'the little beginnings of human society in the West.' We shall notice the curious foreshortening of Cather's historical view, not only in terms of the contemporary scene, but in terms of this frontier period which she has chosen for herself and made her own. We shall trace the increasing sense of disenchantment in her work, and the final sense of complete spiritual defeat and withdrawal which is recorded in *The Professor's House*—that familiar Catheresque wound, 'healed and hardened and hopeless,' which begins to throb all over again. And certainly the religious pilgrimage of her middle period: this voyage of a spiritual malaise which pushes its way back from the epoch of the pioneers and the empire-builders to the New Mexico of the eighteen-fifties and to the French Quebec of the early seventeen-hundreds, and even there, with the passing of the 'old order,' yearns for a still earlier time, a still more absolute cosmos of authority and faith, since on this rock, too, there are shadows—certainly this is one of the most curious of all those curious spiritual pilgrimages in the late nineteen-twenties.

As a matter of fact, Willa Cather's is one of the most complex, if not difficult and contradictory, minds in our letters. If we must admire the conscience, it won't always be easy to follow the logic of this artist. (We shall notice that this sophisticated lady is also an advocate of the primitive impulses, or, at least, of those more direct, unprincipled, and ruthless 'feminine' impulses which mark her most memorable heroines.) And it is, after all, as the work of a talented and tormented woman that her literary world takes on its particular glow and interest. Among the whole group of our feminine novelists, Willa Cather is in some ways the most interesting of them all: less restricted than Edith Wharton, more intense than Ellen Glasgow. And among the circle of novelists under consideration here, she is probably the writer who comes closest to having the sense of a human necessity whose origins are wild and whose destination is tragic.

Is it merely a coincidence, too, that Cather's belated return to the western towns of *Lucy Gayheart* should be coupled with her final declaration of belief in the enchantment *and* suffering of life?—the final acceptance of both the pleasure and pain of ordinary human experience, and the inextricable unity of these two poles of our existence: that old-fashioned 'optimism' of the Middle Generation, which she, along with Sherwood Anderson, and, for all her curious delicacies and restraints, most purely exemplifies.

For this is actually a deeper and tougher sense of life than Henry Mencken or Sinclair Lewis could honestly claim to have, and one which, with Scott Fitzgerald and a new generation of cosmopolitan and primarily urban novelists, almost disappeared for a generation from the American literary scene itself. . . . Between Miss Cather's early western scene and her late return, however, lies another story, and a less fortunate one: to a large degree the story of an evasion of a social environment, of a broken creative framework, and a dissipation of the writer's true energies—a very familiar story in the national letters.

But even the limitations of Willa Cather's work are made more poignant by her long and sustained attempt to deal with them. And as early as her first novel you will realize how sure and sensitive her values are in the human area at least.

2. *The Wild Land*

When she looked back at her first novel, *Alexander's Bridge,* published in 1912, Miss Cather was not favorably impressed by it.

The book was 'external and young,' she says in her 1922 preface and in rather formal auctorial tones. It marked the thrill of novelty and the glitter of the passing show, as opposed to a writer's true 'life-line.' She quotes a remark of Sarah Orne Jewett, her early mentor, 'Of course, one day you will write about your own country. In the meantime, get all you can. One must know the world *so well* before one can know the parish.'

Yet, if there is little of the parish in *Alexander's Bridge,* there is also little of the provincial. It is a remarkably interesting first novel as a matter of fact, and not merely in terms of a prose style that is already supple and fluent, but in terms of the subject matter itself. The scene is set in Boston and in London; the story deals with a successful American architect, happily married, proud of his wife, and fond of their life together, who is nevertheless drawn back into the emotional vortex of a youthful love affair.

The point is that Cather's architect (he is actually a bridge-designer) is one of her most interesting men—one might say he is almost the only interesting man during the whole first period of her work—during the period of the

Pioneer Matriarchy. And her first hero also gives us our first real indication of her own view of experience. For what Bartley Alexander has missed, in the midst of his success and fame, is simply his own former sense of energy and delight: 'the impetuousness, the intense excitement, the increasing expectancy of youth.' What the love affair actually means to him is a return, in the 'dead calm of middle life,' of his own identity. 'There was only one thing that had an absolute value for each individual, and it was just that original impulse, that internal heat, that feeling of one's self in one's own breast.' But there is the equal realization that the full consciousness of self, as it reaches its point of tension, touches the orbit of death.

And just as Alexander's 'affair' with the English actress, Hilda Burgoyne, revives his awareness of the absolute value of life, so it begins to destroy all his formal patterns of living. The increasing recklessness of Alexander's behavior, the sense of his own guilt and folly, the knowledge that the only real emotions he has are those which are destroying him, and, at the same time, the 'sullen painful delight' with which he accepts his impending ruin: these undertones of irony and suffering, which accompany and parallel the notes of an almost lyrical exaltation in the novel, are an unusual achievement for a young writer in the early teens. In the whole group of her pioneer novels, Willa Cather will do nothing better than some of her passages in *Alexander's Bridge;* and what is a little curious, too, is that the older novelist, looking back upon a pattern of feeling which is so intense, intimate, and lived, should dismiss it as superficial or remote

Of course, the English theatrical set through which the early Cather moves here, and the opera cloaks, the calling cards, the 'wonderful little dinners' of ducklings, mushrooms, and truffles which she dwells upon, *are* a little remote from the Nebraska plains; in a way this is an odd vista to be unfolded by the future historian of the frontier, one that is closer to Edith Wharton, even, than to Sarah Orne Jewett. On the London streets, Cather's lovers, in their moment of delight, in their assurance that life is the most indestructible thing in the world, are compared with the gloomy city and with the office workers who have come out to drink the 'muddy lees' of the day. Beyond Charles Street, in Boston, there is apparently not much, too, except a series of labor strikes—'a general industrial unrest' in the American scene which prevents Alexander from completing his new bridge on schedule. It is this Moorlock Bridge, the 'longest cantilever in the world,' which collapses at the end of the novel and, by taking Bartley Alexander's life and his reputation with it, fulfills his convictions of ruin. Yet it is interesting that almost Alexander's last reflections should deal with the industrial masses, with 'all these dirty people' who surround him in the train, these 'poor unconscious companions of his journey . . . who had come to stand to him for the ugliness he had brought into the world.' And it is actually a gang of half-crazed iron-workers who send him to his death, while Alexander, a strong swimmer, tries to beat them off in the swirling waters beneath the doomed cantilever.

In this light the framework of Cather's first western tale, *O Pioneers!* in 1913, becomes more obvious, and even a little stylized. Practically at the start of the novel, one notices the drunken traveling man who tries to flirt with Cather's woman of the plains: that foolish little clothing drummer, who has been knocking about 'in little drab towns and crawling across the wintry country in dirty smoking cars,' and who, when he chances upon a fine human creature, suddenly wishes himself more of a man. Running through the novel, and forming a sort of counterpoint, there are those references to 'the new prosperity' which will come when the wild land has been subjugated by the early generations of pioneers; the new standards in behavior, which will appear with bathtubs and with pianos. 'At home, in the old country,' says Crazy Ivar, 'there were many like me, who had been touched by God, or who had seen things in the graveyard at night and were different afterward. . . . We thought nothing of it, and let them alone. But here, if a man is different in his feet or in his head, they put him in the asylum.'

There are harsher references, too, about the agrarian disturbances which appeared in the eighteen-nineties upon a western horizon that had seemed so illimitable. Politics is the natural field, according to Cather, for such persons as Lou Bergson, who 'has not got a fox's face for nothing'; while the Populist reform movement that centered around Bryan is viewed as a local engagement between the anarchists and J. P. Morgan. In a more notable passage, Carl Linstrum, returning to the prairies from Chicago and New York, expresses the real point of the novel:

> 'Here you are an individual, you have a background of your own, you would be missed. But off there in the cities there are thousands of rolling stones like me. We are all alike; we have no ties, we know nobody, we own nothing. When one of us dies, they scarcely know where to bury him. Our landlady and the delicatessen man are our mourners, and we leave nothing behind us but a frock-coat and a fiddle, or an easel or a typewriter, or whatever tool we got our living by. All we have ever managed to do is to pay our rent, the exorbitant rent that one has to pay for a few square feet of space near the heart of things. We have no house, no place, no people of our own. We live in the streets, in the parks, in the theatres. We sit in

> restaurants and concert halls and look about at the hundreds of our own kind and shudder.'

And this helps to explain the kind of affection with which *O Pioneers!* delineates the background of the first settlers on the windy Nebraska tableland—of those earlier immigrants who owned the land for a little while because they loved it.

For the descriptions of the wild land in *O Pioneers!* and of the half-wild frontier eccentrics like Crazy Ivar who have again become part of the land; and of those first small colonies of Russians, Swedes, Czechs, French, or Bohemians who then set out rigorously, persistently, inch by inch, to tame the land, almost as though they themselves represented an opposing natural force and displayed something of Nature's own relentless will as against the infinite extent of her willfulness—all this is certainly well done here. From that first glimpse of Alexandra Bergson's wagon by night, 'a moving point of light . . . going into the dark country,' to Amédée's twenty French cousins, this is surely the chronicle of 'the little beginnings of human society' on the endless western plains. And in the daily patterns of pioneer activity—the colorful weddings, dances, and costume parties, the all-night gatherings to the tune of a *dragharmonika* or a fiddle, the games, choral societies, and family readings that accompanied the axe, the plow and the Bible—Miss Cather very early suggested the resources of that frontier life which was to seem so harsh and sterile to a subsequent generation of western rebels and expatriates.*

* In a sense one can understand how a Henry Mencken, as a rising Baltimore luminary, an ex-newspaper man with a yen for cosmopolitan culture, and a wit, set the tone for the later movement, while such a writer as the young Scott Fitzgerald, at once innocent and obsessed, was

Such portraits as those of 'Old Mrs. Lee,' or Frank Shabata, for example, are among the first of those vignettes which will add a peculiarly native grace to Willa Cather's frontier tales. The sometimes elaborate, almost Jamesian cadences of her earlier prose ('and however one took him, however much one admired him, one had to admit that he simply wouldn't square') have been refined down to a homelier western idiom. 'He knew the end too well to wish to begin again,' Cather says of John Bergson, dying alone in the wilderness. 'He knew where it all went to, what it all became.' And the unmistakable accents of suffering—

> Spring, summer, autumn, winter, spring; always the same patient fields, the patient little trees, the patient lives; always the same yearning, the same pulling at the chain—until the instinct to live had torn itself and bled and weakened for the last time, until the chain secured a dead woman, who might cautiously be released. . . . How terrible it was to love people when you could not really share their lives!

—the accents of intense suffering, as well as the Catheresque sense of the sweetness and splendor of life, are now linked to the forces of pioneer aspiration and pioneer fate, to the seasons, and almost to Nature itself.

Yet it is interesting that this familiar pattern of feeling, this emotional dualism of the inevitable pain and the implicit ecstasy of life which was the dominating pattern of

a natural victim of the debunkers. More curious is the fact that a Sinclair Lewis, coming out of the prairie towns and dealing, in his earlier novels, with almost the same frontier matrix as Willa Cather, should have had so little regard for it. But possibly the decade between Cather's youth and Lewis's, the decade, roughly, of the eighteen-nineties, actually marked a sort of dividing line between the immigrant settlers and the native realtors.

Alexander's Bridge, is relegated to the story of Marie Shabata in *O Pioneers!*: to a secondary place in the novel, while the heroine, Alexandra Bergson, now wears the mask of the stoic—that 'impervious calm of the fatalist' which, as Cather notes, is always disconcerting to people 'who cannot feel that the heart lives at all unless it is still at the mercy of storms; unless its strings can scream at the touch of pain.' One notices the increasing references to Catholicism and to that little French Church in the wilderness, 'powerful and triumphant there on its eminence,' with its music and pageantry and hallowed rituals of suffering, with the gold cross flaming on its steeple, and offering that kind of rapture in which one can love forever 'without faltering and without sin.' As a matter of fact, Alexandra Bergson, as the central figure of *O Pioneers!*, as the symbolical pioneer woman, and as Cather's superior individual, is almost *too* stoical, remote, and unfaltering. 'What a hopeless position you are in, Alexandra,' says the devoted but ineffectual Carl Linstrum. 'It is your fate to be always surrounded by little men.' In a way, for a woman of feeling, this must be a dull position: at least it begins to seem so in the case of Cather's next and more renowned pioneer heroine.

In many respects, *My Ántonia* marks a gain in Cather's craft. Probably the accounts of the frontier land are even more graceful here; that childhood visit of Ántonia and Jim Burden to 'dog town' is a perfect little episode; while the story of Ántonia's Bohemian family, the Shimerdas, almost summarizes the story of all those 'strange uprooted people' who were among the first citizens of our western plains.* But it is around Black Hawk, Nebraska, that

* Parenthetically, it may be interesting to compare the death of Mr. Shimerda in *My Ántonia* with the death of Addie Bundren in William Faulkner's *As I Lay Dying,* or with Ernest Hemingway's tale of a mountain death, 'An Alpine Idyll.' The literary elements in these three accounts

My Ántonia centers, as Cather carries forward the chronicle of the frontier settlers to the framework of early western town life and the merchants and farmers, the commercial travelers, the eccentrics, and outcasts of what was almost a society of outcasts. Such portraits as Wick Cutter, the dissolute money-lender, or Lena Lingard, the Swedish farm girl; or scenes like those Saturday night operas in Black Hawk or the evenings at the Vannis's dancing pavilion; or frontier legends like that of Blind d'Arnault, the traveling Negro pianist who plays as though 'all the agreeable sensations possible to creatures of flesh and blood were heaped up in those black and white keys': these are among the most attractive passages in Miss Cather's early novels. She is shrewd too about 'the curious social situation' which arose in Black Hawk—that is, the class distinctions which developed between the merchants' daughters and the 'hired girls'—between native refinement and immigrant vitality—and the consequent effect of a whole new ethos of respectability upon the middle-class children. To dance 'Home, Sweet Home' with Lena Lingard, she says, was like coming in with the tide, while the bodies of the town girls never moved inside their clothes, and their muscles seemed to ask but one thing—not to be disturbed.

> The Black Hawk boys looked forward to marrying Black Hawk girls and living in a brand-new little house with best chairs that must not be sat upon, and hand-painted china that must not be used. But sometimes a young fellow would look up from his ledger, or out through the grating

are almost identical. But while Cather includes both an idiot son and a frozen corpse in the ordinary context of frontier life, the later writers isolate one or another of these elements in a context of human degradation—in the milieu of Faulkner's 'poor-whites' and of the young Hemingway's 'peasants.'

> of his father's bank, and let his eyes follow Lena Lingard, as she passed the window with her slow, undulating walk, or Tiny Soderball, tripping by in her short skirt and striped stockings. . . . The country girls were considered a menace to the social order. Their beauty shone out too boldly against a conventional background. But anxious mothers need have felt no alarm. They mistook the mettle of their sons. The respect for respectability was stronger than any desire in Black Hawk youth.

And this guarded mode of existence, Cather's Jim Burden also thinks, was almost like living under a tyranny, where every individual taste, every natural appetite, was bridled by caution. These people tried to live like the mice in their own kitchens; 'to make no noise, to leave no trace, to slip over the surface of things in the dark.'

Yet the middle sections of *My Ántonia,* the sections on the hired girls and on Lena Lingard herself, represent a sort of climax in the novel's action. Cather's narrator is captivated alike by the physical charms of Lena Lingard and the moral stature of Ántonia Shimerda. (And there is that interesting split again between the ostensible heroine, Ántonia, the epitome of the frontier spirit, and Lena, who represents merely the frontier flesh, but who almost runs away with the show.) However, Jim Burden, the descendant of a Virginia family, can never actually make the break, and can never cross that social line which he sees so clearly and despises so heartily. Indeed, as he draws away from the western scene in later life, becomes legal counsel for a big railway, has a wife who plays patroness to the new poets and painters, and himself frequents London or Vienna, Jim Burden's memory of Ántonia becomes more precious. 'She lent herself to immemorial human attitudes which we recognize by instinct as universal and true. . . . She was a rich mine of life, like the founders of the early races.' Very much like Scott Fitzgerald's western observer in *The Great Gatsby,* Willa Cather's narrator, when he decides to revisit the scene of his youth, has the sense of coming back home to himself. 'Whatever we had missed, we possessed together the precious, the incommunicable past.' *

All the same, that closing scene of the novel in which we actually *see* Ántonia has some curious undertones. 'You really are a part of me,' Jim Burden tells her. 'I'd have liked to have you for a sweetheart, or a wife, or my mother, or my sister—anything that a woman can be to a man.' 'Ain't it wonderful,' Ántonia answers, 'how much people can mean to each other?' Is it merely in the shadow of Burden's continental sophistication that Ántonia now seems so much cruder in sensibility and expression, as well as rather battered in appearance—as though she had reverted in some degree to the line of her peasant ancestors while Jim Burden has moved closer to his own more or less aristocratic forebears? The difference between them has never been quite so apparent as it is just when Jim Burden believes that the same road of 'Destiny' which has separated him from Ántonia has now brought them together again. . . . Meanwhile, in 1915, three years before *My Ántonia,* Willa Cather had published a novel in which the pattern of her pioneer tales is defined even more clearly.

In terms of its content, as well as in its actual size, *The*

* The similarity of theme and tone between the closing sections of *My Ántonia* and *The Great Gatsby* has probably not been sufficiently noticed by historians of literary craft: a similarity which extends through phrases and rhythms of the writing to the almost identical 'dying-fall' of Fitzgerald's last sentence in *Gatsby:* 'So we beat on, boats against the current, borne back ceaselessly into the past.' It seems likely, that is, that Fitzgerald drew upon Willa Cather's work for his own development of the theme, although, since both writers also use the structural device of the 'sensitive observer,' there is the common influence of Henry James or the school of James.

Song of the Lark is also, of course, the 'big' book of Cather's first period, and it deserves the wide popular recognition it brought to her work as a whole. (It is no mean feat, incidentally, to choose an opera singer for one's heroine, as she does in the case of Thea Kronborg, and to establish an artist's love for music as the central passion of a novel.) Moreover, when Cather moves southwest to the mining town of Moonstone, Colorado, when her familiar Swedish and German immigrants meet the more volatile Mexicans who, like Spanish Johnny, have learned 'to dive below insults or soar above them,' the early sections of *The Song of the Lark* take on a warmer and richer color, like the sky above the southwestern desert, or like those linden trees of Mrs. Kohler's which have a honey-colored bloom in summer, with a fragrance 'that surpasses all trees and flowers and drives young people wild with joy.' Professor Wunsch, the drunken musician to whom the young Thea recalls 'standards, ambitions, a society long forgot'; Ray Kennedy, the railroad worker who gives his life to the cause of Thea's career; and Thea herself, the gifted, generous child whose close associates were Mexicans and sinners, are all part of this admirable early drama in the dunes. There is the climax of the drama, too: the scene in which Thea, alienated from her home and family by her own 'desires, ambitions, revulsions,' and finding refuge among the Mexicans, realizes for the first time what such a people can give to an artist—feels 'as if all these warm-blooded people debouched into her': that scene in which Cather somehow manages to put the ecstasy and anguish of a whole race of aliens into the description of a soprano voice which leaps and plays about those 'dusky male voices' at night on the desert. *'Die Thea,'* whispers Mrs. Kohler, listening to the music across the gulch. *'Ach wunderschön!'* And so it is.

In passing, it is interesting to notice the descendants of the New Hampshire farmers whom Miss Cather also portrays in *The Song of the Lark* as hard workers and close traders—'with good minds, mean natures, and flinty eyes.' Are these merchants among the citizens who have contributed to the 'general scramble of American life' which Cather's heroine meets in Chicago? For the account of Thea's later musical career in the metropolis is interesting: in these pages, and often very eloquently, Cather stresses her own belief in an individual integrity and personal fulfillment as well as in the technical achievement of the artist. Here are the Catheresque glimpses of those bright moments in life 'which are few, after all, and so very easy to miss,' or of those good things 'which are never complete in this world,' while in the parallel relationships of Harsanyi, who tells the truth to Thea in order to make her free, and of Fred Ottenburg, who deceives her in order to keep her free, we realize again the spaciousness of Cather's view of human relationships.*

Yet it is difficult to ignore the increasing accents of auctorial bitterness, almost of contempt, which mark the story of Cather's heroine's increasing fame as a singer. Is it a Chicago musical society itself, in the days when 'the lumbermen's daughters and the brewer's wives contended in song,' that seems such 'a common, common world' to Thea? Or is it the industrial city as a whole—the rich, fat, noisy city, whose chief concern is with its digestion, as Cather says, whose money and office are 'the consolations of impotence,' and the majority of whose citizens, like the

* Notice the passage in which Ottenburg asks himself whether, between men and women, all ways were not more or less crooked. 'He believed those which are called straight were the most dangerous of all. . . . In their unquestioned regularity lurked every sort of human cruelty and meanness, and every kind of humiliation and suffering. He would rather have any woman he cared for wounded than crushed. He would deceive her . . . to keep her free.'

Poles of Packingtown, live chiefly in the saloons, where one can buy for a few hours 'the illusion of comfort, hope, love—whatever one most longs for'? Certainly the accounts of 'the cosmopolitan brewing world of St. Louis,' or of 'the plunging Kansas City set,' form some of the most acute sections in *The Song of the Lark,* and Cather treats these native manifestations of a *haute bourgeoisie* with a light touch that, from Dreiser to Tom Wolfe, is particularly rare in our social novelists. And yet one notices that the Jessie Darcy who is the operatic darling of the Chicago Northwestern Railroad, or that rather fascinating Miss Beers who is a racy product of 'a long packing-house purse,' or, to some degree, Fred Ottenburg himself, when he uses the tongues of Bayreuth to entrance an interstate meeting of the *Turnverein,* are all more or less dismissed here as being merely 'Stupid Faces.'

Equally so are the native political reformers, those 'few dull young men who haven't the ability to play the old game the old way,' whom Doctor Archie dismisses with some scorn when his mining interests have become so large that his political influence is considerable. And Thea Kronborg herself, having completed her escape from 'a smug, domestic, self-satisfied provincial world of utter ignorance,' as Cather adds in her later preface to *The Song of the Lark,* and having established her place as an artist in 'an idle, gaping world which is determined that no artist shall ever do his best,' is not without a similar element of arrogance, or of a rather complacent provincial ignorance of her own. The material conveniences, the trappings of luxury with which Cather's heroine is surrounded at the end: the fur coat which she leaves for her maid to pick up, the instructions she transmits to her assistant, Mr. Landry, to have tea at five, the cab which is always waiting at her door, the intimate little dinners, or the delicate underclothing which, to her annoyance, has been misplaced by some worthless hotel 'nigger'—is all this a sort of compensation for the travail of an artist in a society of so many material conveniences? And is a mere glimpse of the great Sieglinde, and Thea's gracious bow, quite sufficient to bring happiness to her old friend, Spanish Johnny? Still, that closing section of *The Song of the Lark,* in which Cather's fashionable primadonna chats of London and Dresden with her two rich and devoted masculine admirers, *is* a curious resolution to the tale of an immigrant girl from Colorado. And it is in terms of this scene of wealth and cultivation which Cather dwells upon both at the start of her first novel and at the close of this one, which forms such an elegant framework for her pictures of a more primitive life, that we must consider the work of her first period.

There is no doubt that Cather's pioneer portraits are foreshortened in perspective to a certain degree, a little reduced in size, and also, after one has escaped from the spell of the craft itself, curiously static in their final effect, almost like a tableau of Grant Wood's. Both *O Pioneers!* and *My Antonia* are georgics of the frontier, or idylls of western fortitude, and it seems just as clear that Cather went back to the past, to her childhood memories of the Nebraska plains, to achieve this effect. As early as her first novel we noticed her distaste for the murky cities, the white-collar office workers, and the industrial masses of her time; while the collapse of the defective cantilever which symbolizes the ruin of her engineer-hero in *Alexander's Bridge* is certainly meant to be projected outward into the larger context of an engineering society. In the first of her frontier tales we noticed an almost equally sharp aversion to those modern 'politicians' who appeared on the western horizon so shortly after the first glow of the pioneer effort had faded—those agrarian 'agitators' who seem to be identified in her mind with the unnecessary economic disturbances as well as the increasing standardization of thought and personality in the later stages of her western society. It is against this whole emerging pattern of both rural and urban life in America that Cather has actually set her earlier western individualists, her pioneer makers and ancestors, as an example of a better, a freer, a more heroic and worthy time.

In some part this accounts for both the eloquence of Cather's frontier tales and the final effect they produce of being isolated and almost static episodes, as I say—of being separated *out* of a larger and more complex historical situation. If this is a return to the childhood world of the artist, it is also a sort of childlike return. Moreover, as the chronicle of the pioneers is carried forward through the early western towns of *My Ántonia* to the metropolitan centers of *The Song of the Lark,* there is the same note of isolation and hostility in the later defense of the artist in a purely materialistic society. . . . And yet there are other elements and more curious undertones here. Does the central emotional pattern of Cather's work—that particularly Catheresque sense of an intense splendor in life and of its inevitable loss, of a brief ecstasy and of a long and bitter resignation to suffering—stem back to her first novel, which contains, in fact, not only the fullest statement of this theme, but the most complete human relationship of the first period of her writing? After *Alexander's Bridge* the lyrical note is increasingly subordinated to the stoical, while the line of her superior matriarchs is established, and Thea Kronborg again expresses their central conviction of 'standing up under things,' of 'meeting catastrophe without any fussiness,' of 'dealing with fate barehanded.'

That, too, is admirable, of course, but is it also the fate of Cather's dominant and increasingly inaccessible women to be 'always surrounded by little men,' as in the case of Alexandra Bergson, to be worshiped from afar and to marry for convenience, as in the case of Ántonia Shimerda, and to sacrifice marriage, love, and, finally, friendship in the interests of an artist's career, as in the case of Thea Kronborg? Isn't it something of a catastrophe to avoid all deeper human involvements, as her women really seem to be doing here, though it may be in the interests of the most admirable or illustrious cause? Nor will that life of fame and luxury which Cather returns to and which she conveys so well quite answer this question either, as Thea herself admits when she reflects that the unexpected favors of fortune, no matter how dazzling, do not mean very much in comparison with those things "which in some way met our original want.'

As a matter of fact, one *could* view Willa Cather's representation of her pioneer and artistic heroines as a turning-away, not only from a distasteful contemporary society, but also from a sensitive and crucial area of emotional experience: that is, from all the more or less involved consequences of what we call ordinary human relationships. In any case, the work of her second period will record the stress of an increasingly acute spiritual conflict, if not that of an actual psychic wound. For there, indeed, her figures will learn to live without delight, as she says, and will fall out of 'all domestic and social relations.'

3. A World Above the World

NOT THAT THE HEROINE of 'The Diamond Mine,' for instance, can be viewed as a complete ascetic.

Cressida Garnet is another of Willa Cather's Midland

artists who is fighting for her life, 'for a beginning . . . for growth . . . for eminence and perfection.' But 'Cressy,' hailing from Ohio, plagued by her provincial relatives, and almost devoured by the sycophants who attend upon a glamorous operatic star, is a lighter version of Thea Kronborg, just as most of the stories in *Youth and the Bright Medusa,* in 1920, are more popular and entertaining variations on Cather's central themes up to this point.

I should add that they are very good stories, as well as models of technical competence. (It is interesting to see how she can suggest a milieu or a personality in less than a dozen lines of even the frothiest of these tales.) Quite frankly now within the purlieu of the Wharton-James school, Cather moves about her drawing rooms and salons with a charm that is less evident, perhaps, in the bleak winters and the hot, bursting summers of the Nebraska plains. Those musical afternoons around Washington Square have some attractive moments: the operatic stars, their attendants and satellites, the waiting carriages at dusk, the solid, heavy, cautious American businessmen, and the more generous and reckless artistic heroines, who are, however, not without their own cunning. For what rescues these tales from their own glamour is at once Cather's knowledge of the facts of life, and her realization that facts, after all, are only part of life. And if this lower Fifth Avenue scene of the nineteen-hundreds is to a large degree a sort of cultural climax to a period of material aggrandisement—a little apex of sensibility whose apparently infinite base was the great American fortunes at the turn of the century—it is also true that *Youth and the Bright Medusa* conveys the surface of the scene very skillfully. Perhaps, indeed, these last modulated tones of the Age of Innocence seem more attractive because of their uncertain origins.

In such a 'legend' as that of the Aztec Queen in the story called 'Coming, Aphrodite!' we may become aware of Cather's concern with the more perverse forms of human feeling. And the artist-hero of the story abandons his career for the sake of a capricious and tempestuous girl simply because 'she was older than art, because she was the most overwhelming thing that had ever come into his life.' (It may be worth mentioning that the defiance of social taboos, which seems to be completely outside the ken of Sinclair Lewis's aspiring 'bourjoyces,' and which Scott Fitzgerald's middle-class rebels are constantly struggling to achieve, is almost purely instinctive on the part of Willa Cather's élite.) But this is still the early Cather, the subtle, intense, and entertaining Cather who has so positive a sense of the 'original wants' of her people as well as of their aspirations—and also of those extravagant human impulses that play havoc with our wants and our aspirations alike. Most of the stories in *Youth and the Bright Medusa* were apparently written in the late teens; some of them are reprinted from her first volume of tales, *The Troll Garden,* in 1905.

Even here, though, the western scene of these early tales —this 'borderland between ruffianism and civilization,' this 'desert of newness and ugliness and sordidness'—is presented in a somewhat different light from that of Cather's pioneer idylls. The glimpses of the urban masses or 'the lower manufacturing world' of New York are hardly more reassuring. And, in one of the most interesting tales of *Youth and the Bright Medusa,* there is a curious view of her own cosmopolitan world of art, fame, and enchantment. The young hero of 'Paul's Case' yearns for 'cool things and soft lights and fresh flowers'; the rest of his life is but 'a sleep and a forgetting,' while money is the wall that stands between 'all he loathed and all he wanted.'

Yet the writer regards her hero's early passion for culture as a sort of 'morbid desire.' His visits to Carnegie Hall and the theatrical playhouses of Pittsburgh take on the aspects of an emotional debauch. And he is described, in the end, as not merely a neurotic adolescent, but as an actual criminal who kills himself to atone for his guilt. Is there really such a gulf between ordinary existence—the gray monotony and those 'hopeless, unrelieved years' of existence in Pittsburgh, and the splendid life of Cather's artists and eastern aristocrats? In any case these undertones of remorse and repentance, of almost a religious sense of sin, are to persist in Cather's work, while the split between her two worlds is sharpened in her next two novels.*

There is no doubt that *One of Ours,* in 1922, is Cather's weakest novel, up to this point. The Nebraska countryside from the turn of the last century to the First World War is her scene, as she carries her frontier chronicle a step forward. Her hero, Claude Wheeler, is another western farm boy who is trying to find a direction for his life in a changing society. Certainly the change in the West—the increase of wealth, the establishment of more distinct

* Willa Cather's early poems, which are reprinted in her volume of verse, *April Twilights,* in 1923, are for the most part rather skillful variations on conventional poetic themes and traditional verse forms. In the later poems of the volume, it is interesting to compare her ode to an unknown Roman youth whose look 'arraigns a social order somehow entrammelled with his pain' with her lines on that Packingtown infant, a Polack brat, who 'Twisting a shoestring noose . . . joylessly torments a cat.' Yet such a sonnet as 'L'Envoi,' which opens,

> Where are the loves that we have loved before
> When once we are alone, and shut the door?
> No matter whose the arms that held me fast,
> The arms of Darkness hold me at the last . . .

is an eloquent example of Cather's less sociological emotions, as well as of the sort of despairing wit, curiously close to the Millay-Parker vein, that runs through the love poems of the volume. (*April Twilights* is copyright, 1923, by Willa Cather, and the above lines of verse are quoted by permission of the publisher, Alfred A. Knopf.)

social classes and of increasingly uniform standards of behavior, and the final absorption and evening-out of the original immigrant stocks—this whole 'Americanization' of Cather's original western scene ought to be an interesting theme for the novelist, and, as a matter of fact, the opening sections of *One of Ours* deal with many of its implications. Claude's father, the shrewd and prosperous 'modern' farmer, employs 'the roughest and dirtiest hired men in the country' while he buys every new labor-saving device in order to keep up with 'the bristling march of events.'

The Ehrlichs, the cultivated townspeople who rescue Claude from the 'poisonous reticence' of his family, actually have no more money than the Wheelers. 'They merely knew how to live . . . and spent their money on themselves, instead of on machines to do the work and machines to entertain people.' With prosperity, moreover, came a kind of callousness, so Cather says:

> The farmer raised and took to market things with an intrinsic value; wheat and corn as good as could be grown anywhere in the world, hogs and cattle that were the best of their kind. In return he got manufactured articles of poor quality; showy furniture that went to pieces, carpets and draperies that faded, clothes that made a handsome man look like a clown. Most of his money was paid out for machinery,—and that, too, went to pieces. A steam thrasher didn't last long; a horse outlived three automobiles.

And, as to property itself: 'the people who had it were slaves to it, and the people who didn't have it were slaves to them.' Claude's brother Bayliss, cautious, narrow, mean, 'quick at figures and undersized for a farmer,' with a stock of moral maxims, a notebook of expenses, and a deep-seated sense of injury: this Bayliss Wheeler of Cather's, who is not altogether unlike Faulkner's Jason Compson in *The Sound and the Fury,* and who finally leaves the farm altogether in order to go into the farm-implement business, seems to be the prototype of her new economic man. Down in the Square of Colorado Springs, the statue of Kit Carson still points westward. 'But there was no West, in that sense, any more.'

Apparently so much more secure and easy than her pioneer scene, this whole new western panorama of Cather's actually is more crude, bleak, and hostile. *One of Ours,* slower in pace, bulky in structure, and more realistic in tone, lacks her usual warmth of feeling. The human relationships here are abstract, the episodes of ordinary farm life are flat, just as, indeed, her summary of the 'machine change' in the West is curiously naïve and remote in comparison with Sherwood Anderson's picture of the same historical process in *Winesburg, Ohio,* or *Poor White.* 'There were people, even in Frankfort, who had imagination and generous impulses,' says the country schoolteacher of the Cather novel, 'but they were all, she had to admit, inefficient—failures. . . . If a strong boy like Claude, so well endowed and so fearless, must fail simply because he had that finer strain in his nature—then life was not worth the chagrin it held for a passionate heart like hers.' And the point is that if Cather has very often described, she has never before announced, as it were, the chagrin of a passionate heart.

What we do feel, instead, in the later sections of *One of Ours,* is the familiar, the stereotyped sentiment of the 'Revolt from the Village' which marked our post-war literature: that last discordant cry of an earlier and more genuine rural discontent which now echoed chiefly in the flats and studios of the urban centers.* And it is interesting to realize that the opening pages of *A Lost Lady,* in 1923, contain the first instance of wanton cruelty in Cather's work—the blinding of the woodpecker by young Ivy Peters—the same Ivy Peters, the budding western 'democrat,' who, at the novel's close, will take over Marian Forrester as another piece of valuable property. This is the background of our introduction to a most attractive heroine, and to the Burlington Railroad society which flourished so colorfully in the closing decades of the last century, according to Cather, and which, with its winter seasons at Colorado Springs, its parties, dances, and formal midnight dinners, is as necessary to Mrs. Forrester's existence as money or the jewels her husband bought her 'in acknowledgment of things he could not gracefully utter.'

For Cather's new heroine is by no means another Alexandra Bergson or Ántonia Shimerda. Reflecting as she does the highest gloss of the frontier society in the period when the tycoons had not yet been tamed, and when the women, indeed, were still the most subtle form of booty, and themselves had cultivated, with quite as sure a sense of the market, the charms as well as the duties of their position, Mrs. Forrester is as shrewd as she is gay, extravagant, and vain. Mocking at 'the proprieties she observed' and inheriting 'the magic of contradiction,' she is the best of that whole line of Cather's Edwardian ladies from the

* Similarly, the portraits of both Claude Wheeler's possessive mother and his frigid wife reflect the rather theatrical Freudianism of the early nineteen-twenties, and Claude, confused, ineffectual, the victim of 'a cursed kind of sensibility' in an environment he disdains, may remind you of all those sad young men of the post-war period, from John Dos Passos's musician in *Three Soldiers* to E. E. Cummings's poet-painter in *The Enormous Room. One of Ours* is a mélange of 'modern' trends which Willa Cather handles poorly and never returns to. But her view of the First World War itself is quite different from that of the younger writers. Claude finds his salvation through the war and dies 'believing his own country better than it is.'

Hilda Burgoyne of *Alexander's Bridge* to the Cressida Garnet of *Youth and the Bright Medusa*—a graceful and rather deceptive line of ladies, whose reticence hardly implies innocence. But in the lost lady herself, the sensuous attraction of all these cultivated Catheresque heroines has almost become a form of corruption, while, in terms of the novel's craft, what is remarkable is the technic of exposition by which this is never quite presented and at the same time made inescapably clear. Perhaps only that final and crucial scene in which Niel Herbert, outside of Mrs. Forrester's window and knowing that Frank Ellinger has stayed the night with her, hears a woman's soft laughter, 'impatient, indulgent, teasing, eager,' and suddenly realizes the truth about her: perhaps only that climactic scene of the first half of *A Lost Lady* is too obvious in its implications.

'Beautiful women,' Niel thinks—'Beautiful women, whose beauty meant more than it said . . . was their brilliancy always fed by something coarse and concealed? Was that their secret?' But then he begins to learn the other facts about Marian Forrester: her need for adulation and companionship, her 'power to live,' as she says, which has grown more intense through her solitary existence with a dying man in an obscure country town, and, at the same time, her boredom, her drinking, her desperate little plots to escape from Sweet Water—to see whether she has 'anything left worth saving': all this, which she confides to Niel as, her hand upon his arm, she urges him 'faster and faster up the lane,' and as Niel asks himself what hope there could possibly be for her? It is at this point, as Cather's heroine goes downhill, that Captain Forrester himself, who, as we also come to discover, 'knew everything; more than anyone else; all there was to know about Marian Forrester,' but who has hitherto been a sort of massive and somber backdrop for Mrs. Forrester's deft sallies, begins to figure so memorably in the novel.

Is he typical of those 'dreamers and great-hearted adventurers' who had settled the Old West, a 'courteous brotherhood,' as Cather says, who were impractical to the point of magnificence? At any rate, it is clear that the central human relationship of the novel is meant to represent the dissolution of a society and an age, as well as of the crippled railroad builder and the lost lady. This time, too, Cather's familiar western observer is leaving the West for good. Niel Herbert is going away forever, we are told, and is making the final break with 'everything that had been dear to him in his boyhood.' The people, the very country itself, were changing so fast that there would be nothing to come back to—

> He had seen the end of an era, the sunset of the pioneer. He had come upon it when already its glory was nearly spent. So in the buffalo days a traveller used to come upon the embers of a hunter's fire on the prairie, after the hunter was up and gone. . . . This was the very end of the road-making West; the men who had put plains and mountains under the iron harness were old; some were poor, and even the successful ones were hunting for rest and a brief reprieve from death. It was already gone, that age; nothing could ever bring it back.

And the final 'secret' of Marian Forrester's history, the true cause of her disaster, indeed, is that she prefers life on any terms—that she was not willing 'to immolate herself, like the widow of all these great men, and die with the pioneer period to which she belonged.'

So the meaning of Cather's quotation on the title page of *A Lost Lady* becomes clear: '. . . Come, my coach! Good night, ladies; good night, sweet ladies. Good night, good night.' And the haunting, elegiac tone of the novel, which may recall that of Ernest Hemingway's similar farewell from the green hills of Africa ('Let the others come to America who did not know that they had come too late . . .'); a tone that is not unfamiliar in contemporary letters as a whole, is admirably designed to convey the theme of the novel. Isn't it singular, though, after the wonderful delicacy of the early exposition—and up to this point Marian Forrester is one of the most interesting heroines in our literature—that the account of her disintegration should be so obvious and heavy? Those envious, snooping village housewives who invade the Forrester house when Captain Forrester is dying and after his wife has collapsed; those stammering town yokels with whom Marian Forrester is then forced to seek her pleasure, and whom we see cramming and gorging themselves at the table where Captain Forrester had once so majestically carved the roast; all those ordinary townspeople of Sweet Water, Colorado, who are viewed here with a sort of weary contempt—have they really changed so much from the western types of Cather's own frontier tales? 'She was still her indomitable self going through the old part,' Cather says of the later Marian Forrester, 'but only the stage hands were left to listen to her.' And these less privileged citizens of Sweet Water are now indeed the stage hands in the drama of a dying western aristocracy.

For the Forresters of *A Lost Lady are* meant to represent a superior social caste. Mrs. Forrester is 'one of the rich and great of the world,' as the German tailor's children, the Blums, realize very early in the story, and as, with their feudal European background, they more easily accept the fact that such a fortunate and privileged class 'was an axiomatic fact in the social order'—that 'these warm-blooded, quick-breathing people took chances, followed impulses only dimly understandable to a boy who was wet and weather-chapped all the year.' Or so Cather informs us. But is the history of our western railroad builders—these directors, general managers, vice-presidents, superintendents 'whose names we all knew'—or of the land-grant operators who came along with them, and the large cattle- and grain-shippers who were soon allied to them: is this whole earlier empire-building clan that is described so eloquently and so elliptically in *A Lost Lady* really to be viewed in such terms?

One might say that the chances they took in reality, the impulses they actually followed, are less dimly understandable when they aren't viewed through a child's eyes. These primal spokesmen of the industrial order who stretched their steel to the western ocean and entrenched themselves in the passes and gorges of a new continent, these early missionaries of a new and boundless materialism, were bolder, perhaps. In a sense they were closer to the earth which they divided off and despoiled or to the 'management of men,' as Cather says, than to the issuance of bonds, shares, or preferred stock. Not yet caught up by the inner logic of their own system, they were still adventurers and exploiters rather than manipulators, speculators, or bookkeepers. . . . In plain terms, though, was this 'courteous brotherhood' of hers so completely different from that later generation of shrewd young men 'trained to petty economies by hard times' which she describes with such disdain—or so remote from that whole new business world coming up in the West, in which, so it seems to Cather, it was increasingly difficult for a young man to find an honorable career? For that matter, is Ivy Peters himself, the new type of western trader and 'equalitarian' who takes over the Forrester estate and Mrs. Forrester for apparently the same reason: this coarse and calculating

Ivy Peters, is he so completely different from Cather's Cyrus Dalzell, the president of the Colorado and Utah Railroad, with his private car, his gallant and sympathetic manner, and his little gifts of port and sherry? I mean, if you will ignore for a moment the difference in the bank account and the social poise of her two western figures, and keep in mind the fact that many of our Cyrus Dalzells started out as an Ivy Peters.

In terms of these issues, then, *A Lost Lady* reflects a curious 'sunset of the pioneer'—a prismatic sunset, an almost mythical pioneer. Admirable as the story is with reference to its human relationships and emotional values, and remarkable for its creation of an atmosphere, it is still a kind of touching fairy tale of the more beneficent Robber Barons, or their second and third cousins. It is a reflection not of a society but of a point of view that, increasingly narrow, selective, and fanciful, is actually retreating further and further from society—an auctorial point of view that becomes evident in the next and crucial novel of Cather's work in the middle twenties.

At the outset, however, *The Professor's House,* in 1925, hardly deserves this distinction. Its hero, Godfrey St. Peter, a rather effete professor in a commonplace hinterland college, may remind you of those *academes,* the perpetual Rhodes Scholars, who have set up their private little worlds of taste, their oases of sensibility, in the midst of the arid western plains, and the opening sections of *The Professor's House* probably are a little too fastidious. They mirror the delicacy of the indoor arts; they offer a little sermon on manners for less enlightened midlanders who can't manage to serve rare sherry, or have a sailboat on Lake Michigan and a wife as beautiful as Lillian St. Peter and such well-bred daughters. Even more than Claude Wheeler, in *One of Ours,* Cather's new hero represents that aesthetic revolt of the middle twenties which regarded our materialistic civilization with contempt when it regarded it at all. In the central story of the novel, it is a scientific invention, commercialized and exploited, which has actually corrupted the campus where St. Peter has taught, the old friends with whom he has worked, and even his own wife and daughters; which has destroyed the professor's house, the very source and symbol of his existence.

But *The Professor's House is* a symbolical novel, and in the framework of allegory which we gradually catch on to, even the apparent flaws in the story—the exaggerated finesse of the St. Peter household, the curious sense of remoteness from the world—take on a certain validity. Probably the name of Cather's professorial hero is not to be taken in vain, while the pervading tone of the novel, reticent, elliptic, and mysterious, has also been devised to suit the theme. At least here, in terms of the central human relationships of the novel—husband and wife, parent and child, brother and sister—are some of Cather's most sensitive and acute observations on the human family in general: and here the persistent undertones of suffering in these human relationships, of thwarted desire, of broken delight, of jealousy, malice, and actual anguish, become more marked. That familiar wound of Cather's, 'healed and hardened and hopeless,' begins to throb. In a remarkable series of minor episodes, an underlying pattern of emotional despair becomes dominant, as, step by step, *The Professor's House* records the process of St. Peter's withdrawal from his scholarly work, his academic position and associates, his own home—from the whole nexus of those close family relationships which have always, in the past, sustained him through their warmth and friendliness. 'He did not regret his life,' Cather's hero thinks, as he prepares himself to leave it. 'He did not regret his life, but he was indifferent to it'—

> There must, he was repeating to himself, there must be some way in which a man who had always tried to live up to his responsibilities could, when the hour of desperation came, avoid meeting his own family . . . In great misfortunes, he told himself, people want to be alone. They have a right to be. And the misfortunes that occur within one are the greatest. Surely the saddest thing in the world is falling out of love—if once one has ever fallen in. . . . Falling out, for him, seemed to mean falling out of all domestic and social relations, out of his place in the human family, indeed.

Thus, while *The Professor's House* is an allegory of human imperfection in terms of its outward scene ("My fortunes have corrupted honest men"), it is even more clearly a chronicle of inner defeat and spiritual withdrawal. In this context the curious episode in the novel which is called 'Tom Outland's Story,' and which transfers us from the St. Peter household to the ancient Cliff Dwellers of New Mexico, this irrelevant episode contains the crux of the novel's meaning. For it is on the Cliff Dwellers' mesa, up there in the stone city of the dead which Tom Outland has discovered and which, in a way, has brought about his own destruction—up there, after his friends have deceived him and the city itself has been looted and stripped, that Cather's spokesman experiences a sense of almost mystical exaltation: 'that glorious feeling that I've never had anywhere else, the feeling of being *on the mesa,* in a world above the world. And the air, my God, what air!'—and realizes that the mesa is no longer an adventure, but 'a religious emotion.'

For the Parable of the Mesa is at once the climax of Willa Cather's search for a sort of transcendent splendor in life and the most extreme point of her own withdrawal from all domestic and social relations—and I mean, of course, that whole industrial and engineering society from which, as we saw, the first period of her work already represented a sort of escape into a more heroic or idyllic past. In terms of the pioneer novels themselves, we noticed her hostility to the increasingly respectable age of rural wealth and machines which, in *One of Ours,* she is not only scornful of but hardly tries to understand. And if *A Lost Lady* depicts the 'sunset of the pioneer,' not indeed in terms of fact, but in Cather's own view of the facts, isn't it clear that the glow, the intensity, the actual 'magic' of her last frontier tale, come out of a more intense need for mystery and enchantment in the face of her growing disenchantment about contemporary life? A disenchantment that is marked precisely by the increasing sense of weariness and frustration, and by that final acceptance of spiritual defeat and withdrawal which is recorded in *The Professor's House.*

In a way, what technical achievement could better convey the discordant emotions of a writer at once so quick and alive in the best of her work and so well acquainted with pain and suffering, so much in love with life and so completely estranged from the life of her own time, than that final image of the solitary individual among the ruins of an ancient culture? This very Catheresque individual, who has the sense of both an irremediable disaster and a unique exaltation; who is marked at once by the conviction that he has nothing more to lose and by the realization that, through escaping from his merely human ties and obligations, alone in space and solitude and under the 'consuming light' of the southwestern skies, he has, as

Cather says, 'found everything.' From this eminence, indeed, the Washington society which is contrasted with the mesa in *The Professor's House:* the assortment of self-seeking bureaucrats and servile clerks, the hundreds of 'little black-coated men pouring out of white buildings'—is quite inconsequential.

Yet there are some curious elements in the crucial episode at the middle of Cather's career. Is it, in fact, a conversion or a trauma? For the transfiguration on the mesa also seems to answer that more obscure sense of guilt and retribution which is evident in her work from her earliest short stories and which parallels her search for a special splendor and enchantment in life—a desire *for* an irremediable disaster. And the final realization of the search, the glorious feeling of a world above the world, the marvelous air, the consuming light of the mesa—are they, after all, too much for a single individual to bear? In any case it is while Cather's St. Peter is absorbed in his reflections about the mesa that he attempts to commit suicide—and is rescued by the Augusta of the novel, the faithful Catholic seamstress with her 'little religious book.'

And this singular spiritual ambivalence, this equivocal dialogue between the forms of life and the forms of death—and by now it is difficult to say which is which—is carried on into the period of Cather's better-known and more strictly religious novels. Nor can we afford to forget her ambiguous alliance with the great American fortunes.

4. My Chamber, My Terrestrial Paradise

In the sequence of Cather's novels, however, there is no doubt that *The Professor's House* is a novel of death and rebirth—of a spiritual purging and regeneration, and of that second coming which, formalized in the central rituals of religion, is actually part of the deepest experience of man. Although the literary work reflects rather than conveys the experience in this case, and its real nature still remains obscure, one can't doubt the validity of the conflict, nor, in the next period of Cather's work, the interest, one might almost say the charm, of her catharsis.

The first of these new works, *My Mortal Enemy,* in 1926, is hardly more than a long short story, a novella. The simplicity of its form, the perfection of its finish may remind you of *A Lost Lady;* its heroine is another one of Cather's attractive and willful women—those Madame Bovarys of the western plains. But the account of Myra Henshawe's wild and glamorous youth, her unhappy marriage, and her final return to Catholicism is a sort of postscript to *The Professor's House,* and the ambiguous elements of that struggle become more apparent now. The little town of Parthia, Illinois, where the story opens, is homely and unlettered; by comparison, the New York scene of the nineteen-hundreds is cultivated to the extreme.

For a moment the city itself, like the seasons of Cather's earlier novel, seems to have been brought indoors:

> It seemed to me so neat, after the raggedness of our Western cities; so protected by good manners and courtesy—like an open-air drawing room. I could well imagine a winter dancing party being given there, or a reception for some distinguished European visitor. The snow fell lightly all the afternoon, and friendly old men with brooms kept sweeping the paths—very ready to talk to a girl from the country, and to brush off a bench so that she could sit down. The trees and shrubbery seemed well-groomed and sociable, like pleasant people. . . . Here, I felt, winter brought no desolation; it was tamed, like a polar bear led on a leash by a beautiful lady.

Or so Cather's 'Nellie' thinks about Madison Square in the days when, half commercial and half social, it was at the parting of the ways. For this is again that 'Bohemian' society of *Youth and the Bright Medusa,* a Bohemia of the élite, of talent *and* money, of jewels and flowers and double-breasted morning coats as well as one's artistic integrity—of an earlier, more elaborate, formal, and decorous lower Fifth Avenue society, that is, which isn't lacking in an instinctive and generous vitality, or, as in the case of Cather's heroine, a 'hidden richness.' For the salons of Myra Henshawe's group take on a more brilliant and exotic tone here, the musical and theatrical celebrities glitter ever more brightly. 'Their talk quite took my breath away; they said such exciting and fantastic things about people, books, music—anything; they seemed to talk together a kind of highly flavoured special language.'

Probably the rhythms of Cather's own prose in turn have never been so delicately balanced between exaltation and sobriety. 'You send a handsome fellow like Ewan Gray to a fine girl like Esther, and it's Christmas Eve, and they rise above us and the white world around us, and there isn't anybody, not a tramp on the park benches, that wouldn't wish them well—and very likely hell will come of it!' The opening invocation to this shining eastern scene in the days when the *Wilhelm der Grosse* was sliding up the Hudson, and when, at twilight, Saint Gaudens's Diana stepped out freely against a violet sky, is a remarkable episode in Cather's work, just as the New Year's Eve party at the Henshawes', only some fifty-odd pages later, marks the collapse of this whole wonderfully glamorous, thrilling, and mysterious eastern world of wealth and cultivation. 'When kindness has left people, even for a few moments, we become afraid of them, as if their reason had left them. When it has left a place where we have always found it, it is like shipwreck; we drop from security into something malevolent and bottomless.' The light and vibrant eastern air now seems still and cold—'like the air in a refrigerating room.'

Moreover, while the ostensible theme of *My Mortal Enemy* is that of Myra Henshawe's religious conversion, and the latter half of the story is heavily weighted with the ecclesiastical symbolism of the conversion, the real achievement of the novel is the account of an intense and destructive human relationship. 'People can be lovers and enemies at the same time,' says Cather's heroine. 'A man and a woman draw apart from that long embrace, and see what they have done to each other. . . . When there are children, that feeling goes through natural changes. But when it remains so personal—something gives way in one. In age we lose everything; even the power to love.' Does the ebony crucifix which Myra now keeps constantly beside her compensate in some degree for her sense of loss? Is religion itself different from anything else, because in religion seeking is finding? 'Light and silence,' Cather says, 'they heal all one's wounds—all but one, and that is healed by dark and silence.' These are hardly the accents of discovery or of joyfulness, of course, while even Myra's final realization that her mortal enemy has always been herself, that she is 'a greedy, selfish worldly woman,' carries a curious note of lamentation, rather than of repentance. 'It's been the ruin of us both. We've destroyed each other. I should have stayed with my uncle. It was money I needed. We've thrown our lives away.'

Very early in the story it was this same uncle of Myra's, John Driscoll, the rich man of Parthia, Illinois, who declared that 'a poor man stinks and God hates him.' Was it money, also, that helped to make his departure from the world so impressive to Cather's western observer—

> From the freshness of roses and lilies, from the glory of the high altar, he had gone straight to the greater glory, through smoking censers and candles and stars. . . . Was it not better to get out of the world with such pomp and dramatic splendor than to linger on in it, having to take account of shirts and railway trains, and getting a double chin into the bargain?

And is it possibly the pomp and dramatic splendor of her place in society which Cather's religious heroine still yearns for, instead of a more rigorous régime of poverty and humility, which she has apparently espoused? In any case, it is interesting to notice that the formal mode of religious salvation which brought her earlier hero only to the bloomless side of life and 'the taste of bitter herbs' should lead here to smoking censors and the sweet-smelling flowers of death.

As a matter of fact, *My Mortal Enemy* is a sort of farewell to Cather's earlier American scene of wealth and cultivation. This is her last story to deal with it for almost a decade, and her return to it, in the *Lucy Gayheart* of 1935, will be under quite different circumstances. It is worth noticing, too, that the central theological image of *Death Comes for the Archbishop,* in 1927, should be that of the Virgin Mother ('Only a Woman, Divine, could know all that woman can suffer'), while the central psychological image should again be that of the Rock. In these pages, whatever doubts we may have had as to the significance of the Mesa in Cather's work are clarified by her reflections on the Cliff Cities of the Acomas—those primitive Mexican Indians, 'born in fear and dying by violence for generations,' who had at last 'taken this leap away from the earth,' and on their rock had found 'the hope of all suffering and tormented creatures—safety':

They came down to the plain to hunt and grow their crops but there was always a place to go back to. If a band of Navajos were on the Acoma's trail, there was still one hope; if he could reach his rock—Sanctuary! On the winding stone stairway up the cliff, a handful of men could keep off a multitude. The rock of Acoma had never been taken by a foe but once,—by Spaniards in armour. It was very different from a mountain fastness; more lonely, more stark and grim, more appealing to the imagination. The rock, when one came to think of it, was the utmost expression of human need; even mere feeling yearned for it; it was the highest comparison of loyalty in love and friendship. Christ Himself had used that comparison for the disciple to whom He gave the keys of His Church. And the Hebrews of the Old Testament, always being carried captive into foreign lands,—their rock was an idea of God, the only thing their conquerors could not take from them. . . . The Acomas, who must share the universal human yearning for something permanent, enduring, without shadow of change,—they had their idea in substance. They actually lived upon their Rock; were born upon it and died upon it.

Here the Mesa has become identified with the Rock: stark, grim, enduring. Isn't it curious, though, that Cather's Sanctuary should be so clearly now a leap *away* from the earth, a barren mesa, indeed, on which there is "not a tree or a blade of green . . . not a handful of soil," except, perhaps, the graveyard? Here, too, her hero has lost that first mystical exaltation, the sense of a final and absolute freedom, of a communion with space and solitude in a world above the world. On the mesa of the Acomas, in fact, the Father Latour of *Death Comes for the Archbishop* feels that he is celebrating the Mass for antediluvian creatures—'for types of life so old, shut within their shells, that the sacrifice on Calvary could hardly reach back so far.' The descendants of the Acomas are like rock-turtles on their rock. 'Something reptilian he felt here, something that had endured by immobility, a kind of life out of reach, like the crustaceans in their armour'—in contrast, as Cather says, to European man 'and his glorious history of desire and dreams.' Just as clearly, then, if the Rock has become her central image of survival, it represents *mere* survival, without everything that makes life pleasurable and livable. If the Rock represents the utmost expression of human need, its safety has been achieved at the expense of all other human wants. This may recall another celebrated land of 'rock without water' in the very midst of the American twenties, that of T. S. Eliot himself, and from this vantage-point we can more easily understand Cather's 'historical' novel of New Mexico in the nineteenth century.

For the 'Amérique' of *Death Comes for the Archbishop* is a New World indeed. That opening scene of the novel, in Rome, in the eighteen-forties, with Cather's three Cardinals and a missionary Bishop from the Great Lakes ('Their manners were gentle, their voices low and agreeable.'), is quite a move East for the Anguished Lady in the land of Dos Passos's Power-Super-Power, as one might say; while these low and agreeable tones may also be compared with what a Tom Wolfe was just then calling 'the loud raucous voice of America.' And surely the accouterments of Cather's new western settlers: the burning piñon logs, for instance, that produce 'a perpetual odour of incense about us,' or the soups and salads that are the quintessence of 'a thousand years of history,' as Father Joseph Vaillant informs the newly appointed Vicar Apostolic of New Mexico; or that remarkable mission bell of Cather's, whose tone, 'full, clear, with something bland and suave,' each note floating through the air like a globe of silver, brings back to her Bishop the sudden, pervasive sense of the past, of the Holy Land, the Orient itself—these typical accouterments of her new western settlers are of a different order from the axe, the plow, and the Bible of *O Pioneers!* . . . Among these French and Spanish missionaries and explorers of the southwestern territory in the mid-nineteenth century, the 'simple hospitality of the frontier' includes clerical cassocks of violet silk, military coats of buckskin and velvet, hoopskirts from New Orleans 'all covered with little garlands of pink satin roses'—while outside the party which Doña Olivares has arranged for the officers of the Post at Santa Fe, quite like the mob that swirls around Delmonico's in Scott Fitzgerald's 'May Day,' the drunken American cowboys riot and plunder. You may also notice the series of acrid references to the Ohio countryside from which Cather's missionaries have emigrated: the 'hideous houses and churches, the ill-kept farms and gardens,' for example, or 'the slovenly, sordid aspect of the towns.' Or the description of her own Denver City, Colorado, during the throes of the gold rush: a city of tents, shacks, saloons, and gambling houses, and of ignorant wanderers and wastrels who are 'adrift in a lawless society without spiritual guidance.' In a way, Cather's whole new view of the nineteenth-century American scene is encompassed in this glimpse of an obscene mining town, just as the poor-white 'Smiths' of her narrative, the leaders of a small group of 'low-caste Protestants' who are notable chiefly for their low habits and evil tongues, almost come to represent the entire American populace of the period.

For the time and place of *Death Comes for the Archbishop* represent not merely a drastic move away from the modern American scene, but also a changed view of the American past—of the frontier itself. Isn't it clear, moreover, to what degree Cather's rejection of her native scene is marked by a kind of infantile malice?—while in turn those impoverished Mexican peasants, who were treated so well in *The Song of the Lark,* and who became a source of human warmth and of life itself for her earlier heroine, at least as compared with the cold, sharp Yankee traders, now are altogether too sweet, loving, and pious. Were they *all* such willing and eager converts to the New Faith? Just as there are no tyrannical missionaries to speak of in Cather's historical chronicle, there are few examples of native resistance to Catholicism. The religious conquest of the New World becomes a rout, or a sort of transcendental triumph. And the pagan rituals of the Indian tribes—the fertility festivals or the sacrificial dances and scourgings of the Penitentes, the whole sexual and semi-orgiastic nature of these primitive religious forms: all of this, which makes such a fascinating chapter of the religious history of the New World, is softened and sweetened in Cather's account.

In just those sections of *Death Comes for the Archbishop* which deal with the meeting of different cultures—'The Legend of Fray Baltazar,' or 'Snake Root,' or 'Padre Martinez'—Cather almost denies her own persistent concern with the 'darker' instincts: that is, with those temptations and acerbations of the flesh which have rested beneath the cultivated surface of her art, and have actually been responsible for the tension of her work. And is her emphasis here on the more formal emotions of the Church, and on its apparitions and 'miracles'—is this really an adequate alternative for the artist? 'Where there is great love there are always miracles,' Cather's Bishop declares—

> 'One might say that an apparition is human vision corrected by divine love. . . . The Miracles of the Church

> seem to me to rest not so much upon faces or voices, or healing power coming suddenly to us from afar off, but upon our perceptions being made finer, so that for a moment our eyes can see and our ears can hear what is there about us always.'

We may still be affected by the cadence and tone of such passages as this, just as it is the perfection of the craft as a whole in *Death Comes for the Archbishop* that obscures the real loss in Cather's art and, in a way, her humanity too. For isn't it just that 'human vision' of hers which is lacking for the most part in this chronicle of divine love?—while human perceptions, in turn, can be made so fine that the eye no longer sees and the ear no longer hears what is there about us always. It is this ever more restricted spiritual course, at any rate—this movement *back* in terms of time and place, this movement *away* from the real areas of human feeling—that brings us finally in *Shadows on the Rock,* in 1931, to the French Quebec of the late seventeenth century: to the 'well-ordered universe' of the Ursulines and Hospitalières:

> this all-important earth, created by God for a great purpose, the sun which He made to light it by day, the moon which He made to light it by night,—and the stars, made to beautify the vault of heaven like frescoes, and to be a clock and compass for man. And in this safe, lovingly arranged and ordered universe (not too vast, though nobly spacious), in this congenial universe, the drama of man went on at Quebec just as at home, and the Sisters played their accustomed part in it. There was sin, of course, and there was punishment after death; but there was always hope, even for the most depraved; and for those who died repentant, the Sister's prayers could do much,—no one might say how much.

—and also to the Convent of that attractive young recluse, Cather's Jeanne Le Ber, who believes that '*ma chambre est mon paradis terrestre; c'est mon centre; c'est mon élément . . . Je préfère ma cellule à tout le rest de l'univers.*'

There are very attractive things in *Shadows on the Rock,* to be sure. The descriptions of Quebec and of the Canadian wilderness around it, the changing seasons, the long ice-bound winters, the coming of the square-riggers in spring, touching, with their provisions and gossip from the court of Louis XIV, 'a goal so tiny out of an approach so vast'; the brief incisive portraits of French sailors such as the Saint Malouins, and trappers like Cather's Antoine, of suffering missionaries like Father Chabanel, and 'unfortunate' sinners like Blinker, formerly the king's hangman at Rouen—these are skillfully joined together to form a panoramic view of the 'graces and traditions' of the early French colonists in the New World. And such studies as that of 'Toinette, the gay woman of the Lower Town, or of the dying Count Frontenac, for whom, in the loneliness of the conqueror and the disenchantment of royalty, the world 'was not what he had thought it at twenty—or even at forty,' may remind us of a more familiar Cather.

In a sense, too, although Cather's intention isn't entirely clear, *Shadows on the Rock* may be viewed almost entirely as a children's story. In any case it is *as* a fairy tale of the Church and the New World—as a glowing account of Christian heroes, saints, and martyrs, and of ecclesiastical legends and miracles—that her last religious novel most clearly shows the direction of her middle period and the true nature of her goal. Just as the central spiritual vision of *Shadows on the Rock* is that altogether safe, soothing, and ornamental universe of Cather's Ursuline Sisters, the actual psychological scene is centered around the proper and tidy home life of the apothecary Auclair and the apothecary's daughter, the gentle, sweet, and pious Cécile herself; this innocent and untouched heroine of Cather's, who, without passion or the capacity for passion, grows up in a well-ordered sphere of loving-kindliness and cleanliness. Even her Pierre Charon, the hero of the fur trappers and the *coureurs de bois,* the free Frenchman of the forests with 'the good manners of the Old World, the dash and daring of the New': even this resourceful and subtle adaptation of Rousseau's noble savage who, it is true, does sometimes squander all his pay 'on drink and women and new guns, as his comrades did,' must finally surrender to the prevailing ethos of the respectable affections in *Shadows on the Rock.* Similarly, one of the loveliest lyrical passages in the novel, after Cécile has visited a family of ignorant country people, and at the moment when she actually reaches her maturity and no longer feels 'like a little girl, doing what she has been taught to do,' turns on this motif of, as it were, indoor bliss:

> They had kind ways, those poor Harnois, but that was not enough; one had to have kind things about one, too. . . . These coppers, big and little, these brooms and clouts and brushes were tools; and with them one made, not shoes or cabinet-work, but life itself. One made a climate within a climate; one made the days,—the complexion, the special flavour, the special happiness of each day as it passed; one made life.

'Oh, Father, I think our house is so beautiful!' Cécile cries. . . . 'I must have hot water, Papa.'

Isn't such an episode, touching as it is, a curious one to mark the end of Cather's entire religious pilgrimage? I mean, of course, the long and tormented spiritual search which we have followed, and which, after pushing its way back from the epoch of the American pioneers and tycoons to the New Mexico of the eighteen-fifties and the Quebec of the early seventeen-hundreds, has led us finally to a realm of the domestic virtues—to a psychological universe where, if sin and depravity do exist, they are always modulated, where all violence or recklessness of feeling has been finally subdued, and where the emotional norm is mildness, sweetness, goodness. . . . This achievement of Cather's has its own validity—this is a realm of feelings which can't be hurt. In a way, too, we must admire the resolution of her spiritual turmoil which has been achieved in both *Death Comes for the Archbishop* and *Shadows on the Rock*—a resolution, as we have seen, which encompasses both her yearning for tradition and her attraction to the frontier, Europe *and* America, and which has allowed her to move with grace from Rome or Fontainebleau to a Mexican pueblo, to be at ease with Pope Gregory XVI or a Madame de Maintenon and to be concerned with the most primitive Navajo or Iroquois tribesman. Moreover, hasn't she combined not only pomp and humility, the great and the obscure of this world, but even this world and the next world? At least she has managed to combine asceticism with the best French cuisine, and a renunciation of life with all the comforts of home in the very midst of the southwestern desert or the dark, interminable northern forests. This is surely a woman's way of salvation. But only a talented woman could so subtly join her need for spiritual absolution and her craving for worldly comfort and elegance in that final fusion of the Mesa and the Salon. This fusion has brought together all these psychological extremes in Cather's work at the cost, perhaps, of only one element in her art—her own underlying sense of life and reality, of passion and suffering.

For it is equally true that Willa Cather has achieved a

sentimental 'harmony' at the cost of all real emotional vitality. Both *Death Comes for the Archbishop* and *Shadows on the Rock* are tracts of divine love and of golden goodness which exclude just that uncertainty and anguish of human love, or that deeper sense of good and evil, which have been the distinguishing mark of her best work. By now the emphasis on religious ceremony has almost taken the place of the original emphasis on religion, while the artist's stress on the rich surface of things only serves to remind us of a lost richness of feeling. That 'mortal enemy' of Myra Henshawe's—that vain, selfish, worldly woman—was also in a sense her truest friend, for wasn't it out of this sort of emotional matrix that Cather had formed her true art? To a certain degree the salvation of the *religieuse* meant the destruction of the poet, and the chamber of Cather's Jeanne Le Ber, which is the nun's center, her element, her terrestrial paradise, almost marks the final subjugation of the wild land.

The story of 'Neighbour Rosicky,' in *Obscure Destinies,* in 1932, comes close to being an agrarian idyll. The accent on gaiety is a little forced in this account of an ordinary western farmer's tribulations and triumphs, and of Papa Rosicky's 'special gift of loving people.' Similarly, in the second of the three tales in the volume, 'Old Mrs. Harris,' Cather's heroine has all the virtues of age with few of its less ingratiating mannerisms, while the heroes of 'Two Friends' represent 'solidity, an entire absence of anything mean or small, easy carelessness, courage, a high sense of honour' in the daily affairs of an average Kansas community. *'Le but n'est rien; le chemin c'est tout,'* says one of Cather's personages here in the words of Michelet, but, as a matter of fact, the 'goal' of *Obscure Destinies* has pretty nearly fixed the course of its path. We realize that the volume is intended to indicate the whole range of her new values and beliefs and to present her mature view of the contemporary American scene. And this somewhat overpowering emphasis on the nobility of her literary spokesmen marks an odd return to that human family whose corruption and malice the Willa Cather of *The Professor's House,* just seven years before, had condemned, and all of whose social relationships she had apparently renounced.

Still, this *is* a return—and not merely to the artist's own environment, but to precisely that area of her society which she could hardly tolerate in her earlier work: to the less glamorous, common ordinary life of humanity, I mean —to what you might call its domestic existence. If the whole course of Cather's development over these seven years can be summarized by that leap from the earth to the rock, and from the rock to the dais, the final step of this whole curious circular literary pilgrimage is nevertheless a descent again: from the dais to the kitchen. Does one still have to have those 'kind things about one'—those coppers, brooms, clouts, and brushes which make the special happiness of each day as it passes for her last religious heroine? Does it almost seem, indeed, as though Cather has had to bring something of the dramatic splendor of life directly into its more prosaic affairs—has had to adorn as well as exalt the obscure scene of her return, and provide domesticity itself with the trappings of royalty? All the same we must acknowledge the instinctive realism, or even the *conscience* of the artist which, however fanciful its logic, has brought her back home again, closer to her native origins and ties, and the original sources of her art.

Moreover, there are less benevolent emotions in *Obscure Destinies,* and more familiar undertones and asides, and both here and in Cather's remaining works of the nineteen-thirties we shall follow up the central pattern of her writing. 'And yet, down under the frozen crusts, at the roots of the trees'—a more youthful heroine of hers has told us—'the secret of life was still safe, warm as the blood in one's heart; and the spring would come again! Oh, it would come again!'

And after this long solstice of the emotions, and this formal and ceremonial abdication of the writer's true temperament, we shall notice a curiously intense return to the patterns of her earlier work, to that warm 'secret' of her creative life.

5. *The Tragic Necessity*

FOR THE THREE TALES in *Obscure Destinies* are an exposition of those ties with the earth and the farm animals and growing things 'which are never made at all unless they are made early.' If they center around an idyllic agrarian existence, however, they also present glimpses of a sort of industrial inferno.

'To be a landless man was to be a wage-earner, a slave all your life; to have nothing, to be nothing,' Neighbor Rosicky thinks, while in the country what you had was, after all, your own—

> You didn't have to choose between bosses and strikers and go wrong either way. You didn't have to do with dishonest and cruel people. . . . In the country, if you had a mean neighbour, you could keep off his land and make him keep off yours. But in the city, all the foulness and misery and brutality of your neighbours was part of your life. The worst things he had come upon in his journey through the world were human,—depraved and poisonous specimens of man. To this day he could recall certain terrible faces in the London streets. There were mean people everywhere, to be sure, even in their own country

> town here. But they weren't tempered, hardened, sharpened like the treacherous people in cities who live by grinding or cheating or poisoning their fellow-men.

And you cannot miss the bitterness of this indictment; the whole mixture of contempt and frustration which has been absent from Cather's work during the long sabbatical from her own society.

It may be worth mentioning that Cather's 'Old Mrs. Harris' is no longer living among the southern gentry of her youth, 'where there were plenty of landless people glad to render service to the more fortunate,' but in a snappy little western democracy 'where every man was as good as his neighbour and out to prove it.' In turn, the Mr. Dillon and the Mr. Trueman who represent success and power in a little wooden town in a shallow Kansas River valley at a time when 'business was still a personal adventure,' who, indeed, inhabit a Main Street that Sinclair Lewis never knew, long before the period of pushing and boasting, of 'efficiency and advertising and progressive methods,' are contrasted with the little 'hopper men' of the new economic order. Are these 'Two Friends' rather quaint figures to serve as Cather's spokesmen for the depression years—to appear at almost the exact time when business had become a sort of national calamity? All the same, she has managed to suggest the end of an epoch in the break-up of the old friendship during the political disturbances of the eighteen-nineties. In these final reflections of the story on an old 'scar,' an old uneasiness—'the feeling of something broken that could so easily have been mended; of something delightful that was senselessly wasted, of a truth that was accidentally distorted'—you may catch the haunting refrain of an entire line of American writing which, from Howells to Hemingway, has been confronted with the latest developments of American life.

On a worldly level, the essays and sketches which are collected in *Not Under Forty,* in 1936, throw further light on a special literary temperament. This is Cather's only volume of non-fiction, and even the title which our author has selected for her first major public appearance indicates a deliberate and stylized retreat to the past, and to the recusant stand of 'age'—

> This book will have little interest for people under forty years of age. The world broke in two in 1922 or thereabouts, and the persons and prejudices recalled in these sketches slid back into yesterday's seven thousand years. . . . It is for the backward and by one of their number, that these sketches were written.

In much the same vein the essay on '148 Charles Street' deals with the salon of Mrs. James Fields, where the young Willa Cather first met Sarah Orne Jewett and a whole circle of cultivated personages who assembled under the shadow of the distinguished Boston publisher and were held together by the firm social tutelage of the publisher's widow. Is this harmonious drawing room—'an atmosphere in which one seemed absolutely safe from everything ugly'—a little remote from the true creative sources of the New England tradition it represents: from Thoreau's hut, or the booms and jibs of Melville's whalers? Is it really essential for Cather to tell us that 'nobody can cherish the flower of social intercourse, can give it sun and sustenance and a tempered clime,' without also being able very completely to dispose of anything that threatens it—'not only the slug, but even the cold draught that ruffles its petals'? Now, indeed, the Lady in the Wilderness is almost completely the Lady. And yet that cultivated Boston home of Mrs. Fields's had, at least for the older novelist who looks back upon it, another and deeper meaning. It was not only a place where the past lay in wait for one; it was a place where the past lived on, 'where it was protected and cherished, had sanctuary from the noisy push of the present'—where the ugliness of the world, and "all possibility of wrenches and jars and wounding contacts" seemed securely shut out.

These wrenches, jars, and wounding contacts are familiar to us. Are they *all* encompassed by that garage which now stands at 148 Charles Street, which has 'altogether taken the place of things formerly cherished on that spot,' and which, as Cather adds, seems to represent the only real development in our national culture since that earlier flowering of learning, of talent, and of the finer amenities of life? In any case, what is interesting to notice is the change in the volume's tone after the crack-up of this earlier and in a sense rather derivative and second-class drawing room society. Thus, by comparison with the Salvini or Modjeska of Mrs. Fields's group, the appeal of Dickens or Scott is primarily for 'the great multitudes of humanity' who have no feeling for the form of any art, who, indeed, do not want quality but quantity, change, a succession of new things 'that are quickly threadbare and can be lightly thrown away.' * The younger generation is interested only in contemporary writers, 'the

* In terms of Cather's evaluation of her own European literary models in *Not Under Forty,* Turgeniev is listed as her favorite among the 'great group of Russian writers,' while Doestoevski isn't mentioned. Just so, Balzac is subordinated to Flaubert in the French group, while Zola is completely ignored. And if Dickens and Scott represent the nineteenth-century English writers, as above, D. H. Lawrence himself is viewed as an example of the distinction 'between emotion and mere sensory reactions.' But the real distinction here seems almost to be that between literary perfection and literary force, or depth, and similarly most of Cather's objections to contemporary realism or naturalism have a concealed bias, and are almost directed at the *existence* of the naturalistic novel.

newer the better,' while the neglect of Sarah Orne Jewett, as we are told in one of Cather's more impassioned periods, implies a growing contempt not only for the English language but for the entire tradition of Anglo-Saxon culture. 'Imagine a young man or woman, born in New York City, educated at a New York university, violently inoculated with Freud, hurried into journalism, knowing no more about New England country people (or country folk anywhere) than he has caught from motor trips or observed from summer hotels: what is there for him in *The Country of the Pointed Firs?*' And furthermore—

> This hypothetical young man is perhaps of foreign descent: German, Jewish, Scandinavian. To him English is merely a means of making himself understood, of communicating his ideas. He may write and speak American English correctly, but only as an American may learn to speak French correctly. It is a surface speech: he clicks the words out as a bank clerk clicks out silver when you ask for change. . . . Moreover, the temper of the people which lies behind the language is incomprehensible to him. He can see what these Yankees *have not* (hence an epidemic of 'suppressed desire' plays and novels), but what they *have,* their actual preferences and their fixed scale of values, are absolutely dark to him. When he tries to put himself in the Yankee's place he attempts an impossible substitution.

Nor is the 'adopted American' alone in being cut off from the old moral harmonies, Cather adds; there is also the new American whom George Santayana described as 'the untrained, pushing cosmopolitan orphan.' It is amusing that to make her point Cather should draw upon the phrase of the Spanish-born philosopher, the uneasy child of mixed cultures who was himself, during the American

Twenties and Thirties, an illustrious example of the gifted and retroverted cosmopolitan orphan. And where else but in some such source as this could you find an appropriate phrase during the entire period when so many 'hypothetical' young men of foreign descent, 'aliens' and adopted Americans, sons and grandsons of immigrants, such as the 'German' Dreiser or the 'Portugese' Dos Passos or the 'Swedish' Sandburg or the 'Irish' Fitzgerald, to name only a few, were making their major contributions to the national letters? Or when, for instance, the cosmopolitan Thomas Mann, to whom Cather pays such a glowing tribute in a neighboring essay of *Not Under Forty,* was drawing upon the great Viennese Jew, Freud, for the core of his own writing; not to mention in this connection any other Bohemian, French, or Scandinavian artisans or farmers who, in her own earlier life, had given her an initial sense of the traditions, standards, and craftsmanship, as well as of the music, dancing, and gaiety of life in those primitive little 'American' settlements on the untamed plains of Nebraska.

But very clearly here, in the uncertain tone of this artist who usually appears so serene, in these more importunate accents of malice and prejudice which recall at once the Continental jargon of Mencken and the cold academic purity of Stuart Sherman's view of our native scene in that strange ethnological debate that raged over the 'New Literature' of the post-war period, we may see the symptoms of a running feminine distemper as it were, which has not yet been soothed by Cather's attempt to achieve a spiritual harmony. You may notice, incidentally, that interesting reference to the rhythms of a new American language that is clicked out 'as a bank clerk clicks out silver when you ask for change'—a reference which stands by itself in the midst of all this veiled racial nonsense. Just so, the peroration to perhaps the most famous of these essays, 'The Novel Démeublé'—

> How wonderful it would be if we could throw all the furniture out of the window; and along with it all the meaningless reiterations concerning physical sensations, all the tiresome old patterns, and leave the room as bare as the stage of a Greek theatre, or as that house into which the glory of Pentecost descended!

—betrays a certain uneasy consciousness of the real truth about Cather's own novels of religious sensations and ecclesiastical trappings. And her later remarks about the artist who spends his life in pursuing 'the things which haunt him,' in having his mind 'teased' by them, are coupled, in the closing essay of *Not Under Forty,* with those extraordinary reflections on the everyday existence of an ordinary 'happy' family, each member of which, as she says, is 'clinging passionately to his individual soul, is in terror of losing it in the general family flavour'—

> As in most families, the mere struggle to have anything of one's own, to be one's self at all, creates an element of strain which keeps everybody almost at the breaking-point. . . . One realizes that even in harmonious families there is this double life: the group life, which is the one we can observe in our neighbour's household, and, underneath, another—secret and passionate and intense—which is the real life that stamps the faces and gives character to the voices of our friends. Always in his mind each member of these social units is escaping, running away, trying to break the net which circumstances and his own affections have woven about him. One realizes that human relationships are the tragic necessity of human life; that they can never be wholly satisfactory, that every

> ego is half the time greedily seeking them, and half the time pulling away from them.

For what one realizes here is the singular nature of Cather's picture of 'reality'—those final overtones of fear or dread which linger on in our minds after this description of normal 'everyday' experience. The disparate nature of our group lives and our personal lives is surely one of the most ironical facts of our existence. Still, is our private life quite so secret, passionate, and intense—*always* marked by this element of strain and tension at the breaking point? Those human relationships which are in fact the tragic necessity of human life, which are never wholly satisfactory, while their continuous imperfections form, indeed, the real dynamics of ordinary affairs—can they never be even partly satisfactory? Moreover, while the ostensible play of this passage is on the attraction, the actual need, of ego for ego, the final stress is on the mutual repulsion of these tormented selves, on an almost frantic clinging to one's own identity, a pulling away from, an actual *breaking* of that net which, indeed, circumstances and our own affections usually weave about us—a stress on fear, on flight, on escape. And this is a passage which comes close, if not to the realities of experience, at least to Cather's view of them; while to a large degree it defines the real psychological milieu of one of her last and most illuminating novels. *Lucy Gayheart,* published in 1935, does mark a return in both theme and tone to the pattern of her earlier writing. But it is very far from the 'lavender and old lace' which has been generally used to describe it.

As a matter of fact, Cather almost deliberately points up both the typical and the incongruous elements in the story. Lucy herself is pretty, eager, 'delighted with everything,' as her surname suggests; the whole picture of the town of Haverford, on the Platte River in Colorado, at the turn of the century, is idyllic, innocent, quaint. Similarly, our first impression of Clement Sebastian, the middle-aged singer whom Lucy meets in Chicago, is not entirely exhilarating. Sebastian is a famous baritone, but he is also plump, his torso is 'unquestionably oval,' and he is married. Moreover, with his valet Giuseppe and his assistant, Mr. Mockford, his morning coats and smoking jackets, his complete aversion to anything that might 'tarnish his personal elegance,' he is an exaggerated and artificial symbol of that cosmopolitan elegance which has figured so largely in Cather's work. On its superficial levels *Lucy Gayheart is* a standard and almost stereotyped story in our literature: the love affair of the young provincial girl who seeks an artistic career and the sophisticated city-man who represents all the glamour of artistic success. We see this very clearly, and then, as it were, gradually stop seeing it altogether.

For what Cather has managed to create in the reader of her story is hardly so much that 'willing suspension of disbelief' which the literary critic delights in, but a sort of inevitable and unwitting acceptance of the artist's intention—an intention that is hardly limited to a picture of love's delights. The Chicago musical world of *Lucy Gayheart* is attractive, to be sure. The descriptions of Chicago, its buildings, streets, crowds, and climate, probably rank among Cather's best recreations of the first mystery and enchantment of the large city for the provincial aspirant: the city of flowers and music, as it first seems to Lucy, in which it was hard to believe that there was anything in the world she could not have—which gave one the freedom 'to spend one's youth as one pleased, to have one's secret, to choose one's own master and serve him in one's own way.'

For here, in this late heroine of hers, are those 'feudal' responses which are the real secret of Cather's women: those deeper and more authoritarian patterns of feminine affection, and that whole underlying view of the love relationship as a deliberate return to the primitive experiences of the individual—as a *willed* bondage between master and servant, or between parent and child. But the lyrical opening of the central romance in *Lucy Gayheart* is soon qualified by the unpleasant revelations of love: by Lucy's 'discovery' that passion, dark and terrifying, can drown like black water. Indeed, her first feeling for Sebastian 'had already destroyed a great deal of her,' as Cather says:

> Some people's lives are affected by what happens to their person or their property; but for others fate is what happens to their feelings and their thoughts—that and nothing more.

Moreover, with Lucy's realization that Sebastian also has been broken by his feelings, that he has in fact resolved that 'nobody would ever share his life again,' and has to a large extent resorted to the refuge of Catholicism; and with Sebastian's sudden death, we reach the real center of the novel.

Now, for such a scrupulous artist as Cather, it *is* curious that the pattern of this love story should be so familiar, not merely in terms of its main elements but as to matters of detail. The repetition, for example, of the scenes in the Chicago Art Museum, where a 'rather second-rate French painting' suggested the title for *The Song of the*

Lark; the return to a musical environment which has been such a central preoccupation of Cather herself, and which here again helps to maintain Lucy Gayheart's belief in 'an invisible, inviolable world,' very much as the religious hymns did for the Marie Shabata of *O Pioneers!;* the sense of personal defeat in the midst of worldly success which marks both the Bartley Alexander of her first novel and the Clement Sebastian of this one, not to mention that final death by drowning, which occurs to her hero in both *Alexander's Bridge* and *Lucy Gayheart*—these are certainly among the elements of a central love story which vibrates and echoes in all of her early works; which has been submerged during the whole period of her own religious refuge, and which here at last has been given its final and fullest expression: its *actuality,* perhaps even down to that odd final touch, that author's warning, used for the first time in the whole span of her work. 'The characters and situations in this work are wholly fictional and imaginary.'

In any case, just as *Lucy Gayheart* contains the most complete love relationship in the range of Cather's work, with the possible exception of *Alexander's Bridge,* it is also among her most convincing works. The sense of immediacy that we have in regard to both the scene and the emotions of the central story is a remarkable achievement for an artist who is approaching her sixties. (You may note, incidentally, that the Chicago scene of the novel is by no means the harsh urban society of *Obscure Destinies* and the later Cather.) And here, as Lucy returns to Haverford on the Platte and struggles to patch up her life after the death of Sebastian, and listens to the advice of such country characters as Cather's 'Mrs. Ramsay'—

> 'Nothing really matters but living. Get all you can out of it. I'm an old woman, and I know. Accomplish-

> ments are the ornaments of life, they come second. Sometimes people disappoint us, and sometimes we disappoint ourselves ; but the thing is, to go right on living.'

—and makes her own decision at last to go back to Chicago, to her work and to life itself—'Let it come! Let it all come back to her again! Let it betray her and mock her and break her heart, she must have it!'—we get that sense of a final catharsis, of a human rebirth, which, as we have seen, Cather has constantly struggled for but has actually failed to achieve in the formal 'humanity' of her religious works. For one may also lose one's soul by gaining it, so to speak, under false pretenses; and it is only here that she has achieved a true as against a ceremonial 'resurrection' of the spirit—a celebration of life in the midst of death, rather than a glorification of life without end.

Yet, on the plane of critical speculation, you might say that the true inner pattern of Cather's early work is that of a kind of traumatic wound; that the whole burden of her middle period is the attempt to reach a spiritual equilibrium through a formal mode of religious conversion—and that it was only *after* this conversion, and within the framework of its security, that the original emotions of the writer could approach something like a full aesthetic expression. . . . You may notice that in the later sections of *Lucy Gayheart* Cather does at last reach down into the mystery and drama, or even the mingled splendor and terror, of that *ordinary* human life, that common everyday existence of humanity which, lying directly between her need for worldly glamour and her sense of religious guilt, has constantly eluded her grasp. The description of the domestic relationships in the Gayheart family, of Haverford society in general, and of such townspeople as

Harry Gordon or Mrs. Ramsay are among the best examples of Cather's realism, just as that brief passage of hers—

> In little towns lives roll along so close to one another; loves and hates beat about, their wings almost touching. On the sidewalks, along which everybody comes and goes, you must, if you walk abroad at all, at some time pass within a few inches of the man who cheated and betrayed you, or the woman you desire more than anything else in the world. Her skirt brushes against you. You say good-morning and go on. It is a close shave. Out in the world the escapes are not so narrow.

—almost summarizes the whole nature of small-town life in America. Here Cather expresses that 'mysteriousness of the general' which is at the center of Sherwood Anderson's study of our earlier form of communal organization, and our older and deeper mid-American roots.

It may be worth mentioning that her next novel, *Sapphira and the Slave Girl,* in 1940, marks a return to her own earliest and hitherto almost obscure origins: to the more or less 'aristocratic,' semi-feudal, pre-Civil-War Virginia society from which she traces her own family ancestry. Certainly she has the material of a rich novel in her picture of a typical Virginia plantation, whose master, Henry Colbert, an upright Dutch dissenter, stands out, against that whole generous, careless, easy, slave-owning, horse-racing Tidewater group to which his wife, Sapphira, belongs. And the central story of the novel—Colbert's increasing affection for the slave girl Nancy, and Sapphira's cold-blooded attempt to ruin the Negress through having her seduced by Colbert's younger brother—deals with a very sensitive area of Negro-white relationships in the South.

In its central framework *Sapphira and the Slave Girl* is

probably Cather's most ambitious book, the first of her novels to attempt to come to grips with a difficult and complex social environment. It is interesting to notice how close she comes to the psychological implications of this environment; that is, to the underlying sexual corruption which was attendant upon the institution of slavery; the debasement of the deepest human drives which was implicit in the buying and selling of human flesh, as well as of human souls, and which in a way did less fundamental harm to those who were the 'material' of the merchandising than to the merchants themselves. For the white male could hardly be expected to attribute a human status to a relationship that, in an adjacent area, could be viewed in such completely different terms, and was, indeed, for economic reasons, deliberately relegated to a subhuman status, while the 'innocence' of the Southern Lady was achieved, in turn, by deliberately excluding from her view everything she knew to be true and saw at every moment around her. At least Sapphira, who has married Nancy's mother to a 'capon man' for her own domestic convenience, and who sets 'the worst rake in the country' upon the track of the young Negress, while she laughs at the 'old jokes' of the Negro slaves who mock at their own sexual inclinations, can hardly be viewed as an incarnation of pure white southern womanhood. And in the 'legend' of Jezebel, the fierce African tribeswoman, who is captured, examined, and sold almost purely for her value as a sexual animal, Cather defines the real background, and the basic moral issues, of *Sapphira and the Slave Girl* in less than a dozen pages. However—there is a curious hiatus in the working-out of her southern story.

It is surely legitimate for the novelist to represent the different points of view in her central situation. But maybe Cather's attempt to give a balanced picture of the

Negro-white relationships in her novel is a little *too* successful. Henry Colbert's daughter, Mrs. Blake, has gone over to the Quakers and Abolishers. Yet Colbert's own conclusion that, although he has a legal right to manumit any of his wife's Negroes, it would be an outrage to Sapphira's feelings and an injustice to the slaves themselves, while, after all, are we not all in bonds?—is a model of private sensibility in the midst of a historical crisis. Those 'good' southern plantation owners of Cather's who never 'sell off their slaves to strangers' may sound, again, rather like the Hemingwayish hunter of the *Green Hills of Africa* who never shoots a kudu he has met before, while there is, in fact, altogether too much stress here on the scriptural appearance, the filial loyalty, and the 'childlike trust' of the faithful Negro slaves themselves. For such a subtle novelist as Cather, it seems odd that the slave girl Nancy, the original inspiration and the chief victim of the story, should turn out to be so timid, superstitious, and hysterical. Her despair at being pursued by Sapphira's agent is not entirely alluring ('I'm goin' to throw myself into the millpawnd, I am!'), just as, at the moment of the novel's climax, when she is being rescued and sent off to the North as a free woman, she turns completely irresponsible and dozes off. Still more curious, it is Sapphira herself, the cold, proud, aristocratic mistress of the house, who emerges, at least in her more benevolent moments, as the real heroine of the novel. 'There are different ways of being good to folks,' Henry Colbert says to his dying and repentant wife. 'Sometimes keeping people in their place is being good to them.'

You may notice other ambiguous elements in Cather's southern story. There is that 'foolish, dreamy nigger-side' of Nancy's nature; or that 'soft darky laugh' which makes her, apparently, more attractive. And the Virginia mountaineers—the hill people who are midway between the plantation owners and the Negroes in the story's social scale—are viewed in a curiously ambivalent light: both as sturdy individualists, like Cather's old-fashioned Mandy Ringer, and as an ignorant and vicious mob, like the young Keyser boys of the story. . . . But isn't the main trouble with *Sapphira and the Slave Girl* the fact that nothing really happens in the end?—that a novel which has the material for half a dozen tragedies, and which is set against the fury, the intrigue, and the rhetoric of probably the most crucial period of our history, should turn out to be so pale and remote? And that the novelist herself, who has constantly reiterated her belief that all that is necessary for a drama is four walls and one passion, should manage to achieve, out of all these conflicting personalities and beliefs, only an unlikely 'happy ending'? Just as clearly here as in the acrid social commentary of *Not Under Forty* we may see the evidence of a final division in Cather's values which hasn't been altogether bridged by the synthesis of extremes at the conclusion of her religious pilgrimage. Only in this case the conflict in her thinking is most sharply revealed in just that muting and softening, that 'balancing-off,' and that final literary stalemate which marks her attempt to deal with the basic historical issues of *Sapphira and the Slave Girl.*

For the whole range of Cather's values, standards, tastes, and prejudices, her tone, is that of an inherent aristocrat in an equalitarian order, of an agrarian writer in an industrial order, of a defender of the spiritual graces in the midst of an increasingly materialistic culture. Miss Cather is quite aware of her predicament. Her work is filled with its intimations. What other meaning is there, indeed, to the series of farewells—to the Pioneers, to the Empire Builders, to the Washington Square society of the early nineteen-hundreds—which constitutes the whole burden of her earlier writing? Yet playing all around the edges of this primary western scene, skipping from the immigrant settlers to the last of the railroad builders, delighted, in the salons of Boston and New York, with the areas of sensibility produced by, and all the cultivated by-products of, the great American fortunes, she has nowhere reached the real center of her material. Selecting and enhancing the most subtle effects of wealth, she has, rather like Samuel Dodsworth's wife, either looked down upon or ignored the whole process of creating wealth. Writing so discreetly about the age when business was a personal adventure, she has neglected to mention the most typical forms of the adventure. And Cather's narrow and almost deliberately naïve view of the past, of history, and therefore of human nature itself, has also affected the whole texture of her work.

As a matter of fact, is it the *instinctive* taste of 'the great multitudes of humanity' which has created that succession of new things 'quickly threadbare and lightly thrown away' that she describes in *Not Under Forty?* Or can this be attributed in some measure also to the economic pattern —if not to the economic necessity—of an industrial set-up whose mechanisms of production have so far outrun its methods of distribution? In terms of an older agrarian order, or at least for its more privileged members, the banking system and the stock exchange may have no proper place in imaginative art, as Cather again declares. But have they no place at all in the imaginative art of a predominantly financial republic—particularly, when, during the years of her own artistic maturity, the banking system and the stock exchange were in fact determining the lives, the habits, and even the mythology of the great multitudes of people who perched, rather uneasily, on the crest of the boom market or wallowed in its trough? Miss Cather's belated return to the soil in those agrarian idylls of *Obscure Destinies* might have seemed a little ironical to the migrant Okies of John Steinbeck's *The Grapes of Wrath,* or to those later immigrants who, unlike Neighbor Rosicky, had not been so fortunate as to remove themselves from the stricken urban centers of the depression years.

Miss Cather's stress on the moral elements of character is important, to be sure. Her emphasis, as a craftsman, on whatever is felt upon the page without being specifically named there—on the 'inexplicable presence of the thing not named, of the overtone divined by the ear but not heard by it'—is admirable. But perhaps her view of both that older American world which, as she says, broke in two in the early nineteen-twenties, and that whole new American world of the corporations and the cartels, and of the untrained pushing orphans of finance capitalism is a little *too* intangible. We have noticed those uneasy glimpses of the 'bosses and strikers' with whom you go wrong either way, or of those 'adopted' Americans who are probably not so different from the admirable immigrants of her youth but who almost come to be blamed, in Cather's later years, for whatever has happened to American life. In these later tones of hostility and malice, of isolation, and reversion to the past, as well as in the reluctance to treat a historical situation whose implications appear throughout her work but whose true nature is never faced, indeed, we may almost see the symptoms of a sort of cultural wound. For the general relationship of the cultural and the temperamental factors in a writer's work is usually clear enough. It is the more precise relationship, the weight, the balance, the interaction of these forces that is difficult to judge.

Was it the intense emotional crisis at the center of Cather's literary work which forced her to retreat so completely from the real issues of her own time? Or was it her initial aversion to the whole context of an industrial and financial society which, as early as 1912, in her first parable of Alexander the bridge-builder, forced her back into such a narrow and intense psychological sphere? . . . In a way, too, as I said in opening, the limitations of her work are made more poignant by her long and sustained attempt to transcend them, as well as by those wonderful areas of sensitivity which we have noticed, and by her actual achievement. If only she hadn't needed to go so far afield for her spiritual sanctuary, when a less remote and less ornate mode of salvation might have done! If only the common people of her tales had been allowed to experience a little more of that exquisite torment of life which she portrays so well—or if, in turn, both the promise and the gallantry of life in America had not disappeared quite so completely with the arc light and the hansom! . . . Then, indeed, which one of our novelists would have served as a better chronicler of that last softly lighted, discreetly sparkling evening scene of the great American fortunes at the turn of the century?

Meanwhile, though, we shall continue our study of these key figures in the Middle Generation by an appraisal of another western townsman who speaks directly for that democratic and equalitarian order of things which Willa Cather herself was less articulate about. As you will see, we might call Sherwood Anderson the last of the townsmen.

Chapter Four

Sherwood Anderson: LAST OF THE TOWNSMEN

◇

Chapter Four

Sherwood Anderson: LAST OF THE TOWNSMEN

1. *Ishmael, from Ohio*

IN A WAY, Sherwood Anderson became an ancestor before he became mature. Wasn't *Winesburg, Ohio,* among the magic titles which announced, in 1920, the end of a sterile epoch in American letters, the coming of age of a true American culture? Just as *Main Street* stigmatized our raw commercialism, as *This Side of Paradise* emancipated the flappers and philosophers, and as *Jurgen* pointed, a little coyly, toward the new sophistication, that little group of Ohio tales first revealed the uneasy and distorted recesses of our provincial soul. Thus the early post-war generation invoked Sherwood Anderson as a pioneer and prophet. He became a protagonist of the New Realism, with its resolute and even grim insistence upon the *fundamentals* of life, and especially the unpleasant fundamentals, and especially of American life.

As a standard-bearer, Anderson has suffered the fate of most standard-bearers. Tagged as a figurehead in the Life of Realization, he is apparently fated to remain one—at least for the commentators who fail to read his work very attentively.* Yet just to look at the copy of Ander-

* See, for example, Lionel Trilling's commiserative essay on Anderson in the *Kenyon Review,* Summer, 1941. But Mr. Trilling is typical of the group of academic critics whose chief interest has been in English literature and who believe they can deal adequately with American writing through such essays or through book reviews.

son's first novel, *Windy McPherson's Son,* in 1916, which is in the New York Public Library, is to get a better indication of his quality. Many hands have turned the pages now dismissed by the critics; the publisher's name, the place of publication, are missing from the volume—it seems all the more, perhaps, to belong to the people for whom Anderson wrote it: 'the living men and women of my own middle-western town.' A quarter of a century later, near the close of his career just as at the start, Anderson's *Home Town* was to echo this inscription. 'What's the matter with Oak Hill? Why not Oak Hill?'

Anderson's lifelong dedication to the towns, made as it is in all devotion, and quite special in our literary annals, is not a form of worship; nor is it without conflict. Even in his last work, the *Memoirs* of 1942, there will be intimations of a new moment of crisis for the aging middle-western editor: a new impasse in the series of impasses which constitute Anderson's history. Like the hero of *Beyond Desire,* who lays down his body for a common cause while his mind is still debating the merits of the cause, Anderson will undergo many spiritual metamorphoses in his attempt to understand the meaning of his time. As a matter of fact, Sherwood Anderson is a sort of Wandering American who well fulfills the rôle in the old non-Aryan myth as he seeks again, at the end of his days, the answers he knows he may never know, and the Second Coming in the national life. But this ever-searching, vainly seeking wanderer is a typical figure in contemporary writing. You may remember the Jimmy Herf who ends Dos Passos's *Manhattan Transfer* with the declaration that he is on the road. '"How fur ye goin?" "I dunno. . . . Pretty far."'

Even the facts of Anderson's life are affected by the sense

of permutation that marks his career. He was born, so he tells us, in Camden, Ohio, in 1876. But was it really Camden, or another of those innumerable small middle-western towns through which Anderson's family kept moving? Was it Canton, maybe? Or Clyde? Anderson's mother was 'a beautiful and energetic girl of Italian extraction'—but she was much more than this, as we shall notice—while some members of the family have denied that she was this at all. The 'ruined Southern dandy' of a father is also to be a recurrent concern of Anderson's, and his literary view will change here, too: from those early embittered adolescents, whose minds are filled with fantasies of patricide, to that rebellious, middle-aged businessman of *Many Marriages* who finally accepts himself as a braggart, a liar, a faker, as, in short, one of those disreputable figures in life of whom Anderson's father may remind us.

Anderson himself had become a sort of small-town industrialist. A newsboy, whose parents had never owned 'a square foot of the vast American earth'; a stable boy around the race tracks (Anderson always loved horses—and bands); he worked in the cabbage fields of *Poor White* and in the mills of *Marching Men*. He was an ordinary laborer in Chicago, a G.I. of the Spanish-American War. It was after this that he became a successful advertising man and a manufacturer in Elyria, Ohio. And it was then—half mad, or else, like a certain melancholy noble with whom he had other traits in common, 'counterfeiting madness'—that, at forty, he left his family, his factory, his business associates and all, to end his long apprenticeship to Mammon, to begin to woo the Muse: this foxy publicity man turned fumbling poet, this perverse American entrepreneur turned cornfield mystic. And in the Chicago of the Nineteens—the Cliff City of Sandburg and Dreiser and Masters, of Margaret Anderson and *The Little Review,* of the Revolt of the Flesh in *Winesburg* itself—he established his position in our letters.*

But just when Anderson's troubles might well have begun to end, they began. Was he now as 'successful' in the artistic area as he had been in the economic—a man of some reputation, of leisure, and, once more, of money? Then why does Sherwood Anderson still prowl along urban boulevards and blind alleys; why should he, sleepless, listen to the mechanized heart of the New World in anxiety and fear, and feel himself rootless, placeless, 'a thing swinging in air'? You will see that Anderson's whole creative record is not at all the record of a purely personal life of self-realization; he will discard this notion almost as fast as he had previously thrown over the life of material aggrandizement.

In the long, circling personal search that marks his middle period, a search, rather like that of Tom Wolfe's to follow, often blundering, untutored, particularly native in essence, Anderson is trying to find something different: to find, through his own origins and memories, the meaning of existence in the contemporary United States: 'the right place and the right people.' We shall follow this search, at first through Anderson's voyages to the 'imaginary' towns of his middle-western childhood, and then through his actual journey to the contemporary town itself, to Marion, Smyth County, Virginia.† Yet the bulldozer will reach down to the foundations of Sherwood's second home, too. The chronicler of the machine-change in America who opens his work with the coming of Industry

* Harry Hansen's *Midwestern Portraits* is an interesting and informative account of the Chicago group in its heyday.

† As almost everybody knows, Anderson owned and edited two newspapers in Marion, one Democratic and one Republican.

to the towns will record in turn the final seizure of the town by that mechanized New Order against which he has fought so long. This mid-American provincial who inaugurates his career so bitterly in the mills must return to them again toward the close of his career. In his mid-fifties, and in the nineteen-thirties, the decade of industrial crisis, Anderson will look down once more, from his southern hills, upon those shining glass-brick factory walls which have contained so much anguish for him.

But this record of ceaseless and circling permutation in a changing America, this apparently ironical history—is it as pointless as it is circular? Was Sherwood Anderson fuzzy, muddled, 'eternally confused,' as some of our literary commentators have alleged? He had something, as you will see, to be confused about. And never knowing the answers, he was saved, at least, from the folly of those who know the answers. From these early origins of isolation and bitterness, he emerges as perhaps the most balanced, communal, and sympathetic American writer of two decades—marked by a maturity that, coming to him almost a decade after *Winesburg,* is rare in his generation and that gives his work a special sort of solidity.

Through his circuitous progress, the Last of the Townsmen will reach a special vantage-point among the literary workers of his time, caught as they all are in the historical flux—and to really know them, you ought to know him.

2. *The Deserted Village*

Windy McPherson's Son, in 1916, opens with the portraits of Anderson's western townspeople. John Telfer, the intellectual of Caxton, Iowa, delivers a lecture on poetry to the local butter-and-egg merchant and the village blacksmith. Mike McCarthy, the town rebel, proclaims himself 'socialist, anarchist, atheist, pagan' for the sake of public furor and delivers a public prayer: 'Oh Father! help us men of Caxton to understand we have only this, our lives, so warm and hopeful and laughing in the sun. . . .'

But our lives are not always the way they should be, and Sam McPherson's father, 'Windy,' is the butt of Caxton. The realization that his father was 'a confirmed liar and braggart' throws a shadow over Sam's early life; his days are colored by misery, his mind is filled with fantasies of revenge. 'I could repay all of the years . . . by just one long, hard grip at his lean throat.' Nor are they always fantasies, for Sam actually tries to murder his father when he realizes what is happening to his family. The portrait of Windy McPherson as a ne'er-do-well and exhibitionist is really quite appalling, and Sam's hatred reaches another climax during the illness and death of his mother, while the drunken father wanders off. 'Like the Roman emperor he wished that all the world had but one head so that he might cut it off with a slash. The town that had seemed so paternal . . . now seemed horrible.'

On this note—disowning his father and mourning his mother—Sam leaves Caxton and sets out for wealth. 'Make money! Cheat! Lie! . . . Get your name up for a modern high-class American,' John Telfer has advised him, and he does. 'To be poor was to be a fool'—and Windy McPherson had been a fool. In the pursuit of power, and somewhat like his literary predecessors in Horatio Alger, Sam helps his Boss, marries the Boss's daughter, and gets his fingers on the armament industry. Then, like his successors in the work of John Dos Passos—and Anderson's critique of our national Success Story will anticipate, and in some respects will balance, that of Dos

Passos—Sam betrays his boss, his wife, and himself in order to control the industry. 'Instead of another Windy McPherson . . . he was the man who made good, the man who achieved, the kind of man of whom America boasts before the world.'

As the tone of the quotation suggests, however, the final conquest of power, around which Sam has centered his existence, hardly satisfies him either. Successful at last, he finds around him only warped forms of human activity: he tells himself (as Bryllion Fagin notices, in a rather eccentric but acute study of Anderson) that life in the United States is abortive, that on all sides it wore itself out in little futile efforts, and that nowhere did it seem to give point to 'the tremendous sacrifices involved in just living and working the world.'

Awkward as it may seem today in its technical aspects, *Windy McPherson's Son* is still an interesting novel; abused by time and circumstances it is still going; and this early analysis of a new American materialism was part of the celebrated gesture of renunciation which brought Anderson into prominence during the nineteen-twenties—and left him there. Yet the very different meaning of Anderson's history is foreshadowed in his next work, which gives the other pole of his revolt. In a sense, *Marching Men,* published in 1917 and dedicated to 'American Workingmen,' is a pioneer labor novel. More than a decade before the emergence of 'proletarian writing,' and belonging as he did to no political cult, unacquainted with Bakunin or Bukharin, uninformed as to ideology or dialectic, Anderson—this solitary middle-class businessman—plunges headlong into a major literary current of the nineteen-thirties.*

* The progressive tradition in American letters extends, of course, as far back as the transcendental socialists of Brook Farm, or farther, and it cen-

Here are none of those proletarian saints who came into vogue with the later tradition; in fact the Anderson hero, Beaut McGregor, has an acute antipathy for his fellow-toilers of Coal Creek. 'It was the quality of intense hatred for his fellows in the black hole between the Pennsylvania hills that marked the boy and made him stand forth among his fellows.' And hated in turn by the miners, who have ridiculed his father, and who come to fear the hideous son on whom they have fixed his derisive nickname, 'Beaut' struggles to escape from the horrors of Coal Creek—

> Coming from a community where no man rose above a condition of silent brute labor, he meant to step up into the light of power. Filled with hatred and contempt of mankind he meant that mankind should serve him. Raised among men, who were but men, he meant to be a master.

The image of the Menckenian Superman haunts the early Anderson too. Beaut dreams of Nietzsche, and, seeing around him only the disorder of the American industrial processes, is filled with contempt for democratic society.

In all this one notices the resemblance to Windy McPherson's son. Like Sam, Beaut is a rebel escaping from an unbearable situation: the struggle is again based on hatred, the solution is personal power—the power to dominate the situation. And, although Anderson has now placed his hero among the proletariat, the change in Beaut's social status is matched by the greater intensity of his bitterness. *Marching Men* is filled with bitter and

tered, during the nineteens, in Chicago. But, while *Marching Men* shows the general influence of this tradition, and of Norris and London, it is actually, as I shall indicate, much closer to our own day in its central preoccupation.

acute observations about our industrialized culture: Chicago, the center of it, is 'one vast gulf of disorder,' and Anderson notices that 'vacant purposeless stare of modern life' which marks Henry Miller's portraits of our society. So it isn't surprising that this early Anderson, motivated by revenge and contempt, infatuated with power, and with 'discipline' and 'order,' should arrive at an early brand of Fascism in the last half of his novel.

What *is* surprising, though, is the precision and eloquence of his portraits, as Beaut McGregor works out the pattern of his 'Workingman's Party.' The touch of shoulder to shoulder, the submergence of the frustrated individual in an 'all-powerful mass-hypnosis,' the pseudo-religious exaltation of the group movement and the blind trust in 'the mind of leader'—in these and a variety of other details, Anderson presents the technics of modern tyranny and all the psychological weapons that have been used by the lawless to manipulate the defeated—complete with a Marching Song. Anderson's second novel demonstrates how he can reach into the racial as well as the societal mind, and how close his intuitions are to the crucial matters of today. *Marching Men* is riding the 'wave of the future,' as some see it, that is, and such as it is.

But it is not for Sherwood Anderson. Even while the final sections of his book develop the egomaniacal pattern of modern dictatorship, the writer draws back from the consequences of his own imagination. The more fully Anderson projects this mechanized future, the more reluctant he is to accept it. The superhuman leader and the subhuman mass can achieve a sort of order—but can they achieve good? Ormsby, the puzzled plow manufacturer, who prevents his daughter from marrying Beaut McGregor—and the 'future'—while simultaneously he grows more doubtful about his own capitalistic solutions, emerges as the genuine hero of *Marching Men*. Dismissing his own suggestion of a possible salvation for an increasingly industrialized society, Anderson falls back on his central symbolic figure of a puzzled interlocutor who is no Sir Oracle.

All the same, this figure has already changed in its proportions. While Sam McPherson was marked by a purely individualistic revolt, Beaut McGregor shows equally clearly the individual's need to *belong:* to a movement, a group, a society—and between these two poles of revolt and belonging Anderson is to oscillate for some years. What was there in the American scene that might nourish a human being more fully than the dominant egotism of a competitive society or the submergence of self in the anonymous mass? And in his next two works Anderson will turn to the American past.

He was never at his best as a professional poet, however; he is perhaps only worse when he is being 'poetic.' *Mid-American Chants,* stemming from the Chicago of 1918, is valuable chiefly in so far as it recalls that midwestern revolt of the flesh against both Calvin and Armour, both the Pulpit and the Stockyards; and for its record of Anderson's thinking. One notices again that factory soot which stains the face of America and darkens its spirit—

> Crush and trample, brother, brother—crush and trample 'till you die.

Industrialism is 'a long house of hate,' whose mistress is 'gaunt and drear,' and whose muse is a hoarse and terrible singer—

> Kneeling prayer I shall forget you not, grim singer.
> Black bird, black against your black smoke-laden skies
> Uttering your hoarse and terrible cries.

Yet a sort of descant in these verses has already found new sources of hope. The fertility and peace of the cornfields are contrasted with the crushing and trampling of our competitive ethics. Although the modern mistress dwells in a house of hate—

> Our fathers in the village streets
> Had flowing beards and they believed.

—while in 'Song of the Soul of Chicago,' one of the homeliest and best of the chants, Anderson almost seems to come to a decision about his own artistic rôle. 'I'll talk forever—I'm damned if I'll sing. Don't you see that mine is not a singing people? We're just a lot of muddy things caught up by the stream.' What's more, he will stay along with the other Americans, because—

> There can't any poet come out here and sit on the shaky rail of our ugly bridges and sing us into paradise.

Nevertheless, in some way, a better American meaning will work its way through. 'By God, we'll love each other or die trying.' And with this, we are at the edge of Anderson's first famous work.*

But does *Winesburg, Ohio,* belong, then, to the 'literature of revolt,' as Ernest Boyd says—a revolt against 'the great illusions of American civilization'? Is it a chronicle

* And still perhaps his best-known work: for *Winesburg, Ohio,* while it established the early Anderson, has overshadowed the rest of his career. It is true he was never to equal *Winesburg* in its own vein; he was not, as we shall see, interested in equaling it. But in other areas he was to produce such first-rate books as *Death in the Woods,* or *Puzzled America,* or the *Memoirs.* In point of fact he is one of the relatively few American writers whose later work seems to *be* later work: that is, shows evidence of growth. . . . What stopped many readers of Anderson was his work during the middle twenties.

of those 'cramped spirits,' as Carl Van Doren says, who have been 'repressed by village life'? On another level, does *Winesburg* deserve the charges of sexual perversion hurled at its author when the book appeared—was Anderson really the 'Phallic Chekhov'? ('Was I a goner'? Anderson kept asking himself.) There were other charges, too, almost as horrific, which accused him of dealing with 'commonplace people'—and certainly, for the conservatives of 1919, *Winesburg* may have appeared to be tunneling under all the established values of American life. And for some of the radicals of the day, *Winesburg was* exposing the sewers, and opening for public inspection the inadequate drainage system of the luxurious American psyche.

Contemporary judgments of an important book usually reveal more of the contemporary than of judgment. Perhaps there was something 'revolutionary' in these brief sketches of some Ohio townspeople: dentists, telegraph operators, run down hotel-keepers, misunderstood grocers, and mournful mechanics. In the past our writers had often turned in dismay from such average figures of an average American order: inconsequential lives which Anderson set up against the Shakespearean nobles and the 'super-subtle fry' of Henry James. To make matters worse, these obscure personages had even more obscure maladies, which, once recognized, were to persist and infect all future chronicles of small-town life from a sentimental *Our Town* to a sensational *Kings Row*. The hero of 'Hands,' for example, is a champion strawberry-picker —but Wing Biddlebaum is an inhibited champion, a homosexual strawberry-picker. His profession and his repressions may have seemed equally curious to some readers in the early twenties; and this array of ailing ordinary souls in *Winesburg* culminates with Anderson's tormented preacher who gazes out from his church upon an almost naked female schoolteacher—a teacher, moreover, who is *smoking*. In these respects, *Winesburg* does help to inaugurate a decade of revolt. It foreshadows the imminent crusade against bourgeois, Victorian, and puritanical taboos: it sets the stage for O'Neill's entrance.

Yet, preoccupied as Anderson may seem to be with sexual maladjustment, very early in the book you realize that his concern is not with human copulation, as it were, but with human isolation: and sex, which is a prelude to love as well as an ending, is the method used by Anderson, like D. H. Lawrence, to convey this isolation.

In 'Surrender,' Louise Bentley gives herself to her lover —because she is afraid that 'there was no way to break through the wall that had shut her off from the joy of life'—

> That was not what she wanted, but it was so the young man had interpreted her approach to him, and so anxious was she to achieve something else that she made no resistance.

Louise Bentley's story, to be sure, is 'a story of human misunderstanding.' But aren't all these stories about an inarticulate human misunderstanding? This 'vague and intangible hunger' of Louise Bentley's for love and understanding in *Winesburg,* a hunger which, misunderstood, leads only to hatred of her husband, her son, and love itself, is symptomatic. In another of the stories, 'Adventure,' Alice Hindman, deserted by her lover, growing 'old and queer,' wants to ask the middle-aged drug clerk, Will Hurley, to sit with her, but again she is afraid he will not understand. 'It is not him I want. . . . I want to avoid being so much alone.' Nor is this sentiment confined merely to women in *Winesburg*. The hero of 'The Thinker,' stumbles forward through the half-darkness feeling himself 'an outcast in his own town.' And in 'Tandy' a visitor to Winesburg voices the underlying if always obscurely felt emotion of the town. 'I am a lover and have not found my thing to love. That is a big point, if you know enough to realize what I mean. It makes my destruction inevitable, you see.'

In a casual phrase uttered by the 'stranger' of the story (as many of Anderson's finest intuitions are likely to appear in these 'unnecessary' characters and oblique references) Anderson gives the crux of his message. The point of *Winesburg* is precisely that, while human understanding is so often disfigured and disjointed here—it is still possible. These people *are* lovers, and if their object of love hasn't been found, it *can* be found. 'People live and die alone even in Winesburg,' Anderson says, and the 'even,' which invites a comparison, embodies the theme. This is surely the central meaning of the volume: the psychological factor that holds these apparently scattered and 'plotless' sketches together and gives them an inner unity, just as the village scene gives them an outward unity.

For is it merely the later decades of chance and change which gives *Winesburg* its haunting and tender quality today—its fragrance of fruit orchards, and its particular affectionate feeling for all the forms and habits of a disappearing rural society? 'In those days,' Anderson is fond of saying when he introduces his village customs and oddities, and how the phrase grows on us as we read the book! In those days when an older agrarian order bodied forth its enthusiasts and visionaries: when 'servants' were unheard of in Winesburg, but hired help sat at table with the rest of the family; when 'ideas in regard to social classes had hardly begun to exist' and all young women were simply 'nice' or not nice. (And who could guess what orgies were held in Sandusky of a Saturday night? although Tom Little knows the people in the towns along his railroad 'better than a city man knows the people who live in his apartment building.') There were trotting races in Medina in those days, when Whitney didn't own the horses, and ball games in which Ruppert didn't own the ball-players, and the farmer by his stove was not yet talking 'as glibly and senselessly as the best city man of us all.' The figure of God was big in the hearts of men in those days, when the Bible was the only best-seller, and in the spring, after the rains, when the country around Winesburg was so fresh and delightful, the wagons of berry-pickers would be going by the Fair Grounds. Only a few, Anderson says, know the sweetness of 'the twisted apples' which are left in the orchards of Winesburg after the best of the apples have been shipped off to the cities—and often the personages of the town, like its fruit, seem all the more tender for their crabbed appearance.

No, *Winesburg* is not a radical but a nostalgic document. This opening gun for a decade of revolt is not an indictment but an evocation of a society.* As you follow Anderson's course to this point—the increasing fear of a standardized American social arrangement and the distaste for contemporary life which pervades his early novels as against the return, in *Mid-American Chants,* to the belief of his fathers in village streets and to those rich midwestern cornfields through which you approach his group of Ohio tales—you see, certainly, that *Winesburg* answers his early conflicts. Like the stranger of his story, Anderson has found his 'thing to love,' the thing for which he

* And it doesn't merely *seem* this way now, but it was planned so. *Winesburg* was written, as Anderson tells us later, in the noise and dirt of a Chicago tenement, and in the midst of his despair as to the industrial metropolis.

has been searching, and without which, so he believes, his own destruction would be inevitable.

There are unpleasant events even in Winesburg. Always defending the part of imagination in his work, and proclaiming the 'fact' to be subordinated to his fancy, Anderson is also firmly rooted in reality. 'Into their lives,' he remarks about one of his families here, 'came little that was not coarse and brutal, and they were themselves coarse and brutal.' Still, these older forms of cruelty sometimes had 'a kind of beautiful childlike innocence'—and in the village life of Winesburg is Anderson's memory of a kind of innocence that marked American society before its descent into sin: with the industrial mistress as the new Eve, and the dynamo installed in the serpent's lair.

All the same—it *is* a memory. However real this village scene in Anderson's thoughts, it is nevertheless remote in fact; and can one live in a state of imaginary innocence? The print of the machine is on Winesburg itself. In 'Godliness,' Jesse Bentley realizes that the atmosphere of old times and places which he had always cultivated in his thoughts 'was strange and foreign to the thing that was growing up in the minds of others':

> The beginning of the most materialistic age in the history of the world . . . when the will to power would replace the will to serve, and beauty would be well-nigh forgotten in the terrible headlong rush of mankind to the acquiring of possessions . . . was telling its story to Jesse, the man of God, as it was to the men about him.

And the pressure of the new materialism grows stronger as *Winesburg* draws to a close, as the earlier compassion goes out of the tales and the stress on human inversion and social disorganization increases. While the neurotics 'whóm industrialism was to bring in such numbers' play out their rôle, the advent of the factories brings to a halting climax this account of an earlier rural existence.

In the final sections of the book, moreover, Anderson falls back upon a sort of literary sensationalism, and this pattern of a weak ending will recur in his work. It is a technical error, but is it a purely personal failing? Anderson is an advocate of the 'plotless story,' but is the story of American life, thus far, a little too plotless? Sherwood Anderson's history, as I say, is to be one of perpetual change, and already, in barely three years of a full twenty-five-year span of literary work, we have watched his transformation from a rebellious and power-seeking individualist to the lover of his communal Ohio tales: what he started out by condemning, he has already come to cherish. Yet the central issue remains: when Anderson turns from this rural scene, what is there in his own age that he can equally give himself to and belong with in order to avoid the threat of spiritual destruction?

We shall watch his next attempt to solve this problem while he traces the history of his native heritage under the pressure of social change, and leaves these tender and disappearing memories of Winesburg, Ohio. 'Let peace brood over this carcass,' says the young preacher of the tales in a testament to his dead father, and Sherwood Anderson might echo the sentiment as he mourns the passing of provincial life.

3. Out of Nowhere into Nothing

THAT ANDERSON INTENDED his next novel to be a sequel to his story is clear from his own words. 'The town was really the hero of the book. . . . What happened to the town was, I thought, more important than what happened to the people of the town.' And just as *Winesburg* ends with the anticipations of the machine-change, *Poor White,* in 1920, describes the full impact of the factory system upon our agrarian-mercantile patterns of behavior.

Bidwell, Ohio, had flourished, Anderson tells us, during one of those rare moments when our national preoccupation with 'doing' had yielded to an interest in 'being.' There was a pause between the pioneer rigors and the new industrial rigidity. . . . Meanwhile, in all the towns of midwestern America it was a time of waiting—

> In all the great Mississippi Valley each town came to have a character of its own, and the people who lived in the towns were to each other like members of a great family. A kind of invisible roof beneath which everyone lived spread itself over each town. . . . Within the invisible circle and under the great roof everyone knew his neighbor and was known to him.

Thus summarizing Bidwell's past, Anderson gives the final verdict on his famous chronicle of 'cramped spirits.' And the early sections of *Poor White* have all the warmth and humanity that go with this sense of an 'invisible roof'—a roof that has hardly spread itself over our national letters.

But Judge Horace Hanby, another of those provincial philosophers whom Anderson delights in describing, takes a look into Bidwell's future:

> 'Well, there's going to be a new war here. . . . It won't be like the Civil War, just shooting off guns and killing people's bodies. At first it's going to be a war between individuals, to see to what class a man must belong; then

it is going to be a long silent war between classes. . . . It'll be the worst war of all.'

Just as the novel opens with the last echoes of a society that fused a necessary—and fruitful—collectivism with a more genuine—and rounded—individualism, the worst war of all breaks across Bidwell's horizon. A slick provincial entrepreneur, the Jay Gould of Hicksville, persuades the town to set up a factory for a cabbage-picking machine. With the final success of the factory (after a series of failures during which its control passes from the townspeople as a whole to a group of bankers)—and as Industry comes to Bidwell, and the young mechanics become factory hands, and labor trouble starts—the New Age dawns. Bidwell, Ohio, which starts as another Winesburg, ends as a sort of baby Zenith.* In its panoramic view of a country town during a moment of changing values, *Poor White* is an interesting volume—and it is chiefly the central character study, the long and rather heavy account of Hugh McVey, that has kept the novel from being sufficiently appreciated.

Why does Anderson take such an interest in this cumbersome hero whose history twists and sprawls through the book? Awkward, inarticulate, groping, feeling his own social degradation, McVey is another outcast—and one who never forgets his origins. The 'Mudcat Landing' of his youth, with its smell of dirt and of drink and of fish,

* A collateral reading of Sherwood Anderson and Sinclair Lewis is highly illuminating: while one writer was portraying 'what happened to the town,' the other, in precisely the same year, 1920, was presenting Main Street, and what Lewis pictures satirically with undertones of tragedy, Anderson records as tragedy with overtones of farce. In one sense the two writers are a necessary complement to each other in order to evaluate this area of American life. But in another sense they seem to derive from different centuries—and, as a matter of fact, they almost do: for what Lewis is mainly describing is the final step in the industrial triumph: the pillage of the town.

is a quagmire of despair and defeat which sucks McVey back to it. There is a desperate and nightmarish quality in his efforts to escape from it: to educate himself, to make something of himself, to find, as he hopes, 'the right place and the right people.' Although Hugh McVey reminds us in his temperament and origins of the earlier Anderson heroes, he is no longer seeking power through a personal revolt, but a meaning for his life through a connection with the life of others. And when he has at last found this in the village life of Bidwell, and when it vanishes again as the town vanishes, perhaps you can appreciate the meaning of the recurrent dream which comes to him. It is a vision of a swelling and raging river that uproots the homes along its course, and of the white faces of drowning men and women, and of darkness descending on the land—'on the hills that were torn open, on the forests that were destroyed, on the peace and quiet of all places.' * And this dream, in which the dreamer feels himself a part of 'something significant and terrible that was happening to the earth and to the peoples of the earth,' but throughout which he lies prostrate and powerless and unable to force his way back to consciousness, is a summarization of the novel and a prelude to the short stories that follow it.

Between these Anderson wrote *Many Marriages* (1923), one of the weakest of his books, but nevertheless one that occupies a special place in his work. The story deals with the thoughts and deeds of Anderson's familiar businessman, family man, and respectable citizen, who leaves his business, his family, and his place in the community. But this time with what thoughts!—colored as they are by the sensibilities of a publicity agent and projected by the tech-

* This was actually Anderson's own recurrent dream, as he tells us later.

nics of a publicity campaign—and with the deeds that, semi-erotic and almost wholly embarrassing, seem to appeal to all the more infantile aspects of the post-war literati as well. Confronted by the corn-fed Casanova of *Many Marriages* and his narcissistic orgies—by this incestuous manufacturer of washing-machines who parades naked and alone before his plaster virgin and burning candles; and then continues this act before his stunned wife and daughter while he endeavors (in an interminable discourse) to persuade them, and particularly the daughter, and her by more than strictly verbal argument, that he has found the New Life—confronted, as I say, by these amorous whimsicalities of a frustrated Rotarian, we hardly know whether to laugh at the John Webster of *Many Marriages,* as he sometimes does at himself, or to join with an astounded citizenry and lynch him, as at moments he thinks they will, or merely to clothe and gag him.

In a way the novel is a potboiler, the first of Anderson's bids for popular attention in the nineteen-twenties, as the second is to be *Dark Laughter.* If Anderson belongs so clearly to his native scene, I can't deny either that he has some of its less flattering traits. In his rebellion against a commercial ethics which he knows more directly perhaps than any other comparable American writer, this ex-advertising man will sometimes use a hair of the dog that he bit. . . . At least the sentimentalities of the early Anderson and of his period show up here: these are in part the lamentations of a backwoods savior, this is the Black Mass of an Elk—for paraphrasing as it does a sort of *fin-de-siècle* decadence in the setting of a midwestern capitalism, *Many Marriages* invokes the ghost of Huysmans over the waters of Lake Erie.

Still, Anderson is half-aware of the novel's folly and his own absurdity, and the tale serves to remind us of the commercial background from which he is struggling to free himself, and also of the incipient Jazz Age, which here and elsewhere skirting, he will, in the end, similarly escape. If *Many Marriages* is merely a popularized declaration of the Aesthetic Revolt, how can you account for the human compulsions that it reveals and that give it, despite its grotesqueries, a serious and in some respects a profound emphasis? * Underneath the elucidations of free love and beautiful white bodies, what is the 'passion for explanation' that drives Anderson's hero to explain his own rôle in life? And what is this rôle if not that of a family man who is willing to sacrifice his family, a lover who is willing to sacrifice his beloved, a businessman who is willing to sacrifice his business (and his creditors) in order to further his own half-mad revolt? And why does the John Webster of the novel accept such a rôle, ironically and bitterly, and yet with a sense of self-liberation; and gladly confess (in some of the best passages in the novel) his kinship with the reprobates of this world?

To what degree this view of Anderson's hero is related to Anderson's own view of himself, we shall learn a little later. In its intimations of certain patterns of personal conflict, *Many Marriages* forms an interesting prelude to the more directly autobiographical work of Anderson's middle period. Very different in tone are the two volumes of short stories, *The Triumph of the Egg,* in 1921, and *Horses and Men,* in 1923, which summarize the themes that have preoccupied Anderson up to this point and take him one step further.

Both volumes contain some of Anderson's best-known tales and are a solid achievement. But just as the village framework of *Winesburg* has been broken here, the stories

* Anderson tells us that he had an 'irresistible temptation' to amplify the short version of *Many Marriages* that appeared in the *Dial.*

themselves are uneven in quality; there are also so many *almost* fine stories in these volumes as to leave one half in exasperation and half in despair. The artist seems to rush from one episode to another: and beneath this nervous restlessness there is an increasing element of despair. 'There is something essentially dirty about life,' says the heroine of the last story in *The Triumph of the Egg,* and in one form or another this lament is echoed by all the stories and epitomized in the lugubrious chant of 'Senility.' 'Have you any coughs, colds, consumption, or bleeding sickness?'

There is the factory foreman of 'Brothers' who kills his wife and unborn child 'for no reason,' as he says, except that the room was dark. 'I could never have done it had the gas been lighted.' There is the hero of 'The Door of the Trap,' who spends his life waiting for a meaning to his life, or the lonely old man of these tales who crushes and kills his frowsy little puppy in a final warped display of affection. Just as in the Ohio tales, Anderson is the spokesman of the inarticulate and of the meek. But these obscure existences have become more twisted and tormented: through the quality of their desperation we are approaching the revolt of the meek.

In this context the famous hero of the title story in *The Triumph of the Egg*—Anderson's provincial hero who is infected by 'the American passion for getting up in the world,' and who cherishes 'all the little monstrous things' that are born on his farm in the hope that he will make his fortune by producing a five-legged hen or a two-headed rooster: this hero becomes more than merely a farcical character. . . . Moreover, in the second of these two volumes of tales, *Horses and Men,* the undertones of revolt grow stronger as Anderson moves directly into his Chicago scene. 'We lead such damned lives,' says the burlesque queen of 'Milk Bottles.' 'We do, and we work in such a town. . . . And now they are going to take booze away from us too. . . . I won't stand it! I got to smash everything!' (As a precursor of the contemporary misogynists, Anderson also uses love as a trap in these stories, and women as bait, and liquor as an opiate.) And with 'A Chicago Hamlet' the theme becomes explicit. 'Millions of us live on the vast Chicago West Side, where all streets are equally ugly and where the streets go on and on forever, out of nowhere into nothing.'

Out of nowhere into nothing. This conviction is surely at the root of the restlessness in all these stories, and in this framework of an increasing anxiety there are the disturbed accents of Anderson's more directly personal utterances. 'I have a wonderful story to tell,' says the 'Dumb Man' in the prelude to *The Triumph of the Egg.* 'But know no way to tell it.' In the foreword to *Horses and Men,* Anderson asks whether, 'with these nervous and uncertain hands,' he may really reach 'the form of things concealed in darkness.' Very likely the memorable portrait of Dreiser that opens the volume—a Dreiser 'who does not know what to do with life'—is in part a self-portrait of the Anderson of this period, who also does not know what to do with life in America. And you may now feel the special weight of the three notable stories of horse-racing that Anderson includes here—perhaps the three best of his stories.* All are tales of childhood romance and love (and how tenderly Anderson treats a vanished youth in a vanished past) and all three end in a sad coming of age. The last of them, indeed, is the most bitter in its comparison of human and animal life. 'A race horse isn't like a

* 'I want to Know Why' and 'I'm a Fool' are the best-known, and almost standard models of the American short story, but 'The Man Who Became a Woman,' as I suggest above, is almost as good.

human being,' thinks the young hero of 'The Man Who Became a Woman.' 'He won't stand for it to have to do his work in any rotten ugly kind of dump the way a man will, and he won't stand for the smells a man will either.' And as for this hero himself—a young boy who imagines that upon reaching puberty he is mistaken for a woman, and is attacked by two criminals—Anderson could hardly have found a better fantasy to convey the symptoms of the Danish Disease that pervade all these stories: the quality of an impotent and bitter introspection and of a trapped and inverted virility.

But Hamlet is no stranger to our writers—he is a stock character today. And the *Notebook* of this period* also displays the growing bitterness of Anderson, the anxiety, the nervous depressions, the feeling of instability just when he is being recognized as a 'successful' writer. He knows a man, Anderson says, who would give anything for fame. 'Well, I have had a little of that. He may have mine. Let's trade.' The volume gives us happier views of the writer: his love of luxury and of splash ('I would like a string of race horses, a farm, a yacht.'), his vitality and curiosity ('Presently I shall die with a thousand, a hundred thousand tales untold. People I might have loved I shall not love.'), along with his warmth and humility. Yet all the new places, people, experiences that Anderson tries to enter into—these too are affected by his sense of impermanence and failure; this whole inexhaustible hunger for life is to some degree fanatical and obsessed. Somewhere here —in these trees, rivers, buildings, in these children, servant girls, factory workers, prostitutes, perhaps, in all these crafts and sciences, races and religions of a modern America—can

* Published in 1926, *Sherwood Anderson's Notebook* is a collection of his sketches and articles over this period and a particularly illuminating source-book on Anderson himself.

he find the answer to his dilemma? These are all possible clues, partial escapes, slippery niches. The Negro, in particular, seems to be farther removed from the machine age, and—'for whole days I try being a black man.' Anderson listens to their songs; perhaps here? But in the end, he thinks, they will be caught up also. 'The whites will get us. They win. Don't turn your back on the modern world. Sing that too, if you can, while the sweet words last.'

In an essay like 'I'll Say We've Done Well,' the elements of Anderson's personal anxiety are inextricably joined with the predicament of his society. For isn't it his own Ohio, Anderson asks—isn't it just this stronghold of an older provincial life that has become a citadel of modern industrialism?

> Have you a city that smells worse than Akron, that is more smugly self-satisfied than Cleveland, or that has missed as unbelievably great an opportunity to be one of the lovely cities of the world as has the city of Cincinnati? . . . I claim that we Ohio men have taken as lovely a land as ever lay outdoors and that we have, in our towns and cities, put the old stamp of ourselves on it for keeps.

These are bitter tones for the communal lover of the Ohio tales, and the pages of the *Notebook* hold many such sharp and bitter indictments of the industrialized America of Anderson's maturity—of 'the apparent meaninglessness of individual life against the background of something huge, uncontrolled, and diabolically strong.' In 'King Coal,' the last of the sketches in the volume, and one of the best short pieces Anderson ever wrote, he reaches the crux of the matter. There are some questions, he says, that keep coming back to him—

> It seems to me that love has much to do with the fiber and quality of men as citizens of a country, and the whole matter of hustling pushing coal-mining factory-building modern life for the most part remains in my mind in the form of annoying and to me unanswerable questions. I find myself going about day after day and asking myself such questions as these, 'Can a man love a coal mine, or a coal-mining town, a factory, a real-estate boomer. . . . If a man lives in a street in a modern industrial town, can he love that street? If a man does not love the little patch of ground on which his own house may stand, can he in any sense love the street, the city, the state, the country of which it is a part?'

And, because he would not like to see love of country become in the end a thing like modern religion, occasionally pumped into temporary life by 'some political Billy Sunday and by propaganda in the newspapers,' such questions, Anderson adds, are disquieting. And indeed they are. For what Anderson has been recording is, of course, the fundamental impasse of the nineteen-twenties in American literature. Though some of our writers, like Scott Fitzgerald, will be only partly conscious of the true nature of their predicament and some, like Henry Mencken, only too aware, pushed the issue away from consciousness, the hostility of the American artist to his own society is a central trait of the decade. It is a despair beneath the post-war despair; it is a revolt beneath all the other forms of revolt; whether against the puritan taboos, the Victorian prejudices, or the bourgeois sanctities. . . . And in one way or another it will condition the forms of our artists' activity: their pilgrimages to Spain and Corsica or their exile in Asia and Taos; their delight in such a literary fancyland as Cabell's or their derision of the boobish national circus; their obsessed quest for glamour at the

Ritz or their varying accents of bitterness, such as the masochism of Henry Miller's work or the sadism of Robinson Jeffers's; not to mention that final despairing invocation to the dynamo itself, as in the case of Eugene O'Neill, or the turning worship of Anglo-Catholicism or Nietzscheanism or even, as in the singular case of *Jefferson and/or Mussolini,* of Fascism itself.

As you'll see, Sherwood Anderson also will nibble at many of these 'solutions' to the economic impasse of the American twenties. But never knowing the answers, he knew enough to avoid the easy answers. The Ohio Nada was still from Ohio and, however despairing, it came from the center of mid-American life: Anderson remains the spokesman of the meek even when the meek have become intolerable. These obscure and outraged ordinary American souls whom he has been portraying are so much part of him, indeed, that just *because* of their warped existence, he must believe in them all the more. 'I told my people life was sweet, and men might live,' is nevertheless the concluding note of his Chicago tales, and you are not likely to notice this sentiment in much first-rank American writing for the next fifteen years. If Sherwood Anderson is one of the first social rebels of the early twenties to attack the illusions of civilization in the United States, and in this sense helps to set the tone of the decade, he is also—and this is the main sense of his work as a whole—one of the last to believe in the possibility of civilization in the United States.

Still, was it easy to find a source of life in either the raw Chicago scene or in the gilded commercialism of the new age? 'Did loneliness drive him to the door of insanity,' the Rosalind Wescott of *The Triumph of the Egg* says about her father, 'and did he also run through the night seeking some lost, some hidden and half-forgotten loveliness?' Similarly, the Will Appleton of *Horses and Men,* long after he has left Bidwell, Ohio, and put away his memories of all its 'warm cozy places' and got his job in a factory town, feels afraid of life just when he should be enjoying it most—

> He stood in the hallway of a house hearing two voices. Was he trying to close his ears to one of them? Did the second voice, the one he had been trying all day, and all the night before, not to hear—did that have something to do with the end of his life in the Appleton house at Bidwell? Was the voice trying to taunt him, trying to tell him that now he was a thing swinging in air, that there was no place to put down his feet? Was he afraid? Of what was he afraid?

And perhaps the Anderson of the second period is also afraid he is now 'a thing swinging in air.' At any rate, the passage will stay in our minds as we trace the next phase of his writing: the stopping-short of his narratives of social change and that endless circling in the coils of his own temperament.

4. Search for Origins

At this point, blocked on all sides by the apparently unbeatable America of the machine age, the writer turns in upon himself.

During the years from 1924 to 1929 will ensue that stream, that flood of reminiscences, memoirs, accounts, autobiographies, and barely disguised novels of childhood, adolescence, and maturity—those voluminous introspective studies of Anderson's which have to a large degree obscured his early and late concern with the life around him, and given him the connotation of an egoism which he least of all deserves.

As to other connotations and other human failings, we have seen that he is hardly a Phallic Chekhov—nor is he really a sort of Populist Turgeniev. But, while Anderson's tendency is much more positive, plain, communal, the merit of his attitude is that, after all, he is not *too* positive, plain, and communal. Although his early heroes have already shifted their direction from the pursuit of individual success to a sort of communal belonging—from power to brotherhood—there are still those other elements of bitterness and hostility; one doesn't strangle one's father with the best of intentions. Through Anderson's series of self-portrayals there will emerge some curious twists of the psyche. As in the later case of John Dos Passos, who very similarly throws himself into the search for a better social arrangement, there *is* a temperament here that colors the view of the time.

A Story Teller's Story, in 1924, occupies a transitional place in the shift from social scrutiny to personal introspection. Anderson's first direct autobiography, it opens with the post-Civil-War period of magic-lanterns, village bards, and rural artisans—that day of the County Fair and of Anderson's midwestern 'Tillies' on a thousand midwestern farms. Very shortly, however, these western towns are purged by the emetic of Oil. Had it been foolish, before, for any man to act grand? Now every man might consider himself as 'something special.' A little later, Anderson prowls through urban streets in a time of depression, very much like the later Tom Wolfe in the Brooklyn of 1932, and studies the habits of a new American proletariat (some time before Clara Weatherwax's epics of the underdog), and, sleepless, listens to the mechanized heart of the New World in anxiety and doubt. In fact, most sharply of all his books to this point, *A Story Teller's Story* indicates the quality of Anderson's cultural insight: his feeling for, knowledge of, preoccupation with, that entire American social scheme which just then the more fashionable intellects of the middle twenties were consigning to the categories of farce and fantasy.

However, is it merely because the father of the autobiography is viewed within the framework of this older 'smiling society' that his portrait seems to have changed so? Here he is seen as a mercurial but genial and even heroic vagabond: a 'ruined dandy from the South,' true enough, and still irresponsible, a good non-provider, but also a provincial sport, lover, gay dog, entertainer, and backwoods Mr. Micawber. This is a very different picture from that 'Windy' McPherson who was such a ghastly ne'er-do-well, or from Beaut McGregor's father—the laughing-stock of Caxton—or from the sodden paternal carcass which haunts the memories of Hugh McVey in *Poor White*.

But, then, why does Anderson appear to be still so concerned with the parental image: from the Judge Turner of the autobiography, who assumes the position of a foster-father in Anderson's youth and points the way to wealth and power, to the Alfred Stieglitz of Anderson's later life, who was 'more than a father' to so many puzzled children of the arts? Why is the story of Anderson's actual father so full of references to a sort of common identity of father and son—a not wholly flattering identity? Just as in the earlier novels, the mother of *A Story Teller's Story*, surrounded by poverty and hardship, by a large family and a still unaccountable husband, is to die at thirty—'outworn and done for.' Like the heroes of the ancient myths, who gave themselves a noble descent when they did not actually have one, Anderson devotes many pages here to the kind of parents whom he would have preferred for himself—to a series of imaginary families. 'What is a birth? Has a man no rights of his own?' If *A Story Teller's Story* has summarized the struggle of an American writer to exist in an environment that is hostile to the best sort of human life—this entire cultural birth struggle of Anderson's which we have been tracing—so the autobiography introduces us to another pattern of inner conflict: a personal birth struggle, as it were, which will now preoccupy his thoughts and form the core of his work during the middle twenties.

Whatever the residual conflicts that appear here, though, Anderson *does* draw closer to his family in these pages. Is it a coincidence, too, that directly after he describes his father as a kind of older village bard in the flesh, he should himself assume a very similar rôle in our letters? At any rate, here he is: a true historian of an older mid-American life, a teller of a thousand tales of our agrarian origins, a homely philosopher, pork-and-beans aesthete, preacher, singer, and prophet all in one. . . . This is the form of *A Story Teller's Story*. Sprawling, rambling, often overshooting its mark, and yet turning suddenly to reach it just when we had given up hope—rather like a farmer bargaining for his winter oats—it reflects the talk of Anderson's rural society: a society, resting after its pioneer effort, that valued talk the more and did not set, maybe, too high a standard for it. Conversation was not yet a rigorous occupation in Anderson's midwestern region. The subtle intellectual sorties of the European drawing rooms which so captivated the visiting Americans are some distance removed. All the same, this local gossip has its own flavor, wit, and specifically human bearing that may be a national antidote to publicity slogans as well as continental salons.* And don't be misled. There is an art all its

* It is interesting to remember that Anderson, in the midst of his own success as an advertising linguist, set about deliberately to recapture the casual western drawl of his origins: the apparent *formlessness* of his writing is very often calculated.

own here. If you are willing to return to the kitchen of an Ohio farmhouse and listen to these tales—some of them tall tales and not all of them filled with decorum, some of them traditional and some improvised, some that are never to be finished and some, as it seems, that will never start—you should learn much about an earlier American life and character. Sherwood Anderson is to become one of our prime native raconteurs and *A Story Teller's Story* gives you a first taste of what he is like in this new vein.

His next work, *Dark Laughter,* in 1925, illustrates the contrasts that run through his character—the novel is almost as fancy and 'modern' as the autobiography is old-fashioned and solid. Here are the Sapphic heroines of, say, Dorothy Parker or Edna Millay, wanton by conviction as well as taste, along with the middle-aged young men of Huxley or T. S. Eliot, sexless to their sisters' devout nymphomania: but all living together under the reign of Dada in the post-war realm of drink and despair. 'We were sold out up to the hilt.' Here are the winners of the Dial Prize in their affairs by Freud: human relationships that are irresponsible when they aren't illicit—and it was difficult for them *always* to be illicit—and that are usually without affection, obviously without a future, certainly without consequences. Running through all this in *Dark Laughter* is another favorite motif of the twenties: the noble savage of Harlem. The high shrill laughter of the Negro rings through the white man's troubled house.

A little later, in connection with *Beyond Desire,* I will talk about the tone of all Anderson's popular novels from *Many Marriages* on—their shiny, machine-made veneer that is pasted over Anderson's honest western grain; reminding us of the journeyman artists of his youth whose special talent lay in making oak look like mahogany, and mahogany like pine. . . . But notice meanwhile that if the aesthetic scene of *Dark Laughter* is hardly very convincing, it is also true that Anderson hardly wants to make it convincing. In fact, the novel is another document of renunciation. And this time it is the 'artistic' life of the nineteen-twenties—that is to say, the life of those artists who had been freed from the tribal superstitions, as Van Wyck Brooks pointed out, but who were by no means free men—it is the *Life of Realization* itself that Anderson is renouncing, just as he had previously renounced the Acquisitive Life. Ostensibly a portrait of the emancipated modern ego, *Dark Laughter* is actually a picture of the inadequate modern ego. It is in its way an early debunking of the debunkers.*

Thus, its hero, Bruce Dudley, in despair about the 'artists' he sees around him, and wanting to be 'an artist of another sort,' leaves the bohemian sets of Chicago and Paris to return to Old Harbor, Indiana, just as Anderson's original hero had left Caxton, Iowa, for the industrial and then the artistic centers of the urban metropolis. Anderson is conscious of the irony of this pattern. ' "O Lord! Ring around the rosy. . . . You start somewhere, come back to where you started. . . . Round and round you go. Now you see it and now you don't." ' The novel, moreover, holds other elements of defeat and frustration. 'He would wake in the cold morning,' Anderson says about his central figure, 'having thoughts, too many thoughts.' And this return of Bruce Dudley to his origins, with 'his brain churning—his fancies drifting,' is marked by these ineffec-

* Hemingway's take-off of the novel in *The Torrents of Spring* is therefore almost a burlesque of a burlesque; and similarly Wyndham Lewis, in *Paleface*, uses *Dark Laughter* quite erroneously as a key work of contemporary American romanticism. But it is difficult, in view of the broken form and disturbed emotional context of the novel, not to make this error.

tual and chaotic thoughts, by the sense of a futile backward-circling movement without center or stability, and by a sort of personal disorganization that recalls the nightmarish visions which have pursued a series of Anderson's heroes and is the very opposite of Anderson's earlier stress on power.

Indeed, the central figure of *Dark Laughter* compares himself to a crazy man he had once seen sitting on a Mississippi wharf. '"Keep afloat!" the crazy man had called to a steamboat plowing its way up river.' And it almost seems that Anderson's main objective, like his hero's, will be merely to keep afloat as he pursues the meaning of his personal history back to the childhood of *Tar*.*

It is an 'imaginary childhood,' to be sure. In presenting it, in 1926, Anderson explicitly disavows truth and bows only to fancy. But maybe the denial of the 'fact' in Anderson's second autobiography serves a purpose; at any rate, it is here that he most fully presents the context of the childhood trauma which seems to hang over all his work and the elements of which appear and reappear in his other volumes. And again there are the continual hard times, the changing towns, the large family, the no-account father, the shadowy memory of a mother who is worn out and done for. No two of the Moorehead children, Anderson says, were born in the same house—and what doesn't a house mean to a child? (It is interesting,

* Between these two works Anderson published the first of a series of talks he gave on his craft—although he was never fond of the lecture rostrum, and this prime American story teller, so much at home with all the Tillies and Jacks of our agrarian belt, this incessant colloquist of the hinterland, when he appeared *before* an audience, was likely to stumble and blunder, and, in desperation, invoke and misquote Mark Twain. Thus, *The Modern Writer,* in 1925, is notable chiefly as a source for the later and quite brilliant description of a lecturer's feelings, 'When the Writer Talks,' which ought to be read by every artist who ascends the pulpit.

incidentally, that the Bruce Dudley of *Dark Laughter* returns to the *hotel* where he had spent his childhood, while the central figure of *Winesburg,* George Willard, is also the son of an impoverished hotel keeper.) Tar Moorehead, if he had been born again, would have selected a grocer for his father, 'with a fat jolly wife,' and at night he lies in bed dreaming of a house with laughter in it, and singing—and food. The Mooreheads' place was different—when they had one. 'You could throw a cat through the cracks.' Years later Tar reflects that even as a grown man he had never had any place he could call his own:

> He was an American, had always lived in America, and America was vast, but not a square foot of it had ever belonged to him. His father had never owned a square foot of it. . . . Worthless kind of people in an age of prosperity. . . . If you want to be something in this world, own land, own goods.

Moreover, the physical poverty of the Mooreheads is indicative of a perhaps worse inner poverty. And feeling the social disgrace of his family, and his own isolation even within the family circle—'Tar alone had no comrades'—very early the young boy resolves to create his own life of the imagination. 'If I am shut out of one world there is another.'

To which of these two worlds does the mother of Tar's childhood belong? 'He was in love with her all his life,' Tar says, while he always 'let his father alone.' But his mother, overworked and distraught, seems herself 'such an isolated figure'—a beautiful being to the child, but too distant from him, just as all the world and its people are 'too big, too fast.' Perhaps it is no wonder, under the pressure of this meager and harsh existence with a genially unstable father and a disintegrating mother, that Tar's childhood is broken by periods of illness, of sleeplessness—by his 'bad times,' as he terms them. Or that he should come to have a recurrent vision, by day as well as by night, in which everything escapes from him: the house, the people, the chairs in the room floating away. 'They floated away over the tops of the trees . . . and almost disappeared into the sky.' His own hands, indeed, appear to leave his arms, and something inside of Tar, Anderson says, struggled constantly to bring everything back and put everything in its place. . . . Not to have everything disappear was Tar's problem.'

And so it was. So, too, when we reach the crux of these personal patterns in the 'imaginary' childhood of Tar Moorehead, we may begin to feel the impact of Anderson's conflicts over the first ten years of his writing—not to mention the fifty years of his life.

For, when this older exile looks back upon the exile of infancy, it is difficult not to feel the acute crisis of 'place' in Anderson's history. The cultural tension of Anderson's maturity is doubled by the earlier psychological tension: the writer now without a home in a modern society that is itself 'too big, too fast,' seeks in vain the home of his youth. Here, too, is the source of Anderson's earlier bitterness—Tar's hatred of life, Anderson tells us, was primarily concerned with money: 'He had got a money hunger that ate at him night and day.' Remember the full extent of his original compulsion for wealth and power, the typical form of security in the United States and precisely the one that was lacking in his own early history. It took a certain resolution, no doubt, for Anderson to deny this money hunger just when he had himself become settled in place and power; it took a certain perspective for him to admit the inadequacy of such purely material values—not indeed as a young man, and in a book, but as a man of forty, and in the flesh.

In terms of this personal history, it is worth noticing how Anderson has been reliving his own relationship with his family, and how he has gradually resolved the contempt for and hostility to the parental image which has dominated his earlier literary heroes. And having come at last to understand this image—and to accept his own temperamental affinity with it—it is in *Tar* also that Anderson makes a final identification of his own life with his father's. But was it a simple matter to accept such a rôle? To see himself as another homeless and wandering village bard and folk entertainer, and one, perhaps, with something of his father's 'slickness and plausibility,' with something of the braggart, the theatrical vagabond, and the windy-mouthed story teller—while in his memories, as in his heroes', lies the image of the profligate and the seedy ne'er-do-well? Perhaps this explains the continual note of confession and apology that runs through Anderson's work from *Many Marriages* (in which he first took on the rôle of the disreputable) to *Tar* itself—this 'irresistible temptation' to explain—and explain—himself. And in the continual declarations of love for the mother of these reminiscences, isn't there the implicit admission that Anderson himself, as he draws closer to the patterns of his father's behavior, is forsaking her just as the father did before him? If the child of these chronicles is in effect doubly homeless, it may be that the mother is twice betrayed.

And was it easy, finally, for the mature writer to admit that the western townspeople themselves, to whom he had now dedicated his life and who were his only remaining source of stability, were disappearing in turn—that he was now a folk bard without, so to speak, a folk? Within this entire framework of values we can realize the intensity of

Anderson's search for a more genuine meaning to life in America: for 'the right place and the right people.' The boy who had never owned a foot of the vast American earth, and who had then rejected the concept of a purely material possession, must nevertheless own it all in his spirit—belong to it, become part of it. 'When he grew to be a man,' Anderson says of Tar, 'he saw Europe and liked it, but all the time he was there he had an American hunger, and it wasn't a Star-Spangled Banner hunger either.' No, and it was no longer a money hunger, either —but a longing for the Ohio of his youth:

> Ohio in the spring or summer, race horses trotting on a race track, corn growing in the fields, little streams in narrow valleys, men going out in the spring to plow. In the fall, the nuts getting ripe in the woods about an Ohio town.

It was a longing for the Ohio towns of the nineties and kerosene lamps and threshing scenes in the wheat fields and country people eating and dancing heavily: for the Ohio of the squirrel shooters and of the beech woods. 'There isn't any wood like a beech woods.'

But Sherwood Anderson is still no necromancer. These are also the Ohio towns of closed blinds and curious doings. There were plenty of Madame Bovarys in those towns, Anderson tells us—and brutal characters like the Hog Hawkins of *Tar,* and harsh agrarian epics like that of Jake Grimes and his bound girl, which Anderson afterward rewrote as the story of 'Death in the Woods.' And how much does this love of a former Ohio countryside belong to Anderson's 'other world'? To what degree is it colored by his early and late feeling of social disgrace and personal ostracism—by a longing for the town and countryside *he should have had?* 'The devil!' as Anderson might have said: but all the same, the tender re-creation of the past in *Tar* is tinged by his fear that he is inventing a past. When the boy became a man, Anderson says, and thought of Camden—'the town in which he was born and which he never saw and never intended to see'—there was a reason for his love of the place—

> He owed no one money there, had never cheated anyone, had never made love to a Camden woman he found out later he did not want. . . . Tar was trying, through the creation of a town of his own fancy, to get at something it was almost impossible to get at in the reality of life.

Disavowing truth along with respectability, yielding only to fancy as his mistress—has he now not only taken over but outdone the parental image of an irresponsible story teller? If the personal structure of Tar's life is 'imaginary,' as Anderson wishes us to believe, are the Ohio towns of his memories even more so? If this is a fanciful portrait of an individual's childhood, is it an even more unreal picture of the childhood of the Middle West? This final and corrosive speculation is at the center of all Tar Moorehead's thinking—and with it we reach the end of Anderson's long and circling search for origins.

For, just as *Tar* reaches back into and most fully reveals the earliest patterns of Anderson's midwestern childhood, it is also the last volume of the series of troubled and seeking memoirs which are written over this period—of this tormented American remembrance of things past. The story of Anderson's reversionary quest is almost over; with the *Hello Towns!* of 1929 the final step is taken.*

* Anderson's *New Testament* of 1927, his second book of verse, also records his new decision, although less effectively and in the vein of *Mid-American Chants.*

Late in his maturity, Anderson records his decision to return to the American town life he has loved: to see to what degree the white radiance of eternity *is* stained by life's dome of many-colored glass—to act out now, in person, and day by day, that provincial life he has been retracing in his thoughts over these many years. Here, in the precise year of the Crash, and the start of our most celebrated industrial *débâcle,* Anderson chronicles his return to grass roots: this one-man agrarian resettlement project, which anticipates the FSA, the CCC, and all the other manifestations of a national resettlement project in the nineteen-thirties. 'All right, I will be a country man.'

And the pages of *Hello Towns!*—which is a collection of Anderson's editorials in his Virginia newspapers, along with his running commentary on the town life—are the record of a country man's life. Thus R. L. Brown, town candidate for Justice of the Peace, writes in to the editor of the Marion *Democrat* to deny that he, Brown, is a bootlegger. The preliminary hearing of O. K. Harris for the shooting of Mr. W. A. Sult is to be held Thursday morning; meanwhile young McVey, fifteen, has stabbed his cousin Paul: there seems to be a run of violence in Smyth County, Virginia. Yet the editor of Marion's two newspapers is crusading for a bigger town band, and he wants to clean up the town eyesore, Henry Mencken Park, and to bring about a few improvements in the county jail, also in the Negro school. (In a rather different fashion from that of Sinclair Lewis's sophisticated ladies, Anderson disclaims any intention of 'reforming' Main Street even while he sets about doing it.) Rabbit-hunting in Marion claims another street light—but somehow Editor Anderson takes a rap at the utilities. There will be a checker tournament in Marion next Wednesday, and a greased-pig contest, and, as always, forest fires and family feuds. Next there are pictures of the Marion Fire Department, including Zeb, Joe, and Joe's dog. Miss Ruby Jones comes in to ask whether the paper will print a little account she has written of her new false teeth. And Editor Anderson accepts with pleasure, although he wonders why the town dentist doesn't advertise in the Marion *Democrat.*

It is difficult, though, to record the wealth of such material in the pages of *Hello Towns!*. The volume forms an invaluable record of an average American community. Nor can I easily present the quality of Editor Anderson as, with humility and grace and a rather canny judgment, he becomes the chronicler, arbitrator, cultural center (there are editorials on Van Gogh as well as the Negro problem), and rural confessional of Smyth County. The Marion *Democrat* and Smyth County *News* are in their way a *Tatler* and *Spectator* of the twentieth-century American hinterland, and their pages reveal as much human interest as, if a little less literary finesse than, those of Addison and Steele or Pope and Eusden. If Marion, Virginia, is a typical native town, its two newspapers are a special native phenomenon.

No wonder Anderson is outraged, toward the close of *Hello Towns!,* at the suggestion of a journalistic competitor that he should sell his papers. 'It was a good deal like asking "Will you sell your wife?" '—

> Yesterday I drove my car down a street of our town I had never been on before. I did not know the street was there. Men hailed me. Women and children were sitting on doorsteps. 'It is our new editor. . . . Well, you have been a long time getting down here.' When I drive on a country road in this country, farmers or their wives call to me, 'Come in and get some cider, a basket of grapes, some sweet corn for dinner.'

Will you sell your newspapers? What an idea! Anderson says. 'I have a place in this community . . . I have got an occupation here, something to do.' But, as well as 'something to do,' Anderson's life in Marion has come to mean the fruition of his lifelong hunger for the right place and the right people, the climax of that long backward-circling labyrinthine search for origins: it means 'something to be.'

No, Sherwood will never sell his newspapers, his bond with the town's life. Nevertheless, he is to wander once more beyond these town limits, and, a provincial Proteus who disdains the gift of prophecy, to incur again, at the age of fifty-five, the ordeal of still another form of birth.

5. *The Townsman and the World*

As a climax to the American twenties and the material splendor which Sherwood Anderson has loved and repudiated, the three years after his return to grass roots are marked by smaller pieces of work which appear in handsome limited editions, but in which *he* appears more Andersonian than ever, rambling on through these precious pages,* genially indifferent to the conspicuous waste that may be embodied in each passing fancy.

Whatever the edition, though, when it comes to horses and men, Anderson is likely to be good. In *The American County Fair* (1930), for example, when he talks about

* See the Grabhorn Press edition of *Nearer the Grass Roots* (1929), or the even more striking *Alice and the Lost Novel,* Number Ten of the Woburn Books, hand-printed in London in 1929 by Elkin, Mathews and Marrot.

those old-fashioned country tradesmen who used to own and race their own trotters and mentions the love affair of one of these merchants with a certain May Rose who goes at 2:18—'Do you think he touches the goods in his store that way? And what about his wife?'—Anderson throws off one of those wonderful sketches that make all the special editions worth their slender weight. For this is a 'fragment' that contains the whole structure of a vanished society. With another talk of Anderson's—the one in *Harlan Miners Speak,* in 1932—the wide margins drop away; and as John Dos Passos, who is to continue and to elaborate Anderson's American critique on a wider and bolder scale, if sometimes on a less secure base—as Dos Passos joins Anderson on the speakers' platform, the older age merges with the new. 'I want to be counted,' Anderson says in opening his talk. (The volume is a collection of talks which were given in support of the Harlan coal strike.) And with this announcement the country editor of Smyth County who had, disavowing any 'reforms,' campaigned for a better band in Marion or a new county jail, plunges into the far swifter, far-reaching currents of a decade of social change. The Last of the Townsmen is going to Washington.

A year earlier, in *Perhaps Women* (1931), Anderson had already scented the new times. Ostensibly the little volume advances the theory that it is up to the women, because they are less estranged from permanent human values, to save modern man from becoming a cog in the economic machine or an expendable unit in a prefabricated set-up. 'For a long time I had been convinced that American life had passed into control of the women.' But if the artist of the Chicago tales had subscribed to the suspicion and hatred of women which permeates modern writing, he has rescued himself from this pitfall, too.* If the women *can* save us, it is all right with Sherwood Anderson. 'I did not resent the fact.' Moreover, when Anderson follows up his notion and visits the southern mill settlements and talks with the workers, the owners, the managers, and those efficiency experts who are taking over Main Street and converting it into the Boulevard of the Industries, it becomes clear that the true emphasis of *Perhaps Women* lies elsewhere.

For the mills have also moved into the southern villages which Anderson has just lately adopted for his own. They have their fingers in the schools, the banks, the political affairs of the towns. 'They build the churches and pay the preachers.' They have distorted the vision of the mill-owners themselves: 'men as deeply in earnest,' Anderson thinks, 'as most of the reformers to whom I have talked'—but men who can no longer see beyond the riot fences which enclose their factories. And they have seduced the affections of the young: these new industrial children, mechanics, engineers, and technicians, to whom Anderson talks, and who, without doubts and without humanity, have based their life on the machine. Are the young radicals much different? Also in the pages of *Perhaps Women* are those political 'men of action' who will figure so largely in the revolutionary writing of the nineteen-thirties, but whom Anderson very early sees, just as a Malraux or Silone or Ramon Sender will afterward come to see them, as being too closely identified with the industrialists they are attempting to destroy: a similarly harsh

* From D. H. Lawrence's devouring women to Philip Wylie's 'Mom,' this motif—which is a rather primitive reaction to a cultural sense of masculine defeat—has become increasingly important in contemporary writing. In the American scene particularly, where the men have been most directly subjected to intense economic competition, and where the women, as early as our Transcendental Zenobias, took over the control of 'cultural' affairs, it is a peculiarly sensitive—and illuminating—subject.

product of the same social values. In short, this is the climax and triumph of William James's Bitch-Goddess Success:

> 'And a good word too,' I thought, thinking of money and success as a bitch, and my fellow Americans having got scent of her long since, they trotting at her heels, that peculiar look in the eyes, the look of humiliation not real, pride not real, hope not real. . . . The bitch was trotting in the South now. She had long since invaded my own Middle West, turning men from the cornfields and the forests to the factories and the factory towns.

The bitch is trotting over the entire American earth now. And the mills, hardly satisfied with the havoc they have already wrought in the patterns of Anderson's America, are setting up their own patterns as Industry, growing ever more powerful, withdraws more and more from the general life. 'Can it be that the instinct, on the part of our industrial leaders, to draw away from towns and cities, to set up separate towns, unincorporated, to build high steel fences about the mills, is an unconscious part of a program to make mill workers beings quite separated from the rest of American life?'

Thus the chronicler of the machine-change in America, who opens his work with the coming of the factories to the western towns, records the final seizure of the town by that mechanized New Order against which he has fought so long. Inaugurating his career so bitterly in the mills, the mid-American provincial must return to them again; and this perennial rebel—this Ishmael in the Land of Honey—who has retreated (as Anderson now admits) 'from the city to the town, from the town to the farm,' finds himself back at the dead center of our industrial arrangement. As you turn the pages of *Perhaps Women,* you may wonder what has happened to the erstwhile country editor of Marion, Virginia. For the little volume, ridden as it is by these lifelong speculations of Anderson as to his own country and time, sounds like the reverie of a condemned man. But the reverie of proscription is a typical literary form of our period just as the perpetually seeking wanderer is a central literary figure from the novels of Knut Hamsun to the acrid and despairing reflections of Anderson himself, standing here once more before the prison-like gates of the mills. And if seldom before has the literary exile seemed so *completely* alone, the seeker so continuously frustrated, as in our own period—if the writer who has so often told the story of the American man 'crushed and puzzled by the age of the machine' is forced to tell it all over again—this time there is the possibility, at least, of a new ending. These southern factory walls themselves, apparently so unshakable, so adamant, are already beginning to tremble before an approaching economic crisis: an economic fissure that will in large part level off the whole new industrial structure at the moment of its total ascendency. Just as the portraits of *Perhaps Women* are prescient of this change, Anderson's next work lands us squarely in the middle of it. 'She was a revolutionist,' Anderson says about the heroine of *Beyond Desire,* and the novel itself, in 1932, is a panoramic study of a southern town about to be plunged into industrial war—that long, unacknowledged war, that 'worst war of all,' which the writer had prophesied in the *Poor White* of 1920.

Yet, coming directly after a volume of first-rate essays and right before a collection of first-rate stories—why is *Beyond Desire* so disappointing a novel? What is the trouble with *all* these novels of Anderson's, from *Many Marriages* on, for which he prepares us so well, and which he usually follows so well, but which are in themselves almost always as disappointing as this one? Anderson was not a novelist. The novel form may have increased his difficulties—his essential gift was that of intuition and a brief and brilliant illumination—and perhaps we should accept the simplest explanation—one, however, that is apt to be a little simple-minded, too. The fact is that *Dark Laughter*—as well as being praised as 'one of the most profound novels of our time' by the urban intellectuals whom our provincial groper must surely have respected—was also one of the most popular of Anderson's books. It was perhaps the most widely read of them for precisely those literary elements which make it one of the least effective of his works; even today it is considered a 'typical' Anderson. Well, if he had wanted to, Anderson could have written a series of novels in the same vein, and it was seven years before his next one. All the same, *is* the next novel, which is *Beyond Desire*—is it, in effect, another of Anderson's bids for that general acclaim and worldly prestige which have haunted and tormented his existence: a temptation resting in the depths of his temperament from his earliest childhood days, repressed time and again, and everywhere else but here—but a temptation to which he must finally yield, if only once in every 'long year' of his life?

And if it is, who can quite blame him? One notices, in any case, that the love scenes here are served up in the popular manner: so daring and free, they have in general that sophisticated modern air which ten years later always seems so antique. Yet both *Many Marriages* and *Dark Laughter* held a genuine emotional crux for all their fabricated finish, and in *Beyond Desire* also the errors of tone are accentuated by an underlying sense of strain. This is an illuminating document of Anderson's last period, and when, in the last half of the novel, he moves toward the acceptance of Communism and a revolutionary ethics, the issue becomes explicit. Something has cracked up in America, the Andersonian heroine tells us, and the older tradition of American values no longer is adequate—

> 'I guess we thought—we Americans really believed—that everyone had an equal opportunity here. You go on saying, thinking that to yourself year after year and of course you come to believe it. It makes you comfortable—believing.'

Nor is this a comfortable admission to be made by the writer who has gone on year after year trying to sustain himself in an older American tradition until he also has come to believe in it. This new and crucial conflict, this apparent yielding up of both the personal ethics and the cultural values which Anderson has finally achieved for himself, would be enough in itself to account for the imperfect quality of *Beyond Desire.*

But Anderson has also been dealing with an industrial proletariat. As a matter of fact, here is a new American County Fair in which the machine girls and machine men of *Beyond Desire* gather around the fakes and freaks at a southern circus to eat Milky Ways and drink Coca-Colas and exchange the latest Broadway wisecracks, and to watch the man on the flying trapeze in a sort of mechanical respite from their own existences on the flying bobbins. There is very little in Anderson's account of either the work or the pleasure, alike harsh and vicarious, of these mass-minded souls to recall that love he could give so freely to his earlier rural mechanics and merchants—or even to the obscure and twisted lives of his Chicago tales. 'Are these people after all worth saving?' the Andersonian hero asks himself in the midst of all his other questions—a doubt which Anderson has never previously expressed about the people in his work.

And a doubt which is swept away when Anderson returns to the towns in his next volume of short stories; although, at first glance, none of the tales in *Death in the Woods,* in 1933, may seem very remarkable. In 'There She Is,' a commonplace little businessman hires a detective agency to let him know whether his wife has been unfaithful to him. But then, overcome by remorse, and realizing that his wife's love affairs are balanced by his own financial involvements, he hires the detective agency again—*not* to let him know. Still, the story is a miniature of the human tragedy inherent in our American success patterns, while Anderson is one of the few radical critics of our mores who can view even a businessman as a human being. In 'That Sophistication,' Anderson's European heroine provides an epitaph for the expatriates of the American twenties: 'I might have saved my husband all this money and got all this sophistication I'm getting, or anyway all I needed, right in Chicago.' In 'Another Wife,' a middle-aged doctor who realizes he is nothing much ('What is called a great man may just be an illusion in people's minds. Who wants to be an illusion?') is smitten by a lovely lady—a lady who is herself not quite so slim and young as she once was. But this *is* desire, if it is desire at fifty, and bound down by the fetters of maturity, and it is beautifully presented here. In 'A Jury Case' the writer simply asks himself whether a man is justified in committing murder. 'How do I know what I think?' And this is a genuine, an indispensable sense of complexity in human affairs, just as, in point of fact, we must sometimes know what we think and sometimes not know, and as Anderson always knows the things he must know in this quiet collection of tales.

Although no separate story in *Death in the Woods* may stand out by itself, and, reading them casually, you may miss the skill with which Anderson transmutes ordinary experience into an art form, the volume as a whole is a notable one. Here is the first play of Anderson's completely mature talent, harder on the surface than that which marks *Winesburg,* calmer, and almost prosaic*—but also more complex and contemplative, and underneath the surface as quick and alive as ever. Probably the clue to the quality of these tales—and a special quality in our letters—lies in the story called 'The Flood,' where Anderson's academic protagonist, who has struggled all his life to formulate his 'Theory of Values,' and who has outworn one family in the process, finally yields himself and his work to another—to the facts of his own temperament, that is, and to life itself. But thus consciously giving up his Theory of Values, perhaps he has unconsciously solved it —since he has surrendered a vision of perfection to the compulsions of experience. The quality of this ironic surrender to life lies everywhere in these tales—a 'surrender' that is full of wisdom and of gaiety; and a sense of life that grows in Anderson even while he resigns himself to life. There is no *reasonable* plan to our existence, says the Andersonian Professor—'there are only floods, one flood following another.' Yet isn't it a triumph of reason to be able to navigate these floods?

* We have seen that the 'formlessness' of Anderson's stories is very often calculated. Just so, the 'flatness' of his prose at its best is a meticulous attempt to reproduce an ordinary American idiom. Anderson gives us many examples of the pains he took to develop this style, and the critics who have stated that he wasn't really *interested* in good writing are simply looking for another kind of writing. *Per contra,* see the late Paul Rosenfeld's *Port of New York* for a sensitive description of Anderson's craft. . . . These western rhythms of Anderson's are also behind Ernest Hemingway's 'plain flat tones,' incidentally, and while the younger writer brought them to a kind of perfection, he probably sacrificed something of their naturalness.

In *Death in the Woods,* though, Anderson is back home, among his own people, once again 'part of the general.' (And how full of the variety and mystery of the general is a tale like 'In a Strange Town,' dealing with these country types, as Anderson says, 'of no importance.') Outside, however, the dilemma of the modern age continues. *No Swank,* in 1934, is a sort of preface to Anderson's final phase.* For here, in another special edition, which is, nevertheless, not quite *so* special, are the first intimations of the Depression of the nineteen-thirties as it begins to break down the rigid framework of the Industrial Separatism:

> I can't help feeling that this thing we are going through, this depression . . . the old prosperous, proud, cocksure American in some queer way blown up . . . that there is or should be at least some chance for something humanizing to grow out of all this.

It is needed, Anderson adds, for the successful Americans of the past have been 'the most lonely people in the world.' Have they, like children, believed in their own invincibility, every man viewing himself as 'something special'? Anderson notices 'the great big glorious' commercial egotism—'every man having the right to trample every other man'—that Ring Lardner, springing from the same western equalitarian roots, also noticed, and crucified. All the same, was there something else that Lardner had not caught?—a curious uncertainty in these prosperous, proud, cocksure Americans, 'a constant assertion of something that none of us really deep down in us believes

* The best of Anderson's work is likely to be in a shorter form, whether in the short stories themselves or in these little volumes of essays and 'sketches' which actually hold the keys to his thinking. See also his advice to himself throughout the Jazz Age: 'Be small.'

in.' For all the American man's particular arrogance, he has an 'almost unbelievable humility'—and for all his pleasure in material pomp, he is after 'something much more gaudy than that.'

This resurgence of Anderson's older American belief, moreover, marks the end of his trial marriage with Communism. To talk with Lincoln Steffens, who met the future and saw it work, says the Anderson of *No Swank,* is to be persuaded as to the value of the Revolution. The Russia of the Czars was very corrupt—'to tell the truth, just about as corrupt as some sections of our own government.' Yet, after all, and in spite of the politicos, the big industrialists and the other American kings, America was still a democracy. 'It really is. Don't think it isn't.' (A good many people, just then, in the middle thirties, were thinking it wasn't.) Yes, Russia is trying something big, Anderson says, and it may succeed—but that isn't our problem. 'Our problem is . . . to lift a whole race of so-called individualists out of individualism into civilization.'

Just here, while the majority of our writers were seeking almost every other form of salvation but this one, or merely standing pat on Sinclair Lewis's 'anarchy and the comics,' Anderson has expressed the renewed chance for belief which the breakup of '29 will give to all the refugees from American life as, more slowly, toward the end of the nineteen-thirties, they will also feel and respond to its impact. But if Sherwood Anderson is a maker and ancestor late in his career, too—if this figurehead in the Life of Realization helps to set the tone for those new literary affirmations, however fragmentary, imperfect, and perhaps, indeed, all too evanescent, which mark the early nineteen-forties—this time he has surely earned his place. For you have seen him transcribe this entire arc of cultural withdrawal and return, and include practically every angle in the arc, some years before his fellow writers. It is illuminating that these final insights of *No Swank* should appear in Anderson's sketch of a political figure who springs from Anderson's own countryside; from

> hot long evenings in Middlewestern towns . . .
> neighbors met and talked to . . .
> something slow, quiet, and nice. . . .

—from those same midwestern roots that throughout his career, the writer has clung to in his own literary campaign against 'the smooth guys, rotten guys, angry guys' of the American scene.

And those roots, 'always being lost and again regained,' now that Anderson has reached them once more in the very midst of social crisis, will sustain him throughout the rest of his career. With this hope, at last, of modifying and to some degree controlling the machine-change that has altered and corrupted his America—with this chance at least 'for something humanizing to grow out of all this'—has also come the resolution of Anderson's long, circling search for the right place and the right people. . . .

But Sherwood Anderson's 'chance' for a better future is still not a blind optimism about it, despite the fact that *all* conviction is a mode of incantation to some of our moderns. The pages of Anderson's next work, *Puzzled America,* in 1935, bear witness to the ravages wrought by a half-century of homage to pure materialism. The volume is a personal survey of the national scene during the depression era: there are, for example, those southern tenant farmers, 'shifting from one hopeless year to another.' Or the tobacco farmers whose months of patient work can be wiped out by a single decision made in New York or San

Francisco. 'The tobacco industry is a big, regulated, controlled industry. But the little farmers feel it isn't controlled for them.' Or those new tyrants who have come out of the oppressed classes; the Huey Longs of fact or the 'Snopeses' of William Faulkner's fiction: hard men surviving in a hard society. 'Men who could make money in hell.'

Yet the story of the agricultural South in *Puzzled America* is the story of the industrial North—and of his own West, Anderson thinks. 'There is plenty to be learned yet.' It is *the* American Story, he says, as he visits the 'disease towns' of the mining belts, established in the very midst of invaluable natural resources. 'There's power, lying asleep in this valley, to run half America,' the miners tell Anderson. While half of the American people, from the empty factories of New England to those vast western plains where thousands of acres of drifting top soil have buried fences and houses and whole villages—while half of the people he has visited during these years, Anderson thinks, have been ill in body and spirit. 'They talk about no work in this country. . . . There's work here for a hundred years, giving life to these millions.'

Few other similar chronicles of the period, in fact—and these firsthand investigations of the native scene are a distinctive *genre* of the nineteen-thirties—convey the sense of our wasted physical heritage more sharply than *Puzzled America.* Still, as Anderson travels among these ruined citizens of the fabulous American earth, he sees around him the evidence of a shifting scheme of values—

> We are people who passed through the World War and its aftermath. We saw the upflaring of prosperity, lived through the Harding and the Coolidge times. We got

> the hard-boiled boys and the wise-crackers. We got, oh, so many new millionaires. As a people now we are fed up on it all.
>
> We do not want cynicism. We want belief. . . .
>
> There is at least a chance to set up the framework of a new thing. Be quiet. Wait! Don't push. Those who have had a strangle-hold upon America have been served long enough.

So there are both the facts of destruction and a sense of resurrection in the United States of the depression years—and also, and always, the antics and escapades of ordinary people: these types and originals whom Anderson meets in the course of his travels and who exemplify again the infinite variety of 'the general': There is the 'rural realist' (female) whom Anderson picks up on the road and who asks him hopefully: 'You ain't a gambler, are you?' 'No . . . I'm a traveling man.' Or the ex-electrician who doesn't mind having become a tramp because 'You get a new picture of life.' Or the newspaper publisher who admits he can't possibly believe the anti-New-Deal bilge he prints in his papers. Or the sick workman who tells Anderson that the only cure for unemployment is to kill the unemployed: 'I never will succeed. I might as well be put out of the way.' Or the 'American Muskrat King' who wants to liquidate the egret as an un-American bird. . . . *Puzzled America* is filled with these fine, half-folkloristic sketches 'of people as I have found them': sketches which, proving the central thesis of the volume in terms of flesh and blood, make it an incisive document of the crucial years of our own revolution by ballot.

But then, who was there at the time able to reach down into these particular American lives so deftly as Sherwood

Anderson, so native himself, and directly after so long a struggle to achieve his nativity: this dirt farmer, mill hand, capitalist, and radical all in one, this perennial American wanderer and seeker—a 'traveling man' indeed in the United States of the cartels and the corporations.

If Sherwood Anderson's touch with his own people is very often superb now, why shouldn't it be? Why, his life has been nothing but a continual effort to come closer to them, as he reflects when a Virginia labor leader inquires whether he 'wants in' to a union meeting:

> Yes, of course. I want in everywhere. To go in is my aim in life. I want into fashionable hotels and clubs, I want into banks, into people's houses, into labor meeting, into courthouses. . . . That is my business in life—to find out what I can—to go in. I did not say all of this. 'Sure,' I said.

And in his next three works Sherwood Anderson 'wants in' to his native scene for the last time.

6. *What's the Matter with Oak Hill?*

ANDERSON'S LAST NOVEL, *Kit Brandon,* in 1936, is cast in that 'popular' mold which we have noticed in respect to *Beyond Desire.* As such it probably represents Anderson's final sidewise attempt to get a little more of that worldly power and place which he has cast off elsewhere.

In terms of the novel's material, too, the central portrait of a glamorous bootlegger's moll in the heyday of prohibition may be an attempt to fulfill, however vicariously, Anderson's lifelong craving for pomp and splash.

Yes, the writer who has tried so often is still trying—and the writer who has learned so much is still learning. Although *Kit Brandon* is not a very good novel, it isn't a bad novel either—it is possibly the best of Anderson's novels.

And just as he had opened his career a quarter of a century earlier with those portraits of town life in *Windy McPherson's Son,* now, at the start of still another tumultuous decade, our own, he returns to the town as the core and bulwark of his values.

'What's the matter with Oak Hill? Why not Oak Hill?' Anderson asks in the preface of *Home Town,* in 1940, and the volume, part of a series that was illustrated by the industrious Farm Security Administration photographers, is a little résumé of American rural patterns in the framework of the changing seasons. What's the matter with spring in Oak Hill?—spring, which changes the faces of the towns, East, West, North, and South, and stirs their blood. 'June will be a great time for marriages.' And summer in the small American towns: the time of 'hot still week-days on Main Street, no coal bills, greens from the garden, roasting-ear time. . . . In the Dakotas and down through Kansas, Nebraska, northern Texas, and in the far West it is wheat-harvesting time. It is hay-cutting, wheat-harvesting time in the small farms about New England and in middlewestern towns.' Hot dusty days, long, hot days . . . and autumn in the small towns. 'Can a man make the old overcoat last through another year, can he get new shoes for the kids, will the town factory run full-handed this year, what about the price of coal——'

> 'Say, have you put anti-freeze in your car yet?'
>
> 'Gee, but the summer seemed short. Seems like a wind just blew it away.'

Is it the texture of Anderson's prose that gives to *Home Town* its particularly touching quality? Is it the lucent flowing rhythms and wonderfully homely bits of dialogue through which he presents his town bullies, clowns, and dandies, scholars, mystics, and merchants: this entire gallery of rural types who have become so familiar to us in Anderson's work, but who seem here a little altered, simplified, clarified, almost translucent, reduced, as it were, to their final essence? Or is it simply the FSA photographs in the book, admirable as they are? What *is* the factor that gives *Home Town* almost the tone of a Currier and Ives, the tone of a day forever past and commemorated in its passing by these haunting prose cadences upon which Anderson has lavished so much care and affection? Then there is Anderson's realization that 'the breakup which came to America in '29'—a breakup whose echoes are everywhere in the volume—that this last and most radical change in the pattern of a changing American life probably marks the final, the ineradicable breakup of the earlier agrarian society he has made his own. . . . 'What's the matter with Oak Hill?' 'Seems like a wind just blew it away.'

But isn't there also, in the lyrical and elegiacal quality of *Home Town*, some instinct of this survivor from the past that his own career, so immutably changeable too, is drawing on to its final change? In this last hail and farewell to the towns, even those perpetually tormenting questions of Anderson about his own country and his time are, somehow, a little less acute—are subordinated to the coming and going of the seasons, to the one immortal constant in an always mortal scheme. It is just this view: a sense of a certain inevitability in human destiny, and of an equal human necessity to make its condition a little less inevitable; it is that final Andersonian 'surrender' to life which we have already noticed, and which is now no less quick and alive and gay—that sets off the *Memoirs* of 1942.

Well, here it is all over again: the hard times in a middle-western childhood, the ill mother and the unwanted child, the imaginative but slippery father. (And when Anderson returns to the southern home of his later years, he completes, of course, the identification with that 'ruined southern dandy' of a father.) The young manhood of the *Memoirs* is familiar, too: the 'imaginary' Ohio countryside and the all too solid mills of the urban metropolis. Once again in these pages the early Anderson prowls along industrial boulevards and blind alleys: those Chicago thoroughfares which, out of nowhere into nothing, run on and on forever. The wonderful story of 'Rice'—the old-fashioned bicycle mechanic of the *Memoirs,* with his contempt for the new mass-production technics and his 'running fits' through which he tries to shake off the endless repetition of his new job—such a story almost contains the whole impact of the machine-change on the America of Anderson's youth. And then comes Sherwood Anderson's own running fit, as he renounces his throne among the new economic kings, shakes off his factory, family, business associates, and all, and, a foxy publicity man, turns fumbling poet. Yes, in these pages, too, he starts out once again upon that revolving lifelong search for a meaning to his own life and to life in America which you have just now finished.

But, if Sherwood Anderson is talking about himself again in the *Memoirs,* you can listen to him endlessly now. Because he is also talking about provincial ascetics and pagans in the Ohio of the nineteen-hundreds; about that Chicago epoch which produced the Little Renaissance and the Children of the Arts in the late teens; about Sandburg, Masters, Dreiser, O'Neill, and Theda Bara; about New

York aesthetes in the nineteen-twenties and about New York revolutionaries in the nineteen-thirties; about automobiles; and apple pie and Herbert Hoover; about a certain large radical delegation which was scheduled to arrive in Washington, out of which there appeared only a Negro, a Jew, and, naturally, Sherwood; and about his own southern countryside and people. Anderson is also talking about American morals, habits, types, trends, and movements over the last half-century—about the American *character*—about, in short, everything but himself—and if you can, you ought to listen to him. For the *Memoirs* are a triumph of tone, of a native tone; of a 'grand style' arising from its natural sources and couched in its natural idiom—and of a maturity difficult to achieve in life, and particularly, perhaps, in American life. Never knowing the answers, Anderson knows enough by now. . . . What a long way indeed he has come: this groping provincial, so full of anguish in an age full of uncertainty, who saw the modern Medusa and turned all the more into flesh. Among all the untaught Americans who make up the bulk of our literary annals, which ones, say, have taught themselves more?

We may think of this again some time later on, toward the close of the two decades of contemporary writing which Anderson has helped to initiate—in respect to Thomas Wolfe, I mean, who most nearly among the newer voices is to carry forward Anderson's communal search. In terms of these larger cultural movements, we have noticed how the artist of the Chicago tales very early met and came to grips with the climactic 'No' of the nineteen-twenties: an Ohio Hamlet who proclaimed the New World's Nada. And then, through that endless and almost frenzied quest for 'some lost, some hidden and half-forgotten loveliness,' how he also helps to set the tone for the nineteen-thirties with his final belief in a chance at least 'for something humanizing to grow out of all this.' And, if just here, in this final conviction of Anderson's, there is still the lingering fever of the condemned, he is, at any rate, a *condamné* who has known the grace of life. . . . 'My luck held,' Anderson was fond of saying. And so it did. Perhaps even—for the last of the townsmen in an urban America—perhaps even as to the moment of his death.

Now, however, we are to listen to the new voices. With Sherwood Anderson we have completed our portrait of the Middle Generation and move on to the Younger; to the later Americans of our first Post-War Period, who, equally or more gifted than their ancestors, will appear at times far more circumscribed in the use of their talents: our very impressive moderns who, often mocking at the notion of a different American past, will sometimes seem unable to imagine a different American future—in fact, *any* future.

A certain tormented sage of adolescence whom you may recall—to wit, H. L. Mencken—has already set the stage for them. With our next figure, the demonic young chronicler of the Jazz Age proper, we enter a new scene.

Chapter Five

F. Scott Fitzgerald: ORESTES AT THE RITZ

◇

1. A Promising Past

2. Far Behind the Veil

3. To West Egg

4. Down the Labyrinthine Ways

5. The Eumenides at Home

Chapter Five

F. Scott Fitzgerald: ORESTES AT THE RITZ

1. A Promising Past

PERHAPS he really didn't invent the Jazz Age. 'Safe upon the solid rock the ugly houses stand: Come and see my shining palace built upon the sand!'

But *This Side of Paradise* was the generation's masculine primer, as *A Few Figs from Thistles* was the feminine—and as *The Sun Also Rises* was the second reader for both sexes. Among those not under forty today—including some who have taken to scolding a frivolous younger generation—almost all who could have read his first novel will have read it. Among the young, who will bother with this encyclical of an antique epoch? Nevertheless, it was hardly considered a novel when it appeared in 1920. It was a manifesto, it expressed one's innermost convictions, it was perhaps the first 'real' book one had ever read. Like most literary landmarks, it was so absolutely convincing as to seem unlike a literary landmark.

Irregular in exposition, broken in context, interrupted by poetic sequences, satiric reveries, charts, here were the authentic and almost secret observations of a typical young person of the age. 'A chiel's amang ye takin' notes'—and, faith, he printed them; and became the Fatal Man of an era. This child was, of course, Francis Scott Key Fitzgerald. . . .

He was born September 24, 1896, in St. Paul, Minnesota, of 'Irish and Maryland English stock—' The simple declarative statement holds a lot of complex grief for him. There was a certain friction in his mind between the 'Minnesota Irish' and the 'Maryland English.' Three impressive beats testified as to the Baltimore Cavalier heritage of gay blades and dancing belles. (Francis Scott Key was a great-granduncle; the family connection might seem a little remote, perhaps, for such nomenclative prominence.) But then there was the unaccented syllable. There were the less romantic, or positively grubby, hinterland origins.

Buffalo, where the future author traveled with his family, was not much better. As we shall see, a later Fitzgerald figure is to disappear in the wilds of this abandoned frontier. The inferior financial rating of the young Midwesterner preoccupied his thoughts too. Was it by a stretch of a somewhat elastic imagination that he considered himself the poorest boy in a school of rich men's sons? Among these eastern aristocrats he hardly needs to be reminded of his Catholic heritage; this is a crucial area of his work.

Fitzgerald went to the Newman School in Hackensack, New Jersey, and—'largely because of the Triangle Club'—to Princeton. In 1917 he joined the army. During the week-ends he began to work on his first novel. In 1919 he took a 'poorly paid' job as advertising-writer, sold a story for thirty dollars, went home to rewrite his novel and—

> In two months he had finished *This Side of Paradise,* which, highly successful, resulted in his selling stories to magazines; and his days of struggle were over.

This is taken from Fitzgerald's account in Mr. Millet's handbook; perhaps no other Contemporary American Author could have issued a statement at once so typical and so incongruous.

Certainly the festive days had arrived. Fitzgerald was 'the brilliant, handsome author,' as he signed his letters, and no longer indeed 'poorly paid.' 'Do you mean to say we have only $600 coming in every month?' cries the young wife of *The Beautiful and Damned* during a financial ebb. 'A subdued note crept into her voice.' These were Fitzgerald's party days; the parties of *The Great Gatsby;* the big parties, as Edmund Wilson tells us, 'at which Fitzgerald's people go off like fireworks and which are likely to leave them in pieces.'

I needn't mention the 'exotic speeds' who flash through the pages of the early Fitzgerald, or the 'young contralto voices on sunk-down sofas' which murmur such devastating remarks. 'I've kissed dozens of men,' says one of these girls in a notorious aside. 'I suppose I'll kiss dozens more.' The sofa was the *mise-en-scène* for the drama of the post-war decade, and the kiss was réveille for a generation that watched twilight fall over cocktails at the Biltmore, and dawn strike the windows of Childs' Fifty-Ninth Street. These are bright, trembling children whose destiny lies on the lips of any dancing partner they might embrace twice on the same evening. No other places are possible for, no other voices can whisper to, the young Fitzgerald.

There were others, however, who also accepted this place for home and these hours for life's hours—the same American reading public which would, just two decades later, and just as eagerly, thumb a ride on the Joads's jalopy and jolt along with John Steinbeck's Okies. . . . But it was the early Fitzgerald's gift to endow his rather unreal creatures with a peculiarly touching reality. While a later sequence of American writers—though not always so convincingly—was to discover the soul of the dispossessed, he provided one for the élite.

Those were the salad days of the American twenties, and New York, as Fitzgerald recalled in *The Crack-up,* had all the iridescence of the beginning of the world. 'The first speakeasies had arrived, the toddle was *passée,* the Montmartre was the smart place to dance and Lilyan Tashman's fair hair weaved around the floor among the enliquored college boys. . . . We felt like small children in a great bright unexplored barn.' People were tired of the proletariat, Zelda Fitzgerald announced in *Save Me the Waltz.* (The early marriage of Scott and Zelda was in the style of the Jazz Age; and without Zelda, it has been said, there would have been no Jazz Age.) Everybody was famous then. 'All the other people who weren't well known had been killed in the war.' The David Knights of her own novel are the idols of a world where 'it was always tea-time or late at night,' and like the Fitzgeralds, they leave New York—everybody was leaving, smelling of orchids and plush—for the French Riviera. And surely the group of tanned aristocrats whom the young American actress encounters in *Tender is the Night:* and their beach-parties and garden-festivals, their casual and instinctive air of possession and command over all the delicacies of existence; the intensely calculated perfection of their lives, like those of the 'older civilizations'—surely this is the apogee of the vision of ease and grace which F. Scott Fitzgerald has pursued from Minnesota to the Cap d'Antibes.

Yet his days of struggle are not over; in the early nineteen-thirties he is just approaching a tortuous hour of decision. The corrosive vein in Fitzgerald's penultimate novel, the reverberations of the crack-up, the cry of suffering—a suffering that has become hopelessly twisted and now finds expression in a deliberate perversion of the spirit: these accents of destruction will become familiar to us in the pages of our writer. They are all the more severe because he has traced a deep groove, and has now reached a maturity he has always feared. They are more intense because they come from precisely that European Riviera which has been a perpetual hope of refuge: a psychological Eden, a shining, scented garden of lost innocence where moral conflicts are out of order.

If the younger writer, then, spoke for a gay and pleasure-seeking youth, it was a demonic youth too; here is a kind of torment, though it has been tutored at Exeter, and the Furies are here, though now stopping at the Ritz. Was there ever a smoother surface to cover the emotional involutions? Yet the coiled emotions are responsible for the tension in Fitzgerald's writing—this is what gives validity to his portrait of the Jazz Age: to such a giddy context and such luxurious monkeyshines. Through these Princeton proms and tea dances at Sherry's and midnight dances in the Plaza, through these cocktails and hobble skirts and sunk-down couches—these cold enchantresses and pure kisses and negative contralto voices—the Fitzgerald hero is looking for his path of salvation: or at least for that form of 'divine drunkenness' which may serve instead. —'There,' said Heine upon meeting Musset, 'goes a young man with a promising past.' And this discerning half-truth about an earlier Child of the Century might apply almost as well to the later one.

We shall notice, too, the curiously involved design of the 'past.' . . . But meanwhile the writer himself is not to remain among those other 'rich ruins and fugitives from justice' who, listening eternally to 'the coarse melodies of old sins,' exist on the derivatives of opium and barbital. From his eastern extreme, he will seek the lost star of his route in the furthermost reaches of the American West—

in the California of *The Last Tycoon*. In one sense to follow his travels from west to east, and east to west, is almost to chart the typical movement of the rest of our American writers over the period from 1920 to 1940: this withdrawal and return is a cultural pilgrimage of some interest.

But the wanderings of F. Scott Fitzgerald are also a form of an older and even more cosmopolitan pilgrimage: one which springs from the hero's consciousness of guilt and his need for expiation. 'The Eumenides seized upon Orestes and drove him frantic from land to land.'

2. Far Behind the Veil

THE AMORY BLAINE of *This Side of Paradise* was enchanting. There is no other word for it, and Fitzgerald uses this one often enough to leave no doubt in our mind. The pages of the novel are lighted up by Amory's 'peculiar brightness and charm' as by the glitter of an Athenian among the barbarians of St. Paul, Minnesota.

Amory is 'typical.' But to be typical in the twenties was to be superior. At St. Regis and Princeton (and of course Amory goes to Princeton) his great struggle is to conceal 'how particularly superior he felt himself to be.' And why shouldn't he? Granting himself physical and social magnetism—'the power of dominating all contemporary males, the gift of fascinating all women'—Amory concedes his own infallible mental powers. . . . There is a certain effort involved here, of course. To live by one's code of 'aristocratic egoism,' to move toward 'a more pagan attitude,' one must be versed in the Byronic dicta, and Keats and Swinburne. Amory has also a rather distant knowledge of Marx, who can be invoked, upon occasion, to put the New Jersey bourgeoisie in its place: that is, the balcony.

Yet, is there any point to such intellectual achievement, or, in fact, to any form of contemporary achievement? The chill of modern times has penetrated the most exclusive walls, has touched the shining tapestries at the Ritz. And Princeton itself, for all its Gothic spires and wild moonlight revels, its mélange of brilliant adventures and well-dressed philanderers, its sparkling big-game crowds and glittering caste system—even Princeton, which Amory loves, fails to give meaning to a barren age. 'Here was a new generation, shouting the old cries, learning the old creeds . . . destined finally to go out into that dirty gray turmoil . . . grown up to find all Gods dead, all wars fought, all faiths in man shaken.'

There is, however, a fairly potent anodyne. The love scenes of *This Side of Paradise* were largely responsible, of course, for the novel's underlying value to a generation which, like Amory, denied all underlying values. Amory saw girls— Does one need to continue the quotation?

> Amory saw girls doing things that even in his memory would have been impossible: eating three-o'clock after-dance suppers in impossible cafés, talking of every side of life with an air half of earnestness, half of mockery, yet with a furtive excitement that Amory considered stood for a real moral let-down. But he never realized how wide-spread it was until he saw the cities between New York and Chicago as one vast juvenile intrigue.

And here they are, Scott's girls. The flapper who is 'justly celebrated' for having turned five cartwheels in succession during the last pump-and-slipper dance at New Haven. The flapper who admits that love depends 'on the things one has always been in tune with'—like, for instance, platinum watches. The flapper who has 'permanently abandoned stockings.' The flapper who is longing for 'a diet of caviar and bell-boy's legs in half the capitals of Europe.' The flapper who divides her time between Anatole France and the Shimmy. —Here are Scott's Flappers: whose usual attire is a diaphanous gown and a cigarette case, and whose usual occupation is yawning; whose favorite sound is a plaintive African rhythm at three o'clock in the morning, and whose favorite argument is 'Shut Up'; whose zenith is a new hair-bob and whose nadir is to be seen *talking* to a boy.

These are undergraduate Madame Bovarys; this is the revolt of some very odd angels. . . . But to summarize the post-war revolt in *This Side of Paradise* is to omit all the virtue of the novel. And when you begin to think about it, the novel is more complex than this glistening and entertaining surface might indicate.

For surely Amory Blaine—the conqueror of the Princeton proms with his 'penetrating green eyes' and blond hair, his intricate knowledge of parlor snakes and kissable lips—is an odd figurehead for the Jazz Age. Does he recall at times a certain 'ultra-poetical, super-aesthetical, greenery-yallery, Grosvenor Gallery, *je-ne-sais-quoi* young man'? Then there is Nietzsche's influence via *The Smart Set,* and the early Fitzgerald drew upon Compton Mackenzie's *Youth's Encounter.* Amory is actually a mixture of literary trends, as he is a dabbler in them. But primarily he is Scott's exotic American child, and certainly Scott draws an exotic American childhood.

The central personage of this childhood is, of course, the glittering Beatrice O'Hara. From Beatrice, Fitzgerald tells us, Amory inherits every trait 'except the stray inexpressible few which made him worth while.' In any case the accent on glamour marks both the mother and the son, but gets the son into scrapes from which the mother might more easily escape. Even in childhood Amory must exert all his legendary charm to escape from the predicaments to which his charm has brought him. If he lies by inclination, he must then lie through necessity, and sometimes, too, in desperation. Already in these early pages of *Paradise,* Amory reminds us of those gifted and devastating persons in life who are always more aware of themselves than we think, and even more incapable of dealing with themselves. In this volatile youth there are intimations of a vicious emotional circle from which Amory's successors in Fitzgerald's work, and Fitzgerald himself, are not to be exempt.

Amory's 'cynical kinship' with Beatrice not only colors all his other early relationships; it is the only valid human relationship he has. His father, Stephen Blaine, is noticeably absent from the boy's scheme of reference, just as the mother herself remains an 'O'Hara.' When Stephen Blaine dies, Amory is diverted by the incongruity of his father's death with the 'remote beauties' of Lake Geneva. What interests him much more than 'the final departure of his father from things mundane'—what interests him particularly is the extent of the family fortune his father has left. . . . In Amory's fantasies of the millions he will inherit, and in Amory's disgust when he learns that these millions have evaporated—here is our first glimpse of Fitzgerald's own curious infatuation with wealth: an infatuation which in Amory's case comes almost to supplant his affection for Beatrice.

There are few family ties which can restrain Amory's appetite for glamour, for drama, and for riches. Similarly, there is little feeling, among all these allusions to European resorts, of a native countryside—or a country—

to which Amory belongs. Minneapolis, whither he repairs after one of Beatrice's breakdowns that 'bore a suspicious resemblance to delirium tremens,' is notable chiefly for 'the crude vulgar air of Western civilization.' While the East, for the infant expatriate, has become chiefly a haven for aliens. At Princeton Amory early notices—and quickly dispenses with—a Jewish youth whose temperament is contrasted with that of truer Princetonians. And the 'tiresome' First World War brings Amory into unpleasant contact with the new Americans. His 'spirit of crisis' soon changes into one of repulsion, surrounded as he is by these Greeks and Russians—

> He thought how much easier patriotism would have been to a homogeneous race, how much easier it would have been to fight as the Colonies fought, or as the Confederacy fought. And he did no sleeping that night, but listened to the aliens guffaw and snore while they filled the car with the heavy scent of latest America.

Yet behind all of Amory's pretense and prejudice—this glittering adolescent surface so narrow in scope and restricted in its values—there are sometimes the more strident accents of a midwestern boyhood, just as a harsher truth—and still perhaps that of childhood—will underlie Fitzgerald's own pretenses in the work to follow *This Side of Paradise.*

Is it curious that a 'vision of horror' should follow hard on the death of Amory's father?—this father who has been a rather unpresentable wraith in the boy's earlier history, and whose demise had seemed so tactless amidst the Swiss beauties? By now such 'visions' have become familiar to Amory Blaine. The death of a college friend who has been killed in an auto accident also haunts him. Like something from a misty tragedy played far behind the veil, and yet, he feels, inexpressibly horrible, 'like blood on satin,' the scene returns to his consciousness. Out on a Broadway spree, Amory is forced to leave his party: the laughter, the liquor, the girls—his partner's 'sidelong suggestive smile'—repel him. On the train for Princeton, the presence of a 'painted woman' across the aisle fills him with nausea. There is a strong sexual coloring, of course, to these fits of revulsion—a revulsion that had seized the early Amory on the occasion of his first young kiss: 'disgust, loathing for the whole incident.'

Yet this is an 'incident' toward which Amory's whole life—his sense of drama and charm, his pretense and prejudice alike, his entire education and his inclination—has been directed. And the underlying ambivalence of *This Side of Paradise* is brought to a focus, just two years later, in Fitzgerald's second novel.*

Less generally remembered today, and without the elements of popular appeal that marked *This Side of Paradise, The Beautiful and Damned* is by all odds a better work. Wealth is still the central aspiration, or obsession, of Scott's second novel: the new hero, Anthony Patch, seems to be merely a later Amory Blaine. Yet the continuation of Amory's story is so much better here, the qualitative difference is so marked, that it is no longer quite the same story. Even more than Amory, Anthony Patch is the product of enfabled luxury. His father dies in the best hotel in Lucerne. This time the departure of his parent from things mundane is accepted less casually by Scott's exotic child:

* *Flappers and Philosophers,* in 1920, a collection of lighter commercial tales, is interesting chiefly for the light it throws on Fitzgerald's own idiosyncrasies, and also, in such 'fantasies' as 'The Off-Shore Pirate,' on the popular notion of the Jazz Age.

> In a panic of despair and terror, Anthony was brought back to America, wedded to a vague melancholy that was to stay beside him through the rest of his life. . . . At eleven he had a horror of death. . . . To Anthony, life was a struggle against death, that waited at every corner.

Oddly enough, however, Fitzgerald transfers Amory's earlier feelings about his father to Anthony's feelings about his grandfather. Old Adam Patch is a robber baron of such magnitude that 'the men in the republic whose souls he could not have bought . . . would scarcely have populated White Plains.' Adam is the source of Anthony's presence in society and of his future expectations, and again the boy, considering his grandfather as—literally—a precious nuisance, 'had hoped to find the old man dead.' But finding Adam in good health instead, he manages to conceal his irritation. Some golden day, Anthony tells himself, he would have Adam's millions. 'Meanwhile he possessed a raison d'être in the theoretical creation of essays on the popes of the Renaissance.'

A theoretical creation: for while Anthony does eventually publish a piece in *The Florentine,* primarily he does nothing—and 'manages to divert himself with more than average content.' (To divert oneself is still the ambition of Fitzgerald's heroes.) If one, moreover, reads a chapter of *Erewhon,* takes a bath (Scott's young men take many baths), chatters about luscious débutantes with Richard Caramel and Maury Noble, has an egg-nogg at five—and if, more soberly, one goes once a week to one's broker and twice to one's tailor—it is still possible to achieve this ambition.

Richard Caramel represents the intellectual pursuits in *The Beautiful and Damned;* through him we get Fitzgerald's view of his own profession—a view that extends from

Amory Blaine's aversion to the 'birds' at Princeton to the odious philosopher of *Flappers and Philosophers.* Both Anthony and Maury Noble are obviously superior to Caramel; he feels it and they admit it. Poor Caramel, whose increasingly vapid literary career shows the futility of all serious work, is in fact a perfect stooge for Maury's 'divine inertia'—behind which lies a surprising maturity of purpose: 'to become immensely rich as quickly as possible.' And as Anthony dines and shops and gossips with these familiar Princeton boys—who are however no longer quite boys—one notices that even the intense and impossible love affairs of *This Side of Paradise* have receded from the horizon. Anthony does have a mildly diverting flirtation with his Geraldine—a 'little usher from Keith's'—a 'woman of another class.' But strange as it may seem, Anthony tells Maury, 'so far as I'm concerned, and even so far as I know, Geraldine is a paragon of virtue.'

What is stranger perhaps in these opening pages of *The Beautiful and Damned,* is the extent to which Scott's hero has withdrawn from even that limited contact with experience which Princeton had given him. Anthony's distaste for the American scene around him has increased. Now the United States almost seems to be personified in the figure of Adam Patch; a grotesque, disagreeable figure who provides Anthony with the means to forget his origins. These American leaders are 'little men . . . who by mediocrity had thought to emerge from mediocrity into the lustreless and unromantic heaven of a government by the people.' Has the Gettysburg talk taken an interesting modern turn? When, moreover, in a fascinating episode of *The Beautiful and Damned,* Gloria Gilbert identifies herself with the American middle class—this *class* (to Scott the word is synonymous with *caste*) with its 'brummagem' clothes and its brummagem manners—Anthony is appalled by such 'blasphemy from the mouth of a child.' And as for the lower orders of American society: why does poor Caramel, in order to prepare his new book on the slums, insist on mucking around with those 'bewildered Italians'—those aliens, the débris of Europe, who keep on arriving, and all 'with the same wrongs, the same exceptionally ugly faces and very much the same smells'?

Yet Anthony Patch's career, which starts out so enchantingly, soon begins to deteriorate. And his eventual marriage to Gloria Gilbert, the glamorous 'speed' of Amory Blaine's youth, but one who is no longer going around with 'first-rate men,' is the marriage of the now anguished egoist with the now distraught narcissist. For Gloria—this 'Nordic Ganymede' with her Gum Drops—is Fitzgerald's full-length flapper, and through Gloria Fitzgerald portrays the true quality of his typical heroine: her impatience with men and her vanity 'that was almost masculine,' her beautiful and immaculate body that is incapable of passion and can hardly tolerate physical contact; the gum drops, indeed, that she must chew to avoid chewing her nails; and by contrast the cool perfection of her brow. 'No love was there, sure; nor the imprint of any love.'

However, as Anthony traces each developing "wrongness in the case" of the Jazz-Age Baby (this is skillfully done in the novel, and here Fitzgerald first uses a Henry Jamesian technic), the unraveling of Gloria's temperament leads him in turn to a parallel realization of his own imperfections. Fitzgerald's mythological reference is apt: and clinging to this shining, hard, dominant Ganymede—a cup-bearer to strange gods—Anthony Patch himself takes on the role of the volatile, uneasy, and even perhaps betrayed, un-Nordic woman.

But then, 'betrayed' by what insatiable demands of his own temperament? Fitzgerald is aware of this too, but records it only partially and imperfectly. Meanwhile, Anthony's 'erotic sensibilities,' which have remained calm before his little Geraldine's eager compliance, are stirred by Gloria's inaccessible coldness. And this desire is matched by a passion 'to possess her triumphant soul'—to humble her, that is: to break her.

Now the narcissism of these two becomes more pronounced. Were they earlier such ecstatic 'twins,' mirrors of each other's glitter, 'stars,' each playing to an audience of two? At this point also, held together by their common weakness while their points of difference become points of friction, they are still 'each engaged in polishing and perfecting his own attitude.' Their pathological interdependence becomes more obvious. —'Her arms sweet and strangling were around him.'—Caught up in their obscure and anguished struggle, their accents of defiance toward the outer world grow harsher, their emphasis on self-gratification—and on the 'gay and delicate poison' of liquor—grows more violent. 'Never give a damn,' Gloria cries. 'Not for anything or anybody . . . except myself and, by implication, for Anthony.'

And soon this 'implication' is barely stressed.

While the love affair in *The Beautiful and Damned* goes downhill, goes into the abyss, Fitzgerald's earlier superior disdain for the United States undergoes its own change. The history of the republic, Maury Noble tells us in a moment of inner revelation, is the history of a usurping vulgarity—

> 'We produce a Christ who can raise up the leper—and presently the breed of the leper is the salt of the earth. If any one can find any lesson in that, let him stand forth.'

Again the World War brings into focus the increasing misanthropy of Fitzgerald's figures. At target practice Anthony recites *Atalanta in Calydon* to an uncomprehending Pole. As a nurse, Gloria's martial ardor is dampened by the fact that she may have to treat wounded Negroes. And in the station, parting for battle, the glances of these contemporary patriots stretch across 'a hysterical area, foul with yellow sobbing and the smells of poor women.'

Similarly, in the increasingly tortured thoughts of Fitzgerald's aristocrats, the American 'aliens' assume a new perspective. Did Amory Blaine quietly dispense with his Jewish youth at Princeton, and the earlier Anthony Patch briefly note the Jewish men 'with their fatuous glances and tight suits'? The later Anthony perceives that these people are becoming at once the maggots and the rulers of 'his' country. New York, he feels, can no longer be dissociated from the slow upward creep of this race, 'slathering out on all sides.' Gloria's friend Bloeckman, the movie magnate who gains wealth and power, takes on respectability, style, and changes his name to Black, comes to stand for the race. In a final scene, Anthony, drunk and despairing, voices his accumulated bitterness: 'Not so fas', you Goddam Jew—' The profound sexual frigidity of Gloria herself—as it becomes quite clear in her thoughts about bearing children: 'Motherhood was also the privilege of female baboons'—extends moreover to the whole concept of fertility, and to these immigrants as the product of a conspicuous fertility.

> 'Millions of people, swarming like rats, chattering like apes, smelling like all hell . . . monkeys! . . . For one really exquisite palace I'd sacrifice all of them.'

And the rest of the Patches' story in *The Beautiful and Damned* is not difficult to anticipate.

There are the continual quarrels that leave Anthony feeling like 'a scarcely tolerated guest' in his own home, and Gloria openly contemptuous of a husband who is 'an utter coward' about the phantasms of his own imagination. There are the parties which these two modern lovers fall back upon, as, losing the last traces of concern for one another, each is more surely tied to the other by a common guilt, a common sense of ruin. —These drunken parties, lasting for days, attended by a shifting stream of friends, acquaintances, and finally strangers, which the Patches endure "as they endured all things, even themselves"—which they awake from, nauseated, capable only 'of one pervasive emotion—fear,' and to which they are irresistibly drawn back.

It is interesting to notice, incidentally, that during the maddest of these brawls, Gloria remains 'faithful,' though 'freshly tinted and lustful of admiration.' And while Fitzgerald strips in the songs—

> I left my blushing bride
> She went and shook herself insane
> So let her shiver back again

and:

> The pan-ic has come over us
> So ha-a-s the moral decline

—with this Jazz Age chorus of dissolution, and with the familiar sense of horror that has come, toward the closing pages of *The Beautiful and Damned,* to settle and spread over the Patches' unique and sparkling love, we reach the end of Scott Fitzgerald's Jazz Age romance.

What a curious romance it is—these two figures favored above all others (in their thoughts certainly, but in fact too) who seek each other above all else, and can barely tolerate each other; and make their love an absolute, and are incapable of love . . . And if Fitzgerald's second novel is marked by a gain in the writer's comprehension of his theme, in a way it is a rather curious gain. The Jazz Age figures in *The Beautiful and Damned* are so clearly the projection of those in Fitzgerald's earlier work, and Fitzgerald sees them so clearly now—it is as though he had quite understood the implications of his material from the start. This maturing step in Scott's craft carries him rather too swiftly across the line of maturity, just as the earlier Amory Blaine and the Eleanor of Romilly County abruptly cross the abyss between youth and age. Where *This Side of Paradise* marked the first brilliant flaring of Scott's talent, *The Beautiful and Damned* is in some respects the sputtering-away of the bright flame. The two brief years which have elapsed between the two novels appear to have encompassed two decades of bitter experience: an experience that has no sufficient counterpart in the external facts of the writer's life over this period.*

For with Anthony Patch's perception of Gloria's true nature, the Fitzgerald hero is brought almost to the last reaches of disintegration—indeed the conviction takes root in Anthony's mind that he will go mad.

> It was as though there were a quantity of dark yet vivid personalities in his mind, some of them familiar, some of them strange and terrible, held in check by a little monitor.

The 'monitor' has of course been Anthony's image of Gloria Gilbert as an absolute ideal to which he can dedicate himself: this absolute and impossible ideal which he has

* Arthur Mizener's essay on Fitzgerald in *The Sewanee Review,* Winter, 1946, has noticed this quality in Fitzgerald's second novel and is in general very sensitive to the emotional undertones of Fitzgerald's writing.

used to shield his own temperament from himself—this image of perfection which has been, as he now realizes, 'the chief jailor of his insufficiency.' But now the monitor, the jailor, has deserted its post; and Anthony has become 'a confused spectre, moving in odd crannies of his own mind'—

> Indeed he seldom made decisions at all, and when he did they were but half-hysterical resolves formed with the panic of some aghast and irreparable awakening. . . .

It is interesting, too, how both the cultural and the more purely personal elements of this rather intricate artistic pattern seem to groove into each other. For a writer who disdained any contact with his own society, and in point of fact had too little, Fitzgerald's opening accent on entertainment—these girls, yachts, dances, and parties—was not inappropriate to the post-war decade of the early nineteen-twenties. This stress on Flaming Youth was the reflection of a generation that had seen its own youth threatened or consumed by flame; a generation that, in whatever new style it may choose, we are likely to meet again in the nineteen-forties.

But the concept of an irresponsible individualism was also the Jazz Age's heritage from the Gilded Age. It was, in its origins, the moral, or immoral, bequest of a new American money society to its children in the second and third generations, just as the nineteen-twenties capped the entire historical cycle from 1860 on, and most sharply illuminated its meaning. And Fitzgerald's accent on youth is also the reflection of a wider cultural background—pioneer and pragmatic, in the forests and in the factories—which has always prized efficiency above sobriety and the effective above the reflective: a society which itself has sometimes believed that maturity is the infinite extension of adolescence. We have noticed how limited a view of youth Fitzgerald shares with his people—and how limited a notion of pleasure these pure pleasure seekers display, their life being centered around their libido, and their libido centered around their lips. The refinements of sensuous excitation in the European tradition, from Sade, say, to the Symbolists, are certainly absent from the American version of the life of the senses.

It should be apparent, too, what a particularly American notion Fitzgerald has of a ruling class without a sense of responsibility for, or even a curiosity about, the country that has furnished the sources of its power. To be sure, he is dealing chiefly with the third generation. He is writing a sort of postscript to the *Great American Fortunes:* he is recording the history of this class as it may occur to a Tommy Manville rather than a Jay Gould. . . . And in some respects one may prefer the crude American ancestors to their cosmopolitan heirs, because a will to power is more diverting, at least, than a whim for pleasure; and maybe a thoroughly bad character is preferable to no character at all. (Although it is amusing to notice what miracles of persistence and ingenuity are accomplished by Fitzgerald's figures in their attempts to get money without earning it.)

And thus accepting all the benefits of their social status without a notion of their status in society, Fitzgerald's young men are no longer even 'wild.' They have lost their initial and rather circumscribed flair for adventure. Like the early heroes of John Dos Passos, they are eminently respectable dilettantes, as nerveless as their grandfathers were nervy. You might say that in some curious form of sociological compensation, the descendents of a financial oligarchy that dealt only with the harsher modes of reality

—survival, cunning, force—have lost all contact with reality.

But have they . . . quite? In the dialectic of Fitzgerald's evolution, the 'thesis' of glamour has its antithesis in the accompanying sense of horror that is always in the background of his work. We shall see how the whole glittering post-war tableau which Fitzgerald has unveiled in the pages of *This Side of Paradise* and *The Beautiful and Damned*—how this whole lucent panorama from caviar to yachts springs in large part from a darker search for deception. 'I want you to lie to me,' the Fitzgerald female will cry—'for the rest of my life.' And the Fitzgerald male will echo this feverish demand for illusion. 'His was a great sin who first invented consciousness.'

The obsessive nature of the enchantment emerges, in fact, as the dominant theme of *The Beautiful and Damned.* (I need hardly mention how the title itself marks this; Scott's titles, usually revealing, are often among the best in our language.) In the forced and rather confused ending of Fitzgerald's second novel, moreover, it may seem that the destructive element has actually broken through the polished surface which has hitherto served as its mask.

In the writer's work over the next decade you will see the continuation of his search and the more hesitant and reluctant attempt to unfold that counter theme of 'some aghast and irreparable awakening.'

3. To West Egg

PUBLISHED IN THE SAME YEAR as *The Beautiful and Damned,* 1922, *Tales of the Jazz Age* contained two notable stories.*

* The *Tales* as a whole are thinner and more popularized than those of *Flappers and Philosophers,* more extreme in their accents of vanity and material arrogance, and in their underlying note of abasement. It is in-

The first of these, 'May Day,' almost summarizes, in sixty pages, the drama of the post-war decade. In 'the great city of the conquering people,' with its triumphal arches and jeweled women, the Yale Men, props of a new American aristocracy, serene in their soft woolen socks and yellow pongee shirts, lunch together 'en masse.' (Whitman's democratic phrase has suffered from an odd dislocation in the modern text.) Warm with liquor as the afternoon begins, the aristocrats gossip: Are narrow ties coming back? There never was a collar like the Covington. —In the Gamma Psi party they scent the fragrance of a fashionable dance—exciting, sweet—and their stimulation is carried over to Fitzgerald's girls—such as Edith Bradin, thinking of her own shoulders, eyes, lips. 'She had never felt her own softness so much nor so enjoyed the whiteness of her own arms. "I smell sweet . . . I'm made for love." '

Indeed, in the concentration of 'May Day,' Fitzgerald has almost turned the paraphernalia of adolescence into the trappings of empire. The description of the Gamma Psi dance is remarkable. But this American undergraduate dominion, hardly established, is already trembling. The turbulent scene of 1919, the scene of Barbusse and Dos Passos, has reverberations even here. Edith's brother is a Socialist who pours 'the latest cures for incurable evils into the columns of a radical weekly newspaper.' Outside of Delmonico's the mob is gathering while 'a gesticulating little Jew with long black whiskers' (Trotsky, no doubt) delivers a revolutionary harangue. Two drunken, clownish soldiers, who accidentally become involved with the

teresting to notice Fitzgerald's stress on youth and on sterility (see his ode to the children of the rich in 'O Russet Witch'). And also on a special sense of magnificence in life, accompanied by a special sense of disaster, or retribution, as in 'The Lees of Happiness,' a tale which, as he says, came to him 'in an irresistible form, crying to be written.'

polished intricacies of the Gamma Psi dance, are the liaison-officers between these two worlds.

Or rather perhaps, in Fitzgerald's eyes, they are some sort of missing link—ugly, ill-nourished 'devoid of all except the lowest form of intelligence.'

> The entire mental pabulum of these two men consisted of an offended nasal comment extended through the years upon the institution—army, business, or poor-house—which kept them alive.

To heighten the deft splendor of his dancing collegiates, what better contrast can the writer find than these two boorish representatives of the people cavorting in the back-pantry of Delmonico's? Here the fraternity life is more elaborate and placed still further outside the currents of ordinary American life: an 'ordinary' life that in turn, exemplified as it is by the aliens and radicals outside of Delmonico's, seems even more rabid or vulgar. . . . Yet it is interesting that Fitzgerald should assign to one of these common soldiers—Carrol Key—the proudest part of his own name, and the central figure of 'May Day' is again not *in* the inner circle.* Fitzgerald's Gordon Sterrett is the exile of Gamma Psi. The urim and thummim of the élite are viewed by the outcast, the children of the rich are richer and more childlike; it is through Gordon's feverish and importunate eyes that 'May Day' achieves its special quality. In Fitzgerald's next tale, moreover, the split in the writer's point of view widens, and reaches a point of tension.

* The heroes of a series of Fitzgerald's short stories—the 'outlaw' Dalyrimple of 'Dalyrimple Goes Wrong,' the 'buccaneer' Carlyle of 'The Off-Shore Pirate,' the Jim Powell of 'The Jelly Bean,' who is 'a running mate of poor whites'—are all outsiders who resort to illegal means of achieving wealth and social position.

The tale was designed, Fitzgerald says, utterly for his own amusement, and certainly 'The Diamond as Big as the Ritz' begins as such. The Washingtons' mansion, perched on a diamond mountain in the Rockies, and first seen beneath a sunset like a gigantic bruise, 'from which dark arteries spread themselves over a poisoned sky': this fantastic property claims luxury enough to satisfy the most insatiate child of our century. This is an 'exquisite château' indeed—with its halls of marble, its furs and jewels and faint *acciaccatura* sound of violins, and silky Russian wolfhounds and many-hued cordials, and its darkies ignorant of the Emancipation and delighted with their lot. This is a Kubla Khan of modern materialism complete with automatic baths and pneumatic lifts, barbed-wire fortifications, anti-aircraft guns, and practically painless lethal chambers.

The point is that the Fitz-Norman Culpeper Washingtons, who are direct descendants of George Washington and Lord Baltimore (as Fitzgerald has linked his name with the vulgarest representative of the people in 'May Day,' he suggests here an association with the extremes of moneyed aristocracy)—the Fitz-Norman Washingtons have cut themselves off from all outside contact in order to preserve their diamond mountain. They have corrupted their government to keep their land. They have turned the clock back to keep their slaves. They have had to 'liquidate' their unwitting guests and the more indiscreet members of their own family: pinned to the altar of their wealth, they have had to become inhuman. In his hour of extremity, and in the general tradition of the Robber Barons, the last of this line, Braddock Washington, tries to bargain with the Lord Himself.

Yes, 'The Diamond as Big as the Ritz' may *start* as a fantasy of extravagant luxury, but it soon becomes a fascinating parable of the American propertied class. The symbolism is curious, too, towards the end of the story, when this apostolic seat of divine fortunes is discovered by some jeering, plebeian aviators. (Again Fitzgerald telescopes two social spheres.) As the 'exquisite château' yields to the exigencies of change, and is blown to bits by its owner's hand, Kismine, alone of the Washingtons to escape, snatches a handful of diamonds to carry her along in the outside world. Only they turn out to be rhinestones.

The parable is all the more interesting because one can hardly tell to what degree it is deliberate. While the Fitzgerald figure moves steadily away in *fact* from his vision of wealth, and becomes more clearly the outsider and outcast in the Jazz Age, he clings to the vision even more avidly in fancy. As the vision becomes more plainly a delusion, the delusion becomes precious. . . . John Unger, who is Fitzgerald's condemned visitor to the Washington's estate, is freed by its destruction to return home to his middle-western town of 'Hades.' But he returns to the sunless abode of the ghosts of the dead with little evidence of exhilaration. Perhaps love is a form of divine drunkenness, John tells Kismine, and youth is a form of chemical madness—but 'How pleasant then to be insane!' For—

> 'There are only diamonds in the whole world, diamonds and perhaps the shabby gift of disillusion. . . . His was a great sin who first invented consciousness.'

Has John Unger forgotten, then, at the close of 'The Diamond as Big as the Ritz,' has he—after his sojourn in the doomed château—forgotten the lights of Hades, U.S.A., which for a moment at the story's opening, seemed to burn against the western sky, 'full of a warm and passionate beauty'?

There is little that is warm or passionate, at any rate, in Fitzgerald's 1923 'comedy,' *The Vegetable—or From President to Postman*. As you might guess, the play is a take-off on American politics in terms which may suggest the later Kaufman-Ryskind musical, *Of Thee I Sing*. Like Wintergreen, the Jerry Frost of Scott's play is a typical citizen snatched from his native haunts in order to be made our Chief Executive. 'Did you ever—did you ever have any ambition to be President?' Jerry asks his brother-in-law, Mr. Fish, who is incidentally an 'undertaker from Idaho.' 'Of a company?' asks Mr. Fish, thus presenting the conditioned reflex of the nineteen-twenties. And while Mr. Fish becomes Senator Fish ('That's where you get the real graft.') and the U.S. Treasury becomes a sort of private checking account for the President and his Pals (Fitzgerald's personal fantasy here is the fantasy of his period too)—the rest of the play elaborates this thesis.

The political material in *The Vegetable* certainly has possibilities for satire. There is a scene on the Supreme Court (led by Judge Fossile) that also foreshadows a section of *In all Countries* by Dos Passos, reporting on American justice a decade later. But Fitzgerald's little comedy too clearly shows his own bias. He is not at all concerned, as Dos Passos is, with the human implications of our cultural patterns. He represents merely the distaste of the moneyed élite for the bourgeois makers of money. Again accepting, and in fact clutching after the spoils, he regards the victors with contempt. His satire of the golden calf is directed against the owners of the herd, not against the animal. . . . *The Vegetable* shows up the complete identification of diplomacy with dollars in the political reign—I should say, the interregnum—of Harding and

Coolidge. But the value of the play derives from the fact that Fitzgerald himself so perfectly and unconsciously illustrates the national trait he is attacking.

With what, furthermore, does the writer contrast the ignorance and avarice of the political bosses in the nineteen-twenties, whom he sees through his own curiously ignorant and avaricious eyes? Jerry Frost—this average citizen who is projected into the climactic American dream of parking his toothbrush at the White House—has a salary of three thousand a year and a wife, 'Charl-it,' whose attractions 'have declined ninety per cent since her marriage.' Just as Jerry's salary represents the financial lower depths to Fitzgerald, and Jerry's wife is a relic of American love, so his father, 'Dada,' is too old even—

> for the petty spites which represent to the aged the single gesture of vitality they can make against the ever-increasing pressure of life and youth.

This is, so to speak, parenthood in a democracy. Charl-it's sister Doris, 'who knows a few girls who know a few girls who are social leaders,' is a member of that portion of the middle class whose single ambition, like that of Scott's shop girls in 'May Day,' is to ape the aristocracy—though again Scott's contention is not that they shouldn't, but that they can't.

And to descend this American social scale from the low to the lowest, Fitzgerald presents, in Mr. Snooks the bootlegger—who looks like 'a race-track sport who has fallen into a pool of mud,' but whose behavior indicates that Scott has never talked with these enterprising middlemen of the Jazz Age—in Mr. Snooks, Fitzgerald presents the American proletarian or criminal class.

This is a far reach from another racketeer, James Gatz

of North Dakota: in the serenity of *The Great Gatsby,* two years later in 1925, the writer achieves a remarkable resolution of these earlier and acrid opinions. While the little play outlines the juvenile and weak Fitzgerald, the novel prefigures the eloquent and mature Fitzgerald. Thus the wonderful opening passages of the novel—the lyric passages on New York in early summer, when nature is doing her chores all over again but in a manner that is just a little hurried and self-conscious, the leaves bursting forth on the trees 'just as they grow in fast movies'—almost come as something of a shock.

At the Buchanans' Long Island "Georgian Colonial mansion" which is framed by a half-acre of deep, pungent roses, Tom Buchanan, the former Yale football hero, powerful, cruel, arrogant—'one of those men who reach such an acute limited excellence at twenty-one that everything afterward savors of anti-climax'—is a little artificial and feverish, too. There is an opening tableau. The 'enormous couch,' the two women in their fluttering white dresses: Daisy Buchanan, with her wealth, the 'singing compulsion' of her voice, and her impersonal eyes 'in the absence of all desire'; and Jordan Baker, motionless on the divan, with her chin raised a little 'as if she were balancing something on it which was quite likely to fall'—this characteristic gesture which Jordan will resume at the close of *The Great Gatsby* though, indeed, whatever she has been balancing has fallen. While outside the Buchanans' place, just across the way, but in West Egg, Gatsby himself, who has met Daisy so many years before, and fallen in love, and built his life around the vision of Daisy's elegance—outside, at night, Gatsby watches the green light on the Buchanans' pier.

In a way this is all familiar, of course. The enormous couch is the one which Amory Blaine viewed as the stage for many an emotional act, and which Fitzgerald himself has used for the central drama of the Jazz Age. But just as the couch has changed its psychological dimensions and has become the center of a more sober scene, and is even faintly suggestive of a quainter, pre-jazz age when ladies more innocently reclined, so this typical Fitzgerald world has changed in all its dimensions. Daisy and Tom Buchanan, who drift from Hot Springs to Palm Beach or to 'wherever people played polo and were rich together,' are certainly the Anthony Patches of *The Beautiful and Damned* or the Jeffrey Curtains of 'The Lees of Happiness.' * Yet why does Fitzgerald's narrator almost immediately notice the 'basic insincerity' of Daisy's warm and thrilling voice, and the fact that her sad and lovely face with such bright things in it seems suddenly to carry 'an absolute smirk'? Tom Buchanan, too, with all the elaborate and aristocratic luggage of 'May Day,' is the Yale man in retrograde, and one who now displays a polished distemper that is a step—an irrevocable step, however—beyond Anthony Patch's anguished outbursts. Where Anthony had pinned his misery on the 'aliens,' Tom argues the necessity for a 'dominant race.' Something, Fitzgerald adds, was making him 'nibble at the edge of stale ideas, as if his sturdy physical egotism no longer nourished his peremptory heart.'

Directly after these opening scenes of *Gatsby,* filled as

* What Fitzgerald has done technically in *The Great Gatsby* is to bring over the tight, well-knit, and sometimes trick patterns of his short stories to the irregular and broken novel form which he has been using in *This Side of Paradise* and *The Beautiful and Damned.* So every symbol and almost every detail here is meticulously plotted, and usually balanced off later on in the story. In fact, *Gatsby* was probably the most perfect example of a *planned* novel in our modern tradition up to this point—planned, I mean, in this mathematical sense of a Bach concerto—though *The Sun Also Rises,* a year later, was to match it and *The Sound and the Fury,* in 1929, was to outdo it.

they are with such promise and splendor and disturbing as they are in their undertones, we are introduced, about halfway between East Egg and New York, to Fitzgerald's 'valley of ashes.' And with this desolate and quite literal waste-land which rims the Buchanans' mansion, and over which brood, from an advertising billboard, the immense and vacant eyes of Doctor T. J. Eckleburg, Oculist—the stage is set for the final tragedy of the novel.

The feeling at once of intimacy and of distance that one has in reading *The Great Gatsby* is due simply to the fact that while Fitzgerald has used all the elements of his hitherto dominant literary pattern, he has broken the pattern and regrouped the elements. So the Buchanans, who are Scott's modern American aristocrats—the élite whom Amory Blaine's every breath was drawn in tribute to, and every talent exercised in pursuit of—are now seen in a sharper, less favorable light. It is in this shifting focus of Fitzgerald's values that James Gatz of North Dakota assumes his importance—this obscure western adolescent whose first glimpse of life came on the millionaire Cody's yacht, whose first glimpse of Daisy crystallized this childhood vision, and who, raising his empire of "drug stores," transforming himself into the mysterious Jay Gatsby—rather as Bloeckman had into Black—now attempts not merely to recapture the past in his imagination but to make it repeat itself in actuality. 'I'm going to fix everything just the way it was before.'

Gatsby's is again an apparently typical design in the writer's work. The early dread of poverty and renunciation of his own origins and family, since 'his imagination had never really accepted them as parents at all'; the search for an elegance that is epitomized, as in 'The Off-Shore Pirate,' by the linked symbols of the yacht and the girl; the fantastic Oxford background that Gatsby claims; the 'universe of ineffable gaudiness' that he sets up and his deep, monomaniacal drive to make the future—at any rate—work; the sense of 'complete isolation,' finally, that surrounds Gatsby in the midst of his prodigious parties ('but no one swooned backward on Gatsby, and no French bob touched Gatsby's shoulder')—all these are familiar symptoms. 'Through all he said,' Scott's narrator tells us, 'I was reminded of something—an elusive rhythm, a fragment of lost words, that I had heard somewhere a long time ago.' Indeed Nick Carraway should remember this, while step by step, at first out of curiosity and amusement, then with a growing concern, he retraces the life of James Gatz. —And his own. For it is Nick's increasing sympathy with Gatsby that brings about his sharpened perception of that aristocratic world toward which Gatsby's lifetime of devotion has been directed. Are Gatsby's parties, like his entire establishment, an appalling display of a 'vast, vulgar and meretricious beauty?' Are the sight-seeing East Eggers, who are drawn to these parties nevertheless, offended by the raw vigor of West Egg, by the fate of its inhabitants herded along 'a short cut from nothing to nothing'? The names of the two towns suggest more than a topographical proximity. Then there are Gatsby's too transparent fictions. 'What part of the middle west do you come from?' 'San Francisco, old chap.' 'I see.' Yet these fictions, and the urgent and desperate conviction behind them—are they really very different from those of Jordan Baker, the socialite golf champion who has also begun dealing in subterfuge because she can't stand being at a disadvantage?

In a remarkable aside, interesting in itself but particularly so for the advocate of Amory Blaine and Anthony Patch, Fitzgerald adds: 'It occurred to me that there was no difference between men, in intelligence or race, so profound as the difference between the sick and the well.'

And which are the sick? Tom Buchanan finally beats down Gatsby's ignorant and impossible dream; but does his 'impassioned gibberish' really mark a triumph of the aristocratic code over the vulgarity of the *arriviste?* The drama of *The Great Gatsby* moves toward a crescendo. Daisy, driving Gatsby's car, kills Myrtle Wilson by accident or intention. Gatsby assumes the blame, and Daisy and Tom Buchanan allow him to. Nick Carraway watches as these two East Eggers are brought together in a bond of common weakness, as Daisy makes her decision to return to her own orbit, 'fresh and breathing and redolent of this year's shining motor-cars and of dances whose flowers were scarcely withered.' And when Gatsby, betrayed, becomes even more urgently aware of 'the youth and mystery that wealth imprisons and preserves,' of Daisy gleaming like silver, 'safe and proud above the hot struggles of the poor,' Nick makes the whole issue explicit. 'They're a rotten crowd. . . . You're worth the whole damn bunch put together.'

What Nick Carraway is 'reminded of' in this story, of course, is the fact that Fitzgerald is working out an underlying but hitherto submerged or 'recessive' thesis in his own work. Jay Gatsby himself is the full projection of those previous adventurers, like Jim Powell, Carlyle, and Dalyrimple, who go beyond the conventions in their single-minded emphasis on the conventional life of luxury. And there is little doubt that *The Great Gatsby* as a whole is a response to a major strain in Fitzgerald's temperament—the strain of the outsider, the strain of the 'unadjustable boy' who hurried down corridors at St. Regis, 'jeered at by his rabid contemporaries, mad with common sense'—the strain of 'May Day' and Gordon Sterrett, the outcast of Gamma Psi. The dissident notes in Amory Blaine's own slavish emulation of the élite have given Fitzgerald's work timbre when it seemed hollowest; here the writer has formed the counterpoint that has been hitherto implicit. In the tale of Jay Gatsby and the East Eggers Fitzgerald has clarified both the goal of Gatsby's struggle and the nature of the struggle itself.

But notice that Gatsby is also a new *social* character—one who has no proper education and not the slightest pretense to breeding, who never grew up in Geneva and never went to Yale; whose only clubs are 'trade associations,' whose clothes are primary rather than pastel, and whose method of conversational approach ranges from 'chum' to 'old chap.' Gatsby is diametrically opposed to all of Fitzgerald's handsome, luxurious, and cultivated young men, and the first of the major figures to flaunt such handicaps. For F. Scott Fitzgerald, in fact, for this prime Muse of the Jazz Age, James Gatz of North Dakota—granting the inevitable exception of his millions—is almost the equivalent of a proletarian protagonist. Yet, as the Great Gatsby, he is more than a class symbol. He is a sort of cultural hero, and the story of Gatsby's illusion is the story of an age's illusion, too. The bare outlines of his career—the upward struggle from poverty and ignorance; the naïve aspirations toward refinement and the primal, ruthless energy of these aspirations; the fixation of this provincial soul upon a childlike notion of beauty and grace and the reliance upon material power as the single method of satisfying his searching and inarticulate spirit—these are surely the elements of a dominant cultural legend in its purest, most sympathetic form. And through a consummate choice of detail Fitzgerald has made the legend live. Gauche, ridiculous, and touching as James Gatz is, he is surely our native adolescent, raised on the western reverberations of Vanderbilt and Gould, entering a new world full of shining secrets 'that only Midas and Morgan and

Maecenas knew'—a barefoot boy in the land of steel, and even, in a rather deeper sense, a cousin, say, of Huck Finn, but now drifting in the eddies and backwaters of the Long Island Sound. Whatever there is of permanence in *The Great Gatsby* derives from the fact that here, by one of those fortunate coincidences which form the record of artistic achievement, the deepest inner convictions of the writer have met with and matched those of his time and place. The 'illusive rhythm, the fragment of lost words' that Nick Carraway tries to recall are the rhythm and words of an American myth. 'But they made no sound, and what I had almost remembered was uncommunicable forever.'

So, too, in Nick Carraway—the cautious observer on the fringe of the conflict of East Eggers and West Eggers, the sober 'narrator of the tale'—Fitzgerald expresses a kind of farewell to Gatsby's illusion and his own. Perhaps it is worth noticing that it is the same crude, vulgar air of Western civilization which had once caught Amory Blaine 'in his underwear, so to speak,' which now gives Nick his sense of perspective. After all, Nick tells us, *The Great Gatsby* has been a story of the West. 'Tom and Gatsby, Daisy and Jordan and I, were all Westerners, and perhaps we possessed some deficiency in common which made us subtly unadaptable to Eastern life.' And when the story of the West is over and the blue smoke of brittle leaves is in the air and the wind blows the wet laundry stiff on the line, Nick decides 'to come back home.' *

As you read it, then, the novel seems superbly done. The spell of Fitzgerald's writing in these passages, the

* It is interesting to notice that here the Fitzgerald figure turns to his father for guidance, while in the two previous novels the background of the hero is always 'European,' the American hinterland is viewed with scorn, and the dominant parent is, as we have seen, the mother. . . . In terms of craft, I have discussed the technical connections between *The Great Gatsby* and *My Antonia* in the passages on Willa Cather's earlier novel of East and West.

delicate evocation of a story behind the story, are quite stunning. And while the development of the craft is a factor in this, there is also the development of a point of view that makes the craft possible. While Fitzgerald has blocked out the discordant areas in his own temperament and objectified them in terms of the characters and groups of characters who form the novel's tension, he himself has gained a serenity and perspective that are remarkable for the tormented, inchoate author of *This Side of Paradise*. And yet, after the novel's closing meditations on time and the past—on 'the fresh green breast of the new world' which had once been offered to Dutch sailors' eyes, and on Gatsby's dream which had always been behind him, 'somewhere back in that vast obscurity beyond the city, where the dark fields of the republic rolled on under the night':

> So we beat on, boats against the current,
> borne back ceaselessly into the past.

—after these lovely dying cadences which bring the novel to its full stop, why do we, all the same, have another and different sense of loss—that this novel, which is so good, could not have been just a little better? . . .

The Great Gatsby is surely a maturing step in Fitzgerald's artistic education; it marks a major shift in the writer's values very much like the one he has showed us in Nick Carraway's human education—but then where has it fallen short? In spite of the advance which it marks over *The Beautiful and Damned,* why does the earlier story still stick in our minds, while this one, like Daisy's perfume, fades? What is the subtle deficiency that the novel shares with its Western characters, and what has gone out of Fitzgerald's work, for all its gains?

Perhaps you should remember that the geographical and

psychological conditions of Nick Carraway's decision to come back home are fulfilled only in *The Last Tycoon* of 1941, and then only partially: the western scene that Fitzgerald returns to is not quite Nick's western scene, the return is not altogether a happy one.

And meanwhile the fifteen years between *The Great Gatsby* and Fitzgerald's last novel are years of continuous doubt, of ebbing vitality, of spiritual trauma.

4. *Down the Labyrinthine Ways*

ROSE-COLORED SABLES, diamond garters, gold-heeled slippers, brooches, pendants, pearls and all, Rags Martin-Jones, slipping in on the Majestic for a look at New York's hot spots, is another one of Scott's glamour girls.

But still engaged in the pursuit of entertainment, Rags is a glamour girl who is rather more decadent than her predecessors and not quite decadent enough to be more interesting. Reminding us of the old Fitzgerald, she serves chiefly as a contrast for the new. While most of the stories in Scott's third collection, *All the Sad Young Men,* in 1926, continue to center around pleasure, their undertones, like their title, are somewhat lugubrious.

Poverty, for the recent spectator at West Egg, has hardly become more alluring. 'The poor go under or go up or go wrong or even go on, somehow, in a way the poor have,' Scott remarks in 'The Sensible Thing.' 'The Adjuster,' too, opens with the refrains of the epoch Scott loved—

> At five o'clock the sombre egg-shaped room at the Ritz ripens to a subtle melody—the light clat-clat of one lump, two lumps, into the cup and the *ding* of the shining teapots and cream-pots as they kiss elegantly in transit upon

> a silver tray. There are those who cherish that amber hour above all other hours, for now the pale, pleasant toil of the lilies who inhabit the Ritz is over—the singing decorative part of the day remains.

And yet the passage itself seems to contain the movement of six years in little more than six lines. The élite who now adorn these chambers are altered in texture; the familiar place has unfamiliar accents. The heroine is barely twenty-three years old, to be sure, but she has a home, a husband, a baby—and the jitters. 'Don't you see how bored I am? . . . I want excitement; and I don't care what form it takes or what I pay for it, so long as it makes my heart beat.' And though Luella Hemple becomes a model wife and tends her husband through his nervous breakdown,* she also becomes a sentimental and unreal figure while, in its labored moral ending, the story shows the uneasy character of all the stories in the volume.

This is the postscript to the Jazz Age. In these tales Fitzgerald has thrown over the thin and shining values of the post-war years; although he still cherishes the lilies who inhabit the Ritz, it is with a sense of their pale and pleasant toil. Still, the accent on 'discipline' in these tales, the recourse to suffering, and the acceptance of martyrdom as a norm of behavior, in tones which are reminiscent of the Louisa May Alcott who was ever 'duty's faithful child'—these show quite as clearly the writer's belief that there is nothing else in life worth living for. The alternative to sheer vanity is apparently sheer tor-

* The heroes of *All the Sad Young Men* are, generally, studies in masculine defeat. The Anson Hunter of 'The Rich Boy,' a later cousin of Anthony Patch and Amory Blaine, takes refuge in a rather sadistic code of honor; while the Fitzgerald figure of 'Winter Dreams'—an interesting and crueler version of the *Gatsby* theme—is ruined by his dream girl ('the most direct and unprincipled personality with which he had ever come in contact') and must finally surrender even his illusion of the past.

ment.* 'I've got theatre tickets,' Luella Hemple finally admits to her husband, 'but I don't care whether we go.' Luella's renunciation marks the apex of an adult life for Fitzgerald, and compensates for the lack of any solid relationship between the Hemples, or between them and the 'two children' who pop into the story and splice the strands of marital felicity.

There are homes, there are marriages, there are children in the tales of *All the Sad Young Men*. The hero of 'The Baby Party' examines his young daughter carefully 'as a definite piece of youth' before turning her back to her nurse. In much the same fashion Fitzgerald now examines the pieces of maturity. And in this context of shifting values, it is not surprising that Fitzgerald should revert to a religious theme which has had its persistent undertones in his work. 'Absolution' is interesting for its view of another youthful hero. Rudolph Miller is 'a beautiful, intense boy of eleven' whose eyes 'like blue stones' may recall Amory's, 'green as emeralds.' (And by and large the Fitzgerald irises are ornamental as well as optical.) Of all the sad young men, Rudolph is perhaps the only one to achieve real stature—he is the saddest and youngest—but his method of achieving it is odd.

He is already absorbed in sex and in sin; he belongs to those, as Fitzgerald says, 'who habitually and instinctively lie'; at confession he accuses himself of 'not believing I was the son of my parents.' Right in the Fitzgerald grain,

* This is also a typical sentiment in the early Hemingway or Elinor Wylie, say, and in the majority of younger writers during the nineteen-twenties. The causes of it, again, are more complex than the post-war weariness and go directly back to the nature of American life over this period. But, in any case, there is not much evidence here of that buoyancy which, in an earlier American generation, had marked Sherwood Anderson's surrender to the vicissitudes—'one flood following another'—of ordinary existence, or Willa Cather's final acceptance of the 'mockery and torment and heart-break' of life.

Rudolph has also presented himself with a more suitable and soniferous name; in this case it is Blatchford Sarnemington. 'When he became Blatchford . . . a suave nobility flowed from him. Blatchford lived in great sweeping triumphs.' And 'Absolution' concerns itself with the curious relations of Blatchford Sarnemington and God—a God whom Rudolph deliberately tricks and who, recognizing Rudolph's talent for deception, retaliates by ignoring him. . . .

> An invisible line had been crossed, and he had become aware of his isolation—aware that it applied not only to those moments when he was Blatchford Sarnemington but that it applied to all his inner life. Hitherto such phenomena as 'crazy' ambitions and petty shames had been but private reservations, unacknowledged before the throne of his official soul. Now he realized unconsciously that his private reservations were himself—and all the rest a garnished front and a conventional flag.

These 'private reservations' are to form the core of the boy's life henceforth. . . . He gains power by the realization of his isolation. He tells himself that 'there was something ineffably gorgeous somewhere that had nothing to do with God' and that indeed God must understand that he, Rudolph, has sinned, ultimately, for the greater glory of God—'to make things finer in the confessional, brightening up the dinginess of his admissions by saying a thing radiant and proud.' —All the same, when Scott's hero walks back to his pew, 'the sharp tap of his cloven hoofs were loud upon the floor, and he knew that it was a dark poison he carried in his heart.' And as Rudolph braces himself in the conviction of his immaculate honor, 'horror entered suddenly in at the open window' of the confessional, while outside—

> For five hours now hot fertile life had burned in the afternoon. It would be night in three hours, and all along the land there would be these blond Northern girls and the tall young men from the farms lying out beside the wheat, under the moon.

The 'horror,' of course, is not unlike that which forms a somber background for Amory Blaine's radiance in *This Side of Paradise,* or the 'enormous, terrified repulsion' which seizes Lois in 'Benediction.' Moreover, the conjunction of sin and sexual fertility in 'Absolution' leads directly back to the strange scene in *The Beautiful and Damned* where another blond Northern girl, Gloria Gilbert, escaping into the dark from her companion's sexual advances, hears Maury Noble confess to his own private reservations. Maury, too, has become adept at fooling the deity. 'I prayed immediately after all crimes until eventually prayer and crime became indistinguishable to me.' In a tortured and confused sermon which at once recalls the Eugene O'Neill of *Days Without End* and follows in some part the career of Fitzgerald himself, Maury describes his flight from a Hound of Heaven who still prowls through the Jazz Age. Seek refuge as he may in beauty or in the intellect, in vice, in skepticism or in boredom, he is still pursued—

> 'Protect myself as I might by making no new ties with tragic and predestined humanity, I was lost with the rest. I had traded the fight against love for the fight against loneliness, the fight against life for the fight against death.'

—and overtaken.

This suave nobility and sense of panic, these private reservations, this flight from life, and premonition of a death that waits at every corner—of a dark poison and of cloven hoofs: it is this entire cluster of psychological elements, presented here in their religious guise, that has rested at the bottom of Fitzgerald's work and that is now rising to the surface. And, though the elements will shift in focus as they have already shifted in each novel of Fitzgerald's, and though now the scene will be remote from the wheat fields of Dakota, it is this cluster of conflicting emotional elements that gives Fitzgerald's next novel its peculiar and fascinating intensity.

For now he tries to penetrate the 'labyrinthine ways' of his own mind—and uncover the mounded dust of the years to where, like Francis Thompson's, his mangled youth 'lies dead beneath the heap.'

The lapse in time between *All the Sad Young Men* and *Tender is the Night* in 1934 is interesting in itself. (*John Jackson's Arcady,* a little pamphlet published in 1928, describes the possible feelings of the father of a member of the Lost Generation, in a rather incredible way.) And through the opening pages of the new novel there is the sense of a sharp change. The young actress who first appears 'on the pleasant shore of the French Riviera' is physically in the direct line of Fitzgerald's girls. She has golden hair, she is eighteen, the dew is still on her.

But Rosemary Hoyt is also quite moral, hard-working, and, with her 'virginal emotions,' specifically 'American.' 'There she was—*so* young and innocent . . . embodying all the immaturity of the race.' She is very different from the anguished butterflies of Scott's youth. In fact she is Scott's first heroine to break from a sharply circumscribed, almost rigid feminine type. So too, Rosemary's mother, the tough and devoted Mrs. Elsie Speers of the novel, hardly resembles the fabulous Beatrice Blaine. And it is against this background of sober American virtue that we are introduced, first to the little group of middle-class

American tourists who rather repel Rosemary, and then to the gathering of bronzed 'aristocrats' who attract her and lead her in turn to Mr. and Mrs. Richard Diver.

The Divers!—so warm and glowing in these opening pages of the novel, with their 'special gentleness' and 'far-reaching delicacy' and their power of arousing 'a fascinated and uncritical love,' not to mention their money, their air of possession and their command over all the amenities of life which, to Rosemary, contains a purpose and direction 'different from any she had known.' With what delight does the dewy young American girl come upon this alluring ménage—recalling perhaps the similar apostrophes of a Eugene Gant upon the first glimpse of that cultivated Rosalind in her feudal castle on the Hudson. Here Scott's Rosemary has a conviction of homecoming—'of a return from the derisive and salacious improvisations of the frontier.' This is a typical and almost stereotyped scene, however, in the annals of provincial American writing. There are also Howells and Garland in Boston, Willa Cather in the musical circles of Chicago, Dreiser among the financial titans of New York. This is indeed the silent wild surmise of our new Cortezes, charting the eastern shores from their frontier peaks. —And surely too the Riviera Divers represent the last and desperate attempt of Fitzgerald himself to grasp that vision of ease and grace he has pursued from Minnesota to the Côte d'Azur.

But it is to Rosemary's 'immature mind' that the grace of the Divers' life is revealed; and Fitzgerald now more specifically defines the nature of this obsessive vision. Nicole Diver is charming indeed, she is the 'furthermost evolution of a class'—

> For her sake trains began their run at Chicago and traversed the round belly of the continent to California;

> chicle factories fumed and link belts grew link by link in factories; men mixed toothpaste in vats and drew mouthwash out of copper hogsheads; girls canned tomatoes quickly in August or worked rudely at the Five-and-Tens on Christmas Eve; half-breed Indians toiled on Brazilian coffee plantations and dreamers were muscled out of patent rights in new tractors. . . . She illustrated very simple principles, containing in herself her own doom.

While the tone is somewhat uncertain here (Fitzgerald is not quite at ease among the industrial processes) we must realize that the writer is developing a sense of his American cultural patterns—these 'very simple principles' which Fitzgerald's people have reflected so beautifully and hitherto so innocently.

The new intellectual framework is clearly articulated in *Tender is the Night.* In fact the novel is probably overloaded with references to the American frontier and the American empire, American ducal families, American men and women, American manners, clothes, faces, and even American trains—absorbed as they are 'in an intense destiny of their own.' Here the writer has not only disentangled himself from his own earlier aspirations and stepped aside, like Nick Carraway, to observe the habits of the American sheltered class. He has stepped *outside* this class. And if here Fitzgerald fails perfectly to convey the elegance of the Divers's circle, it is simply because he has moved too far beyond it. The process of disenchantment has become one of disengagement. For these glamorous aristocrats who are first introduced to us through Rosemary's young eyes are actually a collection of idle and unhappy expatriates; and as for the Divers themselves, of course, theirs is an appalling story of disintegration.

Although part of the novel's interest comes, again, from the delicate unfolding of its central 'mystery,' the plot can be summarized more or less concisely. In the spring of 1917, some ten years before Rosemary's advent, Doctor Richard Diver has arrived in Zurich to continue his studies. But in treating the young Nicole Warren, whose nervous breakdown has resulted from her incestuous relationship with her father, Diver is caught up in her beauty and helplessness. Married to her, he is held at the start by his love for her, and then by her almost total dependence on him. (Nicole has periodic reversions to insanity during the course of the novel.) The Warren millions complete Diver's encirclement—his professional ambitions are dissipated, his talent unravels into the meaningless sort of social charm which has intrigued the innocent American actress.

The theme of *Tender is the Night,* then, is that of the Divers's strange past—and of their equally strange present, for as Dick loses, Nicole gains control of, their life together. This is certainly a full-sized theme, and as Fitzgerald develops this dubious, shifting, intricate relationship, many sections of the novel are illuminating in the extreme. But why is it that the parts are always better than the whole—that the novel, filled as it is with fascinating insights, written very often with all of Fitzgerald's grace, still seems curiously off center?

One should notice the paradoxes. While Fitzgerald's new American sense pervades these pages, it can hardly be said that this sense is either immediate or affectionate. It is more often abstract, ambiguous. Dick Diver's single moment of genuine identification with his native ground occurs, directly after his father's death, in a cemetery in Westmoreland County, Virginia, and Diver's thoughts are of 'the souls made of new earth in the forest-heavy darkness of the seventeenth century.' At last attempting on his foreign shore really to come to grips with his own society,

Fitzgerald does find that distance lends enchantment. But it must be the distance of two centuries as well as the span of an ocean, and what the writer seems to cling to are the mouldering dead of a half-imaginary epoch. 'Good-by, my father—good-by, all my fathers.' Similarly, while Fitzgerald places the scene of *Tender is the Night* in a center of psychiatric healing, and uses a psychiatrist for his hero, and fills his story with psychological lore, he hardly views psychiatry as the new salvation. Indeed, Dick Diver is ruined by the patient he has 'cured'—while Nicole, a perverse phoenix arising from the ashes of her distorted youth, achieves her 'freedom' through becoming vicious.

Certainly, too, it is a series of horrifying episodes which gives the story its underlying power. The savage downward spiral of the musician, Abe North, very early foreshadows the fate of all the major figures in the novel. And even the minor personages—the 'hopelessly corrupt' young Spaniard, Francisco, the decadent English lesbian, Lady Caroline, the exhibitionistic American, Collis Clay, who lies drunk and naked on his bed before the aggressive stare of Nicole's sister, 'Baby' Warren—even these minor portraits, acrid and mephitic, and accompanied by such scenes as those in the nightmarish chambers of Dohmler's Sanatorium—this last resort of 'the broken, the incomplete, the menacing of this world'—or in those other sealed-off chambers near Lake Geneva where Nicole's incestuous father is now dying: all this contributes to the continuous tide of dissolution upon which the Divers are swept outward beyond all chance of rescue . . .

And as these two former lovers still cling to each other in an embrace that has become, however, a paroxysm of self-survival, as Nicole finally reverts to the type of amoral wanton that was implicit in her earlier fantasies of filth, and as Dick, sliding downwards through all the stages of moral collapse, loses even his powers of decision and bodily control, the penultimate accents of *Tender is the Night* are surely those of a blind and frantic death struggle. 'You used to want to create things—now you seem to want to smash them up.' —'You ruined me, did you? Then we're both ruined.'

These accents of destruction are familiar, of course; they carry us back to the pages of *This Side of Paradise* and *The Beautiful and Damned.* But the crack-up in *Tender is the Night* is all the more severe, as I suggested earlier, precisely because it follows such a deep groove, and because Fitzgerald reveals it with the conviction of maturity. It is more intense because it is pictured from precisely within that European Riviera which has always been, as in the case of Anthony Patch, a last hope of refuge. And it is more appalling because it extends, finally, to the craft of the novel itself. The wavering motivation, the artistic confusion in the last sections of the book—the sense one has of brilliant and disordered fragments—make it really seem to *be* the diary of a collapse; a diary written by the subject of the collapse, the one who, viewing all the symptoms so intimately, is the least likely to get at the source of the illness.

Tender is the Night, then, is a novel of lost causes, or lost cures, as it represents Fitzgerald's most precipitous descent into the abyss, and fulfills the pattern of disaster which has been the core of his work. Yet what actually lies in these depths where now the writer wanders, without light, through Keats's 'tender' night? What discordant impulses have led Fitzgerald to make this recurrent plunge into darkness? And what is the nature of that destructive element most sharply felt in these pages, if perhaps even here, towards the end, rather opaquely described? For one has the curious impression at times that the novel is really about something else altogether—and yet *Tender is the Night* is certainly at the center of Fitzgerald's recurrent aesthetic conflict and brings into focus some of the more obscure elements we have noticed in his previous work.

In a way, Fitzgerald's entire story to this point is a postscript to our baronial days that might be entitled 'The Great American Fortunes—Fifty Years Later.' And for the children of the rich it was a simple step to project the new American Success Story completely out of the American scene: to move forward on the one hand, as Fitzgerald did, beyond the spires of Manhattan to the salons of Paris and to the Cap d'Antibes. And on the other hand, and omitting Minnesota entirely, just as T. S. Eliot had instructed a generation in how to omit Missouri, to move backward to Fitzgerald's feudal southern aristocracy. . . . It isn't impossible also, for these two extremes to meet. In the memory of a seventeenth-century Baltimore Cavalier society, with its gay blades and dancing belles, lies the vision of a lost paradise which Fitzgerald revived for the descendants of Morgan and Vanderbilt.

Yet Francis Scott Key Fitzgerald's ties with the South are somewhat more complex than this, too. If he is, in memory and desire at least, a southern gentleman, in a still deeper spiritual sense, and rather in the manner of the Poe whom he invokes in his earliest novel, he is an 'illegitimate' southern gentleman. In *Tender is the Night* the strain of the 'outsider' in Fitzgerald has actually led into the strain of the outlaw and the illegitimate has become the illegal. It is interesting to realize how large an emphasis Fitzgerald has placed on violence, from the earliest fantasies of Amory Blaine to the pirate Carlyle, the bandit Dalyrimple, and the gangster Gatsby. Probably the writer's outward concern with theatrics is matched only by this inner preoccupation with crime.* And these feelings—which have again emerged in the religious stories: in the 'enormous terrified repulsion' of 'Benediction,' in the 'dark poison' of 'Absolution' and in these tales' underlying sense of moral isolation and of hounded flight—are inextricably involved with the sexual issues in Fitzgerald's work. As early as Amory, too, 'the problem of evil . . . had solidified into the problem of sex,' and the profound sexual revulsion of Fitzgerald's heroes had become quite clear.

What shall we say now concerning those sparkling Jazz-Age lovers whose highly tactile bodies are balanced by their quite untouchable emotions, and whose exquisite delight in romance is inevitably accompanied by their acute distaste for passion? Those flappers who are prepared to risk all for an embrace—but an embrace, cold, calculated, and histrionic, which itself risks nothing; who are so full of sensuous attraction, but an attraction apparently as much above natural as it is above social law—and as unfulfilled as it is unobtainable? In essence these are dream women. . . . And Fitzgerald's heroes, from Jay Gatsby to the Munro Stahr of *The Last Tycoon,* still haunted by his dead wife's smile, are, in fact, living in dreams: in an impossible past that denies all the possibilities of the present.

They are lovers, in short, for whom love seems impractical; and the nature of their past may indicate the reasons. You may remember the essentially feminine quality of the young men who stem from the Beatrice Blaine of *This Side of Paradise:* the vanity, the wiles, the delicate sensitivities of these graceful, indolent, clinging young men:

* There is also a concurrent sense of guilt from the first scenes of *This Side of Paradise*—and Amory's visions of a horror 'like blood on satin'—to the final scenes of *The Last Tycoon* where the Fitzgerald heroine will feel the full impact of her father's 'producer's blood.'

their 'charm.' And in turn, from Gloria Gilbert and an array of other early 'Ganymedes' to Nicole Warren, the Fitzgerald heroines have been given essentially masculine attributes.* Following this pattern, the symptoms of sexual ambivalence run through Fitzgerald's work—along with those of a still deeper emotional conflict.

Just as the Fitzgerald heroines are the dominating forces in his work, they are also cast in an almost identical mold. We have noticed the curious resemblance of a whole line of them; while the tonal similarities of their names—Isabelle, Eleanor, Gloria, Nicole—suggest the actual similarity of their temperaments.† Are they dream women, indeed, not unlike Edgar Allan Poe's Eleanora and Ligeia and Madeline? Possibly Fitzgerald drew his names from this source; the reference, at any rate, is illuminating. For Poe is concerned, of course, with the love of 'cousins,' just as Fitzgerald's earlier lovers proclaimed themselves to be 'twins.' Very much like Fitzgerald, Poe is concerned with the mutual adoration of these related, and extravagantly beautiful, and finally altogether perverse lovers: in 'The Fall of the House of Usher' this becomes quite specifically the dark and illegal love of brother and sister. Poe is deeply concerned with this—not to mention the 'nervous maladies' and 'mysterious disorders' of his lovers, or the burying-alive of these bewitching and diseased beings, or that final persistent desire for those now fatally pure and entombed bodies. . . . Poe is directly involved with the

* In this connection Fitzgerald has even further modified the plot of the standard Success Story, since, culminating with 'Baby' Warren—type of the American female who has 'made a nursery out of a continent'—and the later Josephine, the railroad heiress whose every glint is a spike, the Fitzgerald women are actually portrayed as the true heirs of the Robber Barons, dominant though sterile.

† Among the first of Fitzgerald's heroines, the distracted Eleanor of *This Side of Paradise* is already cast in the mold, as is the Josephine of *Taps at Reveille,* one of Fitzgerald's last heroines.

emotional consequences of the incest taboo, in short: a taboo which is hardly less directly *implicit* in the whole range of Fitzgerald's writing.

This may also clarify that 'inexpiable, mysterious crime' of Manfred's to which Fitzgerald's first hero refers, since we know that Byron's emotional life flowed in similar channels. In Fitzgerald's work, however, it is impossible (if it were profitable) to identify the real origins of this intricate web of feeling. Is it simply a final literary identification with Poe himself, the 'dispossessed' Southern writer to whom in other respects Fitzgerald seems to link himself? Or does it derive from some early, unrecorded childhood relationship—a relationship like the central one in Faulkner's *The Sound and the Fury* perhaps, where the child's distinction between the desire and the deed, the 'imaginary' and the 'real,' is uncertain and, indeed, unimportant, and where the stigma of 'sin' eventuates peremptorily from some alien adult orbit?

The Beatrice Blaine of *This Side of Paradise,* from what we know of the writer's history, is a completely fictional mother. Yet does the entire emotional sequence refer back again to some such feminine image of whatever complex origin: an image that in point of fact colors almost every thought and feeling of the young Amory Blaine, that is almost completely expunged at the close of Fitzgerald's first novel, but that nevertheless continues to be prismatically refracted in a series of Fitzgerald's glittering and neurasthenic heroines? —In this event, at least, the apparent obscuritics and discordances of *Tender is the Night* are partially clarified. For the 'hidden' emotional relationship of father and daughter, of Nicole Warren and that mysterious, shadowy father who is the true source of destruction in the novel, becomes a shield for the emotions of a mother-son relationship. Dick Diver's suffering would become in turn an act of penance and purgation —and purged, he is free at last to return to the home of his fathers.

Perhaps you ought to keep in mind that this is a deep and abiding theme in the arts from the time of the Greek 'myths.' A little later we shall notice some of its more uneasy modern manifestations. And in our own artist's last two works, covering the last seven years of his life, this cultural and psychological pattern will be continued. —But notice meanwhile that Fitzgerald's Dick Diver, leaving the festive Riviera shore which has been the scene of his mortification, and having nevertheless blessed this shore 'with the sign of the papal cross,' *does* return to the American earth which has been equally the object of his divided emotions.

This return of the native is not quite in the manner of a Sherwood Anderson figure once again greeting the farming settlements of his youth. Nor is it like Nick Carraway's coming back home to his own Middle West. In fact, Dick Diver has rather the air of a pallbearer than of a prodigal son as he opens his little office in upper New York State, and fails, and moves along from one American town to another, and finally disappears in this frontier wilderness.

Deus misereatur. . . . In the closing passages of *Tender is the Night,* all the same, there is a sense of retribution and of absolution: even in such a return to Buffalo, or Batavia, or Lockport, U.S.A.

5. The Eumenides at Home

TAPS AT REVEILLE, in 1935, is Fitzgerald's last and in some respects his most interesting collection of tales. Where the earlier volumes of short stories have accentuated the note of material splendor, and a sort of spiritual frenzy to possess this splendor, this one is built around the theme of error and remorse.*

In 'Two Wrongs,' Bill McChesney, a handsome and gifted show-producer whose wife has lost her baby while he has been out on a drunken binge, atones by sacrificing himself for his wife's artistic career. There is a God here, though maybe He is somewhat histrionic also. (What is really here is a primitive and almost mythological sense of retribution: the price of a happy soul is a damned soul.) Joel Coles, in 'Crazy Sunday,' is an amplified portrait of McChesney. He has spent his childhood between London and New York, 'trying to separate the real from the unreal.' As a Hollywood script writer he is still cursed by 'the dramatic adequacy inherited from his mother': there is a party scene at which Joel, drunk and exhibitionistic, does a good job of ruining his own career. . . . This is probably the single best story of *Taps at Reveille,* but the point of the volume is in the 'Basil and Josephine' sketches which open Fitzgerald's last collection of tales and in 'Babylon Revisited' which closes it.

It is interesting, too, in so far as *Tender is the Night* marks a point of final dissolution in the series of dissolving experiences which form Fitzgerald's career, that his emphasis should now come to rest on the American origins of his central literary characters. With these eight scenes from the life of Basil and Josephine (they were apparently intended to form the nucleus of another semi-autobiographical novel) we move much more directly into the

* The incidental tales in the collection reflect Fitzgerald's familiar notions. In 'The Last of the Belles,' for example, the South is represented by a delicate lady, the North by an illiterate though engaging ruffian. In 'A Short Trip Home' the Fitzgerald heroine gets mixed up with a ghost—the ghost of a racketeer.

writer's past: into that vulgar midwestern background at which his earlier figures had sneered when they did not shudder. Like Amory Blaine, Basil is an attractive and effeminate adolescent—in a curious transmutation he is phonetically linked with the names of Fitzgerald's major heroines. But where Amory had boasted of, Basil now meditates upon, his exotic American childhood: a childhood which opens, again, with the note of 'sin,' with fantasies of crime and fears of insanity, and with the conviction of being 'morally alone.'

Love is merely another channel for Basil's egocentric charm, and a channel that leads all the more certainly to shipwreck. A curious series of adolescent heroines is listed here, recalling those 'Harrison Fisher girls on glossy paper' to whom Basil, reality continually disappointing him, or he it, has paid reverence: There is the precocious Imogene and her yacht; the dazzling Miss Erminie Gilberte Labouisse Bibble of New Orleans whose imperishable smile conceals the limited mentality that is manipulating a set of priceless molars. Heir to this grimace and to millions of dollars, there is Josephine herself, the beautiful, hard, and almost vicious 'speed' of these tales who, accepting 'the proud world into which she was born' just as her railroad-building ancestors did theirs, moves through it, implacable and unsatisfied—'every glint a spike.'

With these little details, Fitzgerald has placed Josephine in her American cultural context. (Notice how she is dominated by a desire for power over men, not for a relationship with them; or how, again, morally tainted as Josephine is, she is hardly aware, in the American moral framework, of her own corruption.) More precisely here than in the earlier case of Nicole Warren, Scott has defined the real milieu of his heroine—and of the other descendants of the American ruling class around whom his writing has revolved: these sweet-smelling children of the rich who combine their ancestors' social irresponsibility with their own personal irresponsibility. . . . With a smile that is not a smile, a mouth twisted by 'a universal compassion' but an expression not quite that of compassion, and eyes shining as if with fever while she torments her lover for her own altogether empty purposes 'as if they had been two other people,' F. Scott Fitzgerald's Josephine, the Last of the Flappers, is rather different from those first enchanting girls who danced to meet the tinsel dawn of the nineteen-twenties.

The Left Bank is also a ghost town after the advent of the American Depression, and the Charlie Wales of 'Babylon Revisited' is caught up in nightmarish memories of fluttering thousand-franc notes and hangovers that lasted for weeks and screaming girls in public places and men who locked out their wives in the snow because the snow of 1929 wasn't real snow. 'If you didn't want it to be snow, you just paid some money.' Here, too, the big party is over (the elegiac tone is similar to Hemingway's in 'The Snows of Kilimanjaro') and Fitzgerald's hero, who is desperately trying to salvage what can be salvaged, thinks he knows the meaning of the word 'dissipate': 'to make nothing out of something.' Yet Charlie Wales has something of Basil's earlier faith in his capacity to endure and survive: 'to shake off the blood like water' and to carry his wounds with him 'to new disasters and new atonements.' In a way he hasn't an altogether wrong view of his own situation:

> 'I heard you lost a lot in the crash.'
> 'I did . . . but I lost everything I wanted in the boom.'

'Selling short.'
'Something like that.'

And with these tones, and with this touching although hardly very glamorous or glittering middle-aged midwestern character of Fitzgerald's last period, we are on the edge of Fitzgerald's last novel.

It isn't a far jump in one respect from the French to the American Riviera of *The Last Tycoon* in 1941. Still, what an odd itinerary Fitzgerald has followed in order to complete the circuit of his American withdrawal and return. Remember his travels East from the 'barbarian' atmosphere of St. Paul to the Princeton circles of *Paradise,* the New York society of *The Beautiful and Damned,* and the Long Island society of *The Great Gatsby.* And still East: for Nick Carraway comes back to his western people, but his literary mentor travels on to Paris and Cannes and the cultivated sensibilities of *Tender is the Night.* East—but while Dick Diver, fleeing from a dissolute European scene, returns to 'bury' himself in Buffalo, Fitzgerald himself sharply reverses his own course across an ocean and a continent. He crosses the Atlantic, slips by East Egg and Minnesota, and—almost as if he were drawn to the furthermost reaches of the American West by the memory of a lost frontier—arrives for his salvation in Hollywood.

Certainly this is a dramatic design for our whole literary movement in the nineteen-twenties and -thirties. It summarizes a chapter in modern American literature. It telescopes the history of our literary exodus and return during the last half-century from Henry James to Ernest Hemingway. And while Fitzgerald was racing from riviera to riviera, remember also that back home the socioeconomic system whose effects he was in part escaping from, and whose product, in his own cultural innocence and elegance, he most surely was—that back home, during the depression years, the financial order of Coolidge and Hoover—'the great machine,' as Dos Passos said, 'for which they slaved'—was cracking up. And a new generation of American novelists, from Tom Wolfe in the streets of Brooklyn to John Steinbeck and his California Okies, was just then coming to grips with its native land.

In this sense Fitzgerald's return to Hollywood reflects the contrasts of two diametrically opposed periods in our national life. Now, too, that Editor Anderson of Marion, Smyth County, Virginia, was looking down from his southern hills upon those shining, glass-brick factory walls which had put an end to Winesburg, and to an earlier American age. Yet where else, during the boiling American thirties, could F. Scott Fitzgerald go? We have seen the writer's cultural disestablishment from earliest childhood: his almost compulsive fixation on that one-half of one per cent of the American people who themselves have constituted a rootless ruling class; and his earlier ignorance of even the cultural configuration represented by that ruling class. During his growing disenchantment with this class, perhaps his only remaining deep and instinctive contact with all the myriad phases of life in the United States was with the show business. From the Amory Blaine who saw life as a stage to the young actress of *Tender is the Night,* the histrionic impulses of Fitzgerald's people are dominant. In the flux and dissolution of his earlier values, they alone remain stable.

Although Hollywood isn't the most propitious home for an American writer to return to, it was almost Fitzgerald's only possible home. . . . And partly through his own limitations and his increasing awareness of them, who was better suited to deal with the kaleidoscopic Dream Factory of the industrial United States?

As for the sparkling native scene, with its Lions and Wolves and Nymphs, its pasteurized Galahads and coiffured Lady Godivas: Hollywood, the home of the close-up, the build-up, the frame-up; land of frocks and frills where, as Fitzgerald notes, 'a mixed motive is conspicuous waste' and Thorstein Veblen bows to Groucho Marx; where twice daily an altogether new Cinderella turns in her Pumpkin for a Packard (because the glass slipper comes in adjustable sizes) and each night the American Bitch Goddess orders a thousand angels to dance on the brow of a Queen: this, our own Hollywood, the S.R.O. Nirvana of the mechanized opium-eaters where at last Fitzgerald's haunted memory of eastern elegance hits an all-time high as the western star cries Heigh-o Silver—certainly this native scene has been brought to us before, but never more delicately than in these weird episodes which form the running satiric background of *The Last Tycoon.*

Done with a beautiful technical virtuosity, these episodes have all the sparkle of Fitzgerald's earliest novels; and what's more, the glittering surface now belongs, not to a limited and adolescent, but to a relatively complex and adult, world. Against the continuous Hollywood foibles in *The Last Tycoon,* Fitzgerald puts the episodes of Hollywood's ability and ingenuity, all its rich talent, which in the case of Munro Stahr finds a proper direction. In the Heavenly City of a nation 'that for a decade had wanted only to be entertained,' Stahr is also the apotheosis of sobriety. And surely this movie producer who lives completely in his work, whose 'studio is really home,' this gifted and tragic despot is Fitzgerald's most appealing hero.

As the final projection of the child of the Jazz Age, however, Munro Stahr is a particularly curious figure. A poor and uneducated New York Jew who is the spiritual prince of cinema's inner sanctum, Stahr is hardly reminiscent of Fitzgerald's first hero to whom even the cream of the Ritz was watery, or of that Anthony Patch, obsessed by the sprawling, slithering 'aliens,' who finally called Bloeckman—an earlier, less flattering version of Stahr—a 'Goddam' Jew.' It is no less interesting to discover that a Negro is the final test of Stahr's own stature. You may remember the fisherman whom Stahr meets on the beach at Santa Monica, and whose conviction that the movies are worthless makes Stahr revise his whole production schedule—this obscure Negro man who had come out 'to read some Emerson,' Fitzgerald tells us, and who goes off unaware 'that he had rocked an industry.'

This is an odd transformation for a writer who has clung to a feudal southern aristocracy when he wasn't panting after a blond northern élite. It is a transformation which brings into focus the reversal of Fitzgerald's values which is embodied in *The Last Tycoon* and for which his abrupt geographical reversal from east to west was the prelude. It is difficult to ignore Fitzgerald's final stress on poverty as against wealth, on character as against charm, on energy and work as against grace and ease, and even on the alien toilers as against our native Princetonians. Munro Stahr is without doubt an archetypal American whereas a whole row of early Fitzgerald figures have tried desperately to become archetypal Europeans. And just to complete the picture, I ought to point out that Stahr, who is a sympathetic but exacting autocrat, is as clearly the dominant father in Fitzgerald's last novel as the exotic Beatrice Blaine was the dominant mother in Fitzgerald's first novel.

Was F. Scott Fitzgerald the early chronicler of the American Success Story in its purest and most exalted form, moreover, the natural folklorist of the nineteen-twenties, the divine soothsayer of those economic princes and princesses whose kingdom consisted of diamonds? Then notice the stress here on Hollywood's duds, flops, and has-beens. The bankrupt producer Manny Schwartz who opens the novel; the drunken writer, Wylie White, whose career has come to a dead end; the industrial magnate, Mr. Marcus, whose once brilliant steel-trap mind is now intermittently slipping; old Johnny Swanson, once as big as Tom Mix; Martha Dodd, the 'agricultural girl' whose beauty has washed out; and Cecilia herself, the innocent young Bennington girl who during the course of the novel suffers 'an immersion in the family drain'—these are among the Hollywood citizens who walk along 'Suicide Bridge' with its new fence, and give *The Last Tycoon* its own undertones of ruin.

Is there still one remaining constant in all this flux? Has Fitzgerald returned quite deliberately to this California scene for his last portrait of the 'age of glamour'? Even the sparkling Hollywood décor, into which Scott puts his last impulse of enchantment, trembles under the reverberations of time and change. The writer for whom the revolutionary roar of Europe in 1919 could barely stir the drawn curtains of the Ritz, nor the rioting mob outside of Delmonico's mar the light *clat-clat* of afternoon tea—this prime story teller of a boom-town America now speaks of the Bonus Army, of labor troubles and early Fascists, and of the rich who since 1933 'could only be happy alone together.' Indeed Scott's Cecilia returns to Hollywood 'with the resignation of a ghost assigned to a haunted house.' And the driving intensity of Munro Stahr—the preoccupation with his dead wife, the disregard of his precarious health, the half-deliberate 'perversion of the life force'—springs from this inner knowledge. The Last Tycoon is the perfection—and deterioration—of his type.

Thus the firm of Maecenas, Morgan & Fitzgerald closes its doors. This is a final step in the history of our writer's partnership with the American rich—a dissolving partnership, as we've seen, and one that works its way from the top down: from Amory Blaine to James Gatz, the poor boy whose struggle to ape the élite first fully shows them up. Though Munro Stahr represents the positive factor in this radical change of Scott's values—though he represents a natural rather than a ceremonial aristocracy, and a New rather than an Old World order of things—Stahr is meant to portray the historical ending of this order, too. The writer who has fled throughout his life from any contact with a vulgar American social arrangement, has returned home to record its peak and its passing.

Ave atque vale. In the scene with the Communist organizer Brimmer, Stahr loses his control. And with Stahr's surrender, to drink, to his own 'increasing schizophrenia,' and to a future which he must accept but cannot belong to, the story reaches its climax. 'Is *this* all?' Brimmer thinks. 'This frail half-sick person holding up the whole thing?' Stahr, Fitzgerald tells us in his notes, 'is to be miserable and embittered toward the end.' There is to be 'a bitter and acrid finish'—and with this we have boxed the compass of Fitzgerald's wanderings and must take a final reckoning of his entire course.

For the particular sort of ambivalence we have noticed in other areas of Fitzgerald's work operates here also. The 'moral,' even the *fact,* of Fitzgerald's last novel, was predicated in his first novel. Was wealth an absolute goal to the young Fitzgerald? It was a goal which hardly yielded absolute returns—rather, in fact, the contrary. It was only when Amory Blaine lost his money, his social position, his entire career, that he felt he knew himself. As we have seen, the older and wiser Anthony Patch of *The Beautiful and Damned* repeats Amory's pattern even more frantically. ('Do you think that if I don't get this money of my grandfather's life will be *endurable?*') And is Anthony's reward, then, after having finally gained his object, to be bundled off to Europe: a completely disorganized and half-mad cripple? It is a short move from the hero of this parable to the Dick Diver who is clearly ruined by Nicole's fortune.

Furthermore, just as 'poverty,' for the earlier Fitzgerald heroes, meant merely the loss of one's hereditary fortune, so wealth itself represented merely an entrance into the charmed circle of the élite. And we have traced Fitzgerald's underlying revolt against not only money but social position itself—the strain of the outsider and the outcast of Gamma Psi. When Fitzgerald records the antics of the rich in *The Great Gatsby,* it is with the increasing realization that he is as much James Gatz as he is Nick Carraway. Yet the 'western spectator' who returns home at the novel's close is a splitting-off of Fitzgerald's personality—an illuminating flare, so to speak, but one that fades into darkness. . . . The emotional compulsion still persists. Almost a decade after Fitzgerald has reached his conclusion as to wealth and social position, he has become, in *Tender is the Night,* more 'eastern'—and wealthier—and more despairing. The hero who returns home is a shell of Nick Carraway, just as Anthony Patch was a shell of Amory Blaine. And it is only with this second descent into the abyss—the second almost total destruction of his hero—that Fitzgerald reaches a point of catharsis and a sense of a new beginning.

Isn't this a curious sequence of events? Although one

is forced to pursue wealth, it is with the firm conviction that one's true salvation lies in poverty. Although one seeks outward social position at all costs, it can be achieved only by an inner betrayal. Although an unearned fortune and an ambiguous place among the élite are the only ends for the early Fitzgerald protagonist, the same fortune and place are the surest means to disaster. . . . And Fitzgerald continues to cherish these ends—these means—until he comes, indeed, to the edge of disaster.

In this chain of events it becomes apparent, too, that *Tender is the Night* again occupies a central place: here, in this eastern elegance, is the climax of the search: here is the sharpest cycle of destruction; here is the moment of purgation and regeneration.* And whatever the nature of the incest-taboo which is also at the center of the search, the shadow that lies over Fitzgerald's heroes—from Amory's sense of 'horror' to the nervous collapses of Anthony Patch and Dick Diver and the 'increasing schizophrenia' of Munro Stahr himself—is hardly a literary mannerism. This is indeed a distraught Narcissus who gazes down at his shining image.

An image, mirrored in water, which cannot be washed away for all Fitzgerald's equal insistence on a completely

* In its central framework, Fitzgerald's career has the elements of a primitive fable. So it is interesting that the process of atonement in *Tender is the Night* should take place near that Geneva scene where Amory Blaine first announced the fortunate death of his father. It might almost seem that Fitzgerald's dualism of 'East' and 'West'—of Europe and America—is in part a concealed form of a deeper parental ambivalence. At least no one could represent the European mother country more glamorously than the Beatrice Blaine who initiates Fitzgerald's career—and no one embodies the democratic America of the Founding Fathers more fully than the Munro Stahr who closes Fitzgerald's career.

A similar parental conflict, incidentally, can be observed in the career of Henry Adams, and probably the whole cultural conflict of East and West in American literary thinking could stand a closer examination, as Ferner Nuhn has already shown in his excellent study, *The Wind Blew from the East.*

pure body and spirit—his refusal to accept the slightest ordinary human blemish. (Very likely Fitzgerald's addiction to histrionics is a variation on this theme, since the actor playing a rôle can assume a personality to cover his own.) You may remember how the writer's initial aversion to poverty—and the 'aliens'—sprang from this curious fastidiousness. 'It's essentially cleaner to be corrupt and rich than it is to be innocent and poor.' But the paired adjectives here are illuminating. To be rich, then, is to be corrupt? And is it through the absolute pursuit of wealth—through this immaculate materialism, so to speak—that one hopes to escape the tainted spirit? . . . But then, at the same time, by deliberately seeking out corruption, may we not the sooner perhaps embrace the inevitable disaster: the retribution and atonement that we are, in fact, looking for?

It is certain, at any rate, that Fitzgerald's search for glamour, as the writer himself sensed from the start, was hardly a superficial one. Only a ghost-ridden talent could abandon itself so completely to these trivialities, invoke such an odd species of defiance against the stern reckoning of the Rock. Vanity of vanities, all is vanity: then let us exalt vanity alone. . . . Twilight falling over cocktails at the Biltmore, midnight striking for the dancers at Delmonico's, and dawn touching the glass at Childs' Fifty-Ninth Street: these few brief hours alone stand between us and the Furies. And here, too, is our most certain meeting—for in this modern version of the myth, it is just here that the Furies lounge and gossip: it is *at* the Ritz that they have their suite. The method chosen by the writer to drug the moment of awakening is the method that most surely hastens it. The flight from reality is the path of destruction.

Now in truth there is only the alternative of 'diamonds

or disillusion' in the whole world. And if love is a form of divine drunkenness, and youth of chemical madness—'how pleasant then to be insane.' And his was a great sin indeed 'who first invented consciousness.'

Although this deeply felt and disturbing emotional conflict at the center of Fitzgerald's work gives it a hidden force, however, it is the same emotional conflict that finally prevents Fitzgerald from realizing the force and depth that are actually implicit in his work. Thus we have the final cleavage of this tragically divided writer: the cleavage of his writing itself. On the one hand, the 'psychological' novels—*The Beautiful and Damned* and *Tender is the Night*—intense, powerful, and unco-ordinated: the force of their discordant impulses reflected in the ragged ending of the first, and the disorderly ending of the second novel. And on the other hand, the 'social' novels—*The Great Gatsby* and *The Last Tycoon*—very skillful, often superb technically, and yet curiously hollow at times, and in a sense quite 'unreal' underneath, since they reflect without carrying through the real emotions of Fitzgerald's writing.

One needn't labor the loss here, or the wider cultural implications. The young Fitzgerald, disowning his own heritage, leaving his criminals just on the edge of 'crime,' attempting with all his tormented heart to pass as a Nordic—this Fitzgerald was in the American grain.* The rich, too, are an American novelist's natural prey, just as the nineteen-twenties and nineteen-thirties were among the best decades in the nation's history to observe the rich in the polar extremes of their existence. Between the Boom and the Bust, between the billboards and the breadlines,

* American audiences have never been very sympathetic to such themes as incest. Even today the familiar reaction is distaste or ridicule. Yet it is curious to notice how important a theme it has been in our own literature, from Melville and Poe to O'Neill or Faulkner. Perhaps it is such a basic theme that our writers can hardly afford to ignore it.

there was certainly need for a new Henry James: for a post-Versailles, post-Proustian, and thoroughly acclimated James to record the entrance, the strutting about and the exit of the indigenous millionaire. But the writer who was in some respects best qualified to fill this rôle in the younger generation was at once too close to his theme and too remote from it, and meanwhile our true drama lacked its true voice.

Yes, *The Great Gatsby* fades a little with its last 'dying fall'—but it is still the warm and touching chronicle of our deceptive native romance, just as 'The Diamond as Big as the Ritz' is among our best shorter parables of wealth, as 'May Day' has all the faintly bitter fragrance of the age of pleasure, and as *The Last Tycoon* is still the closest that an American novelist has got to the truth about the histrionic home of the Success Story. Although Fitzgerald remains the folklorist of the rich in their more restricted aspects, and, like his own Munro Stahr, who had never learned enough about the feel of America, still retains 'a certain half-naïve conception of the common weal,' there are few others who could have given such a bright and glowing intensity to such a shallow world. Once having known them, is it easy to forget the flappers who dwelt in diaphanous gowns and subsisted on caviar: inviolable and distraught spirits who wavered between the classics and the shimmy? In another respect, moreover, even the account of Fitzgerald's illusions has a memorable quality.

For the suite at the Ritz, the pursuit of a youth without prospects, the slow and tortured realization of 'the wrongness in the case' of the Jazz Age itself—in this respect Fitzgerald's own history provides us with an invaluable natural history of his period. And isn't it possible, in respect to the entire decade of the nineteen-twenties—wasn't *it* a sort of Narcissus, in love with its own glittering image? Our writer's preoccupation with the illegitimate and the illegal is not so remote from the time of Insull and Teapot Dome. As a historical epoch, the American twenties also tried to bargain with God, and who shall say what sense of moral isolation or of hounded flight did not dwell in the blacked-out conscience of the age: this age in itself beautiful and damned, for which horror and death waited at every corner, and whose youth may seem 'never so vanished as now.'

Taps sounded for it, certainly, at reveille. In the shadow of the Second World War, it had its own appointment with the Furies.

Chapter Six

The Years of Loss

◇

1. The Land of Canaan

2. Heralds of Empire

3. The Pharaohs of Detroit

Chapter Six

The Years of Loss

---

1. The Land of Canaan

AND DIDN'T F. SCOTT FITZGERALD have more talent than the rest of the Younger Generation put together, as Gertrude Stein was reported to have said?

At any rate, he was the first of a new literary dynasty: that series of gifted figures who rose to prominence during the middle nineteen-twenties, those 'stars in the new constellation'—to use André Gide's phrase—of strictly contemporary American authors. Just as the typical figures of the Middle Generation had revived a national consciousness of our literature, so the new writers established their work in the capitals of the world—in London and Moscow as well as in Paris. They formed a notable group of writers in the post-war period; they were the founders of a body of literature marked by its technical virtuosity, its vitality, its promise. In a sense Henry Mencken's pronunciamento was justified, and leadership in the arts, and especially in the art of letters, had almost come to rest on the western shore of the Atlantic.

Before World War I, in the teens of the new century, the New Poetry had opened the way. After the war, the poets continued to be in the lead; to a certain degree it was the experiments and discoveries of the Symbolists, the Imagists, the Vorticists, brought over to and elaborated in the area of prose, which set the tone of the new literature, while such more or less established figures as Edgar Lee Masters, Robert Frost, and T. S. Eliot were joined by Vachel Lindsay, Robinson Jeffers, and E. E. Cummings. . . . Elinor Wylie and Edna Millay were among the first of the distinguished literary ladies who played a prominent part in the artistic scene of the middle twenties.

Among the historians, philosophers, and journalists who provided the new movement with an ethos and framework of values, a Lincoln Steffens, an Upton Sinclair, the Beards, John Dewey, and Veblen were followed by such 'promising young men' (in Mencken's words) as Vernon Parrington, Van Wyck Brooks, and Edmund Wilson. (It was in Brooks's slender volumes that the new movement found a source of inspiration, while both Parrington's *Main Currents in American Thought* and Wilson's *Axel's Castle* were to set up a new standard for American literary criticism.) On the theatrical front the Provincetown players were presenting Eugene O'Neill. In the medium of the short story, Ring Lardner, with a remarkable ear for the vulgate, was crystallizing the local idiom into a series of acrid and progressively disenchanted modern episodes.

In the main stream of our prose, the novel form itself, John Dos Passos, William Faulkner, and Ernest Hemingway, along with Scott Fitzgerald and, a little later, Thomas Wolfe and John Steinbeck, formed the first line of native talent.

It was a talent that was varied in achievement as well as in quality. The novelists wrote short stories, of course. In the case of Hemingway's work, the colloquial flat midwestern tones of Sherwood Anderson were refined into some of the most distinguished tales of the epoch. The short-story writers wrote verse and plays, and, meanwhile, the poets had turned into scholars, historians, and literary critics. . . . Furthermore, just as Dos Passos enriched the structure of the novel by a variety of new technics—the 'Camera Eye,' the 'Newsreel,' the 'Biographies'—William Faulkner enriched the novel's content, in such works as *The Sound and the Fury* or *Light in August,* by a consummate use of the interior monologue. And behind the specific achievements and literary temperaments of the decade lay the different literary schools and groups, and also the aesthetic feuds and debates.

In the process of these literary maneuvers and campaigns, indeed, the artistic scene of the nineteen-twenties took on something of the vitality and cunning that had been limited to the purely economic sphere of American life for almost half a century. We have already noticed the opening encounter of the decade between H. L. Mencken and the notables *de l'institut américain.* But the later competition between the exponents of Freud and the psychological novel (a Conrad Aiken or an Evelyn Scott) and the advocates of Marx and the sociological novel (an Ernest Poole, a Waldo Frank, or, in adjoining fields, a John Reed and a V. F. Calverton) was practically unrestrained. If Elinor Wylie belonged to an occult circle, both Edna Millay and Scott Fitzgerald, whose early work had almost transformed them from literary rebels to folk heroes, belonged to the shock troops of the new movement. With the defection of Professor Stuart Sherman, the group of academic critics called the Humanists found themselves in an exposed position; but the younger group called the Southern Agrarians protected their flank and, retreating from the gross clamor of society in general, entrenched themselves securely in the classics.

Meanwhile, an interesting array of primitives, bohemians, and sophisticates, from Mabel Dodge Luhan to

Joseph Hergesheimer and James Branch Cabell, gave the period elegance and color. Such figures as Archibald MacLeish, Matthew Josephson, and Malcolm Cowley numbered themselves among the dissenters and experimentalists who had established the magazines *Transition* and *Broom*. . . . These were among the best-known but not the only important periodicals of the period. Just as the political opinion of the nineteen-twenties ranged from the radical *Masses* and the liberal *New Republic* and *Nation* to the conservative or reactionary *Bookman*, so the literary groups had their own publications. If the *Dial* and *Seven Arts* flourished in New York, so did *Poetry* and the *Little Review* in Chicago, the *Midland* in Iowa City, the *Frontier* in Helena, Montana, and the *Double Dealer* in New Orleans, while the Little Theaters and New Galleries operated in Cleveland, Pasadena, and Dallas, as well as in Washington Square.

In fact, as the literary renaissance of the twenties developed, it seemed to call forth voices from the mountains and plains and bayous of the continent, and it represented, not merely the flowering of our various regional cultures, but the emergence of the new racial stocks which, from the eastern seaboard to the prairies of the eighteen-nineties, had helped to settle the last frontier and to service the young industrial machine. As we have seen, it was from these racial stocks that the new literature drew a good part of its vitality, while, among the arbiters of literary taste at least, it was very often the native 'Anglo-Saxons' who remained the advocates of decorum and sterility. Here, too, the Negro scholars and poets of the twenties opened the way for such later figures as Langston Hughes or Richard Wright.

So it was a bright prospect that the literary heirs of Thoreau, Hawthorne, and Melville looked out upon during the middle nineteen-twenties, and a Canaan that had been promised during the long years of pestilence and drought. (In its scope and variety, as well as the richness of its first achievement, the new movement could well be compared with the literary renaissance of the eighteen-fifties.) Their own Mencken, smiting the rock, had drawn forth water. And at Meribah there was the sound of rejoicing. 'It was an age of miracles, it was an age of art,' said the later F. Scott Fitzgerald, looking back upon the lost decade, and New York had 'all the iridescence of the beginning of the world.' 'Almost everybody had theories,' said Zelda Fitzgerald in *Save Me the Waltz:* 'that the Longacre Pharmacies carried the best gin in town; that anchovies sobered you up; that you could tell wood-alcohol by the smell. Everybody knew where to find the blank verse in Cabell and how to get seats for the Yale game'—

> The city fluctuated in muffled roars like the dim applause rising to an actor on the stage of a vast theatre. 'Two Little Girls in Blue' and 'Sally' from the New Amsterdam pumped in their ear drums and . . . quickened rhythms invited them to be Negroes and saxophone players, to come back to Maryland and Louisiana, addressed them as mammies and millionaires. The shop girls were looking like Marilyn Miller. . . . Paul Whiteman played the significance of amusement on his violin. They were having the bread line at the Ritz that year.

Nevertheless, and almost from the very start, as in the case of Scott Fitzgerald himself, there is a curious sense of dissolution in all this gaiety and expectancy. And the new literary movement of the American twenties was to end almost everywhere on a note of emptiness and bitterness, disease and disaster; negation and exhaustion. Had the pioneer trails moved westward in earlier days: from

Vermont and New York to Ohio, from Ohio to Wisconsin and California, while the frontiersmen longed for the Hawaiian Islands and the New England fishermen brought back trophies from the South Seas? Now, as the literary tide flowed east in the nineteen-twenties, Winesburg, Ohio, gave way to Chicago, and Chicago to New York, and New York to London, Paris, and Capri—and Capri to the Wasteland—

> Here is no water but only rock
> Rock and no water and the sandy road . . .
> Here one can neither stand nor lie nor sit
> There is not even silence in the mountains
> But dry sterile thunder without rain
> There is not even solitude in the mountains.*

Such was the last home of the native rebels and exiles—the true home of these rich and homeless talents. Thus spoke the 'English poet' of the twenties, who was born in St. Louis, Missouri, and who also turned East for his salvation. And the dominant note of aridity in the work of T. S. Eliot—this evocation of a land without water, this dry, sterile thunder, this sandy road—will find echoes everywhere in the writings of the epoch: in the Manhattan Transfer of John Dos Passos and the Long Island suburbs of Ring Lardner, in the deep and nightmarish shadows of William Faulkner's southern lowlands and in the clean well-lighted places of Ernest Hemingway's tales.

We have already seen the pattern of artistic withdrawal and negation established in H. L. Mencken's 'evolutionary' universe, of course—a universe that spawns forth only ghouls and ogres—as well as in Sinclair Lewis's Zip City or that Chicago west-side of Sherwood Anderson's whose

* From: *Collected Poems of T. S. Eliot.* Copyright, 1930, by T. S. Eliot; copyright, 1934, 1936, by Harcourt, Brace and Co., Inc.

streets run 'on and on forever, out of nowhere into nothing,' or on the desolate mesa of Willa Cather's work.

This is actually the unifying pattern of the Middle Generation too, and in the individual studies we have traced its development in detail. It may be useful, though, to summarize some of its general implications.

2. *Heralds of Empire*

IN THESE TYPICAL FIGURES of the Middle Generation, whose values were pretty much established before World War I, we have already noticed the evidence of a sort of dry rot in the national letters.

The period which initiates the literary renaissance of the post-war scene, the years between 1915 and 1925, which mark the publication of Mencken's *Prejudices,* of *My Antonia,* of *Winesburg, Ohio,* of *Main Street,* of *This Side of Paradise*—these years of transition and of a first bold achievement, are also years of loss. In the developing context of our society, these gifted new authors, heralds of empire, are also harbingers of disaster, while that refrain which became the keynote of the movement, that eloquent, almost glorious affirmation of America's coming of age, probably marked the end of the young Republic.

We have noticed the difference in social status as well as in temperament between the members of the Middle Generation. Was Baltimore's Henry Mencken a larva of 'the comfortable and complacent bourgeoisie'? In literary terms at least, the most fervent desire of the early Sinclair Lewis was to escape from those crude frontier settlements of the northern Middle West, while the deepest inclinations, the true instincts of Willa Cather were those of a tidewater artistocracy. In his own mind, Sherwood Anderson identified himself with the obscure and meek of this world, as well as with the braggarts and ne'er-do-wells, the wandering minstrels and village bards of an older agrarian society. And Francis Scott Key Fitzgerald's youthful claim was to have revived the memories of the Cavaliers for the descendants of 'Midas and Morgan.' Moreover, the work of Mencken and Lewis is primarily influenced by social-economic pressures, while the novels of Fitzgerald and Miss Cather are primarily influenced by psychological tensions, and Sherwood Anderson is again somewhere in the middle ground.

All the same, it is interesting to watch the common drift of these writers, in one phase or another of their work, toward that cosmopolitan, urban, eastern, and finally European and Continental 'sophistication' of the nineteen-twenties. This is surely a recrudescence in a most virulent form, if not a climax and summary, of that curious underlying conflict of 'East' and 'West' in our culture from the time of Jefferson, when an American was 'the born enemy of the European,' to the time of Henry Adams or Henry James, when it almost seemed that an American was the born enemy of the Americans. Here, indeed, those 'luxurious fancies which were born of increased wealth' again revived the dying spirit of colonialism, as Henry Cabot Lodge pointed out in respect to an earlier period of our history, and those young men 'who despised everything American and admired everything English' (or in our own day, French, German, Russian, and Italian, too) became the true colonists, petty and provincial.*

* As F. J. Turner has shown in *The Frontier in American History,* the historical conflict represented by 'East' and 'West' was not only between European and American values, but between the eastern seaboard and the frontier settlements from Vermont to Oregon. It was a conflict between established order—a social hierarchy, economic power, cultural standards—and the pioneer emphasis on freedom and independence. As such, it

Obviously it isn't the notion of cosmopolitanism itself that one questions here; it is the curiously limited, naïve, and almost evasive nature of the post-war search for sophistication. Every cultural flowering, perhaps every culture capable of flowering, contains 'national' and 'international' elements, implies the cross-fertilization of ideas as well as the cross-breeding of racial stocks. From the Athenians in the days of Saint Paul, who spent their lives in nothing 'save to hear and see some new thing,' to the Elizabethans or our own Founding Fathers, the vitality of a culture may almost be judged by its receptivity to that which lies beyond its own borders or customs, its curiosity, its tolerance. It is perfectly true, as Sarah Orne Jewett pointed out to her young protégée, Willa Cather, that one must know the world in order to know one's own parish. But one must also know one's parish in order to know the world.* . . . The curious duel in *Tender is the Night,* between Tommy Barban, as the polished representative of the 'older cultures,' and McKisco, the stumbling delegate from the New World—that symbolical duel in which Fitzgerald's own sympathies seem to move alternately and inconclusively from one of the participants to the other, is an illuminating episode in the literature of the nineteen-twenties.

For the cosmopolitan excursions of the period left behind them almost the entire core and the central values of American life. If Franklin or Tom Paine divided their

represented one of the polarizing elements of our national development. From Jefferson and Jackson to William Jennings Bryan, our traditions of social reform, our native radicals and revolutionaries, have been linked to the 'West.' And it is interesting that the literary movement 'East' in the nineteen-twenties should be linked to the end of the frontier in American history. Compare Willa Cather's 'Down in the Square . . . the statue of Kit Carson still pointed westward. But there was no West, in that sense, any more.'

* 'If anyone says, "I love God," and hates his brothers, he is a liar. For how can he who does not love his brother, whom he sees, love God, whom he does not see?' (I John, 4:20.)

time between the world and their country, and Emerson or Thoreau loved New England at least, we have seen how the glory of Mencken's universe is centered around his bachelor's apartment. Nor should we forget, in this connection, that cell of Willa Cather's Jeanne Le Ber which is the nun's center, her element, her terrestrial paradise. The history of the American literary spirit during these years is the history of a spiritual constriction—of a survival struggle, as in the case of both Mencken and Cather, which very often omits the elements that make survival pleasant or even probable. Remember that there was only one thing wrong with George F. Babbitt's house: 'it was not a home.' And so with George F. Babbitt's wife. And with George F. Babbitt's children. . . . Very likely one of the central achievements of Sinclair Lewis's work is its continuous depiction of marriage as a second-rate imbroglio, while the typical human relationship of the period is compounded of narcissism and paranoia. Or compare that melancholy husband of Scott Fitzgerald's later tales, who viewed his young daughter, with some surprise, as 'a definite piece of youth.' As in the case of Lewis, the period which seeks after 'youth' most eagerly probably understands it least, and is forced in the end to repudiate it almost entirely. And as in Fitzgerald's case, once within the framework of any set of mature values, the alternative to sheer vanity is apparently sheer torment.

Do these values mark the triumph of an urban sophistication—and of the 'city-writers'—over those, like Sherwood Anderson, who represented a groping and provincial American hinterland? Four out of five of our authors are Westerners, three came from small western towns. Yet we have seen their almost identical attitude toward that 'crude, vulgar western air' of their own time: toward the prairie settlements of *Free Air* or *Main Street,* the western townspeople of *One of Ours* and *This Side of Paradise*. Had the western earth itself changed so much from the red-grassed plains of Willa Cather's childhood or the fruit orchards and beech woods which, in Anderson's memories, comprised 'as lovely a land as ever lay outdoors'? In the work of Lewis, at any rate, nature has become chiefly a pictorial matter, while in the work of Fitzgerald it all but disappears. Over this period, indeed, the *presence* of the American continent, which, with its forests and rivers and plains, had been so strongly felt in our earlier literature, is altered to suit the yokels and hinds of the Menckenian mythology.*

And wasn't it from the same rural scene and provincial roots that the progressive movement of the late nineteenth century had drawn its strength, as well as its chief literary spokesmen from Ed Howe to Hamlin Garland and the later Howells, penitent and bitter? The Aesthetic Revolt of the nineteen-twenties was a direct descendant of the reform movement of the nineteen-hundreds. But if the ties with the older tradition were finally dissolved by the impact of the post-war disillusionment, we have already seen how the social criticism of Norris and Dreiser's Naturalism became a matter of evasion and escape in our own group of writers, from the 'unembittered laughter' of Lewis to the cynical disdain of the early Fitzgerald. In the terminology of the Nietzschean Smart Set, the American people became the 'masses,' and the masses soon became the 'mob' and the 'aliens.' Wasn't it quite as true of a living society as of a living language that it was 'like a man suffering inces-

* It is interesting to compare Thomas Wolfe's later impression of those Brooklyn children who were 'suckled on darkness, and weaned on violence and noise.' 'They had to try to draw out moisture from the cobblestones . . . they rarely knew the feel of earth beneath their feet . . . their youthful eyes grew hard, unseeing, from being stopped forever by a wall of masonry.'

santly from small internal hemorrhages, and what it needs above all else is constant transfusions of new blood from other tongues. . . . The day the gates go up, that day it begins to die'? And where was a source of new blood in the American society of the nineteen-twenties if not in the ranks of those whom Mencken himself admitted were 'specialists in human liberty'—those new mixed Americans who seemed at times to be the only pure representatives of the older American traditions? There were figures of stature in our post-war period, there were heroes even in the middle twenties who were not 'sentimental fanatics' or 'martyrs.' Yet we have noticed not merely the tones of ignorance and class prejudice in four out of five of our present novelists, but the signs of a curious revulsion from the large sections of the American population which were formed by the industrial workers or the later immigrants.*

As a matter of fact, if some typical members of the Younger Generation were to detach themselves almost completely from the sources and forms of American society, the Middle Generation had initiated the exodus of the artists. This is surely the end of that 'beloved community' of Josiah Royce and the New England tradition of colonization. And that 'falling out of all domestic and social relations, out of his place in the human family, indeed' of Willa Cather's symbolical professor is another illuminating episode in the literature of the period. The development

* We have already seen the distinction in Willa Cather's work between the immigrants of the western plains—and of her childhood—and those of the eastern cities. It may be worth remembering also that there is no significant working-class figure in the whole range of Sinclair Lewis's portraits. It is only after Martin Arrowsmith has been reduced to the verge of moral disintegration by drink and despair that he forms a brief acquaintanceship with those 'shabby young men' who prowl causelessly from state to state and fill up 'the all-night lunches, the blind-pigs, the scabrous lodging-houses' of the nation.

of our literary tradition in the nineteen-twenties—admirable as it was, with all its honors and accomplishments—was also at the expense of a larger human content: both of the communal sense which had moved our older novelists and of that 'nakedness of spirit' which had marked our letters from Melville to Dreiser, and which perhaps only Sherwood Anderson still represented among these members of the Middle Generation. For all the advances in technic, and in both cultural and psychological patterns of behavior, the newer writers would often slight the individual human soul that the older writers had tried to understand.

During these years the pagans danced about the golden calf, while the tablets of the Lord were broken. But maybe the stress on the Aesthetic Man of the nineteen-twenties was almost as misleading as that, in the central area of our society, on the Economic Man. The older writers had called themselves 'students,' or 'scribblers,' the younger ones were definitely 'artists.' And very often they tried *so* hard to be, instead of simply being, artists. There can be a sort of conspicuous consumption in the spiritual as well as in the material realm. Those massive and clumsy Dreiserian tracts which listed every last item in the lower drawer of the financier's desk tried to include the furnishings of his mind and heart too. They were not written as 'stories,' they were meant to represent life, and particularly the realities of life in America, and they represented the ending of an epoch in the national letters.

Yet the Younger Generation, in its own insistence on literary freedom or even anarchy, was to some degree following the tradition of a vanished frontier in a country whose only history had been prophecy. As we have seen in the studies of the Middle Generation figures also, the clock moves faster in the United States; time is the catalyst of the national spirit, and change is the *status quo*. From the Ohio towns at the turn of the century to Akron and Youngstown, from the age of the arc light to that of the neon lamp, from the first federal income tax to Teapot Dome and the Klan, we have noticed the variety of intense social pressures visited upon our typical literary spokesmen. Was it only Willa Cather's world that broke in two somewhere in the middle twenties? It was Sinclair Lewis who pointed out that in the United States a pendulum was not a pendulum—it was a piston. You might say that we have followed our present group of authors through the vicissitudes of not merely two, but three worlds: agrarian, mercantile, and industrial. At least, within the span of half a century they witnessed the transformations of three major phases of modern history, while, between the Spanish-American War and the First World War, 'the States' became the U.S.A., and the children of the western plains became the subjects of oil, steel, and tobacco.

As a matter of fact, considering the nature of their cosmos, it is significant that most members of the Middle Generation kept their equilibrium to the degree that they did, and retained the virtues and persisted in the accomplishments that we have already noticed. —'Let it come! Let it all come back again!' Perhaps all you have to do is to compare Willa Cather's final acceptance of the 'mockery and betrayal and heart-break' of ordinary existence with a statement by the writer who was to summarize the values of the Younger Generation more eloquently than anybody else. You may remember those almost antithetical lines in the peroration to Ernest Hemingway's *Death in the Afternoon*. 'I know things change now and I do not care. It's all been changed for me. Let it all change.'

But the nature of the 'change'—whereby the democratic infant of Walt Whitman's work became the 'great machine' of John Dos Passos's—may also need a word of explanation.

3. The Pharaohs of Detroit

ALTHOUGH many immediate cultural factors appeared to be in favor of the Literary Renaissance of the nineteen-twenties, all the underlying factors of our social evolution were against it.

Certainly the First World War had its place in the sequence of affairs, and the post-war disillusionment is the usual descriptive phrase for the period. Yet we have already noticed the remote quality of some of our typical chronicles of World War I and those disdainful warriors with their Gothic abbeys and their passages from 'Atalanta in Calydon.' Hemingway was to be a notable exception; but in literary terms the enormous room of E. E. Cummings was almost as much of a sanctuary as a concentration camp for the post-war generation.

Among our own group of novelists, you may remember that Willa Cather's view of the war was quite different from that of most of her contemporaries, and even favorable in terms of a national life which, before the war, had become mostly a 'business proposition.' The literary values of Mencken, in some respects the worst war casualty of them all, of Sinclair Lewis, who, as the chronicler of the national manners, almost completely ignores the war, and of Sherwood Anderson, had been developed before the war itself.

No, the First World War may have been the immediate cause of the post-war revolt; it was certainly not the true cause. . . . But it did mark the consolidation of the new industrialism in American life, as Mencken's work shows all too clearly. It marked the triumph of the combines and cartels, the beginning of the end of a free capitalism.

It accelerated all the processes of an era of such 'profound economic and social transformation'—as the conservative historian, F. J. Turner, had pointed out as early as 1903—'as to raise the question of the effect of these changes upon the democratic institutions of the United States.' * It initiated the extreme, one might say the mortal phase of a long-term revolt of our writers against that ruthless and callous industrial order which had evolved out of the throes of the Civil War. And the extraordinary and disproportionate effect of the First World War upon the writing of a whole generation, on whom the literal horrors of the war had had only a relatively light impact, can be explained, as I have said, only in the light of this underlying cultural development.

No wonder Josiah Royce urged a higher provincialism in order to combat the nationalism of our day: the assimilation of all into a 'common type,' the rise of a 'remorseless mechanism—vast, irrational.' In this sense Sherwood Anderson's little group of Ohio tales was an epochal document, the last full attempt to record the variety and mystery of the older village scene before Woolworth's came to Winesburg and the country people danced to the tune of the looms. In Willa Cather's work also we have noticed that 'guarded mode of existence' in Black Hawk, Nebraska, where every individual taste, every natural appetite, was bridled by convention, and people tried to live like the mice in their own kitchens. And you may remember the 'universal similarity' of those smooth, standardized, and fixed American towns which Gopher Prairie is meant to

* In *The Frontier in American History*. By the end of World War II, the movement of monopoly had become even more extreme. According to the reports of the Temporary National Economic Committee and the House Small Business Committee, the largest corporations now hold approximately two thirds of the nation's usable manufacturing facilities. 'Never have so few controlled so much.'

typify: 'the same lumber yard, the same railroad station, the same Ford garage . . . the same standardized, nationally advertised wares.' The chronicle of village life that is presented in the annals of the Middle Generation is the chronicle of its disintegration. As in Lewis's work, the typical citizen of this new society wanders between a hinterland with which he has lost his ties and an industrial order which he cannot come to grips with.

You might say that the celebrated 'Revolt from the Village' which marked our literature in the nineteen-twenties was actually a revolt against the suburbs. Everywhere in the literature of this period we have seen the ascendancy of that new middle-class ethos of respectability, 'success' and privilege, from Mencken's first qualification for happiness (next to a 'superior and disdainful air,' the reputation of being well-to-do) to the luxurious Yale men of F. Scott Fitzgerald's work. . . . In the Cosmic Bourjoyce of Sinclair Lewis's novels, indeed, there is the extension of the Middle-Class Empire from the creation of the Duplex Trailer to the blind, dark bourgeois womb of time. What could be clearer, now, than the fact that this standardized middle-class man who has been cut off, apparently, from all the abiding human impulses, that this latest victim of history's whirl, has become history's only hero? Perhaps never before in literary annals has such a narrow and rigid view of life become such an absolute rationale of existence. And in one of the major literary creations of the period—George F. Babbitt himself—we saw the true outlines of the middle-class colony in the United States: that in-between world of derived goods and derived values which exists on the sufferance of General Motors and General Foods.

'Thank God, these treasures are in the hands of an intelligent people, the Democracy, to be used for the general good of the masses, and not made the spoils of monarchs, courts, and aristocracy, to be turned to the base and selfish ends of a privileged hereditary class.' So spoke the iron-master, Andrew Carnegie, ashamed, on his deathbed, of his wealth and power. Is the western 'optimism' of Willa Cather's Captain Forrester—'What you think of and plan for day by day, in spite of yourself, so to speak—you will get. You will get it more or less. That is, unless you are one of the people who get nothing in this world'—also a residuum of the frontier ethics? Nevertheless, it was an ethic that involved human as well as economic values; it was the survival struggle in the native style, as it were. And, springing from local origins, remembering the 'more or less' in a man's life as well as the distracted creatures who surrounded him, it took cognizance of those who also get nothing in this world.

Yet, as the great fortunes were drawn out of the forests, the lakes, the prairies, and the plains of the western territory, as the tycoons were taken over by the industrial combines, the accents of corruption marked even the national age of innocence, and personal guilt became a matter of corporate management. 'The American people went on believing that they were still what they once had been,' said the virtuoso publisher, S. S. McClure, himself a child of the frontier—'but they were not.' —'Well, I declare to you,' said one of Henry Adams's literary spokesmen, 'that in all my experience I have found no society which has had elements of corruption like the United States.' And what a curious sense of profound and pervasive evil is at the foundation of Henry James's work: the literary proponent of the 'innocent' American of the nineteen-hundreds. . . . Moreover, as the emissaries of copper and silver extended their empire to the Rockies, marking out states for their colonies, perhaps the native disciples of social justice could really be viewed as 'a few dull young men who haven't the ability to play the old game the old way.'

Wasn't it the main paradox of finance capitalism in the United States that, as it developed the resources of a continent, it lessened the stake of the individual in his own little town or city? 'If a man does not love the little patch of ground on which his own house may stand,' said Sherwood Anderson, 'can he in any sense love the street, the city, the state, the country of which it is a part?' In any event, we must recognize the degree to which the portraits of these members of the Middle Generation represent a general dissipation and failure of the older western tradition of social protest. In terms of the established patterns of the national life, this seems to mark the end of our spiritual frontier, too. The voices of communal aspiration have become those of solitary bitterness, of evasion and fantasy, of a desperate hedonism.*

That is not to say that these ancestral voices have been lacking in their own timbre, quality, or significance: you have seen all that already. Where else, indeed, can you find a more perceptive and intimate account of the change in the older national character over these years than in this many-volumed diary of the American mind put together by its typical literary spokesmen?—and the unhappy tone of its final pages may suggest something of the unhappy nature of the contemporary scene. Were the younger writers to be labeled the 'Irresponsibles'? At least they

* This is to be the prevailing tone of the Younger Generation also, as we shall see in what is chronologically the next volume of this series, *Writers in Crisis.* And probably the destructive satire of Ring Lardner, the last member of the Middle Generation to be treated there, can also be traced to the friction of the frontier values with the standards of the big money. Incidentally, it is interesting to notice the similar vein of bitterness and self-hatred that runs through *The Autobiography of William Allen White:* the story of another western small-town boy who made good.

felt the pressures of their age more intensely and acknowledged them more directly than most of their later critics. A Dos Passos, a Hemingway, a Faulkner, served many an eloquent summons upon their countrymen even if they worked in solitude and doubt, and their cultural framework, like that of Willa Cather's, was narrow or broken. 'A second chance—*that's* the delusion. There never was to be but one. We work in the dark—we do what we can—we give what we have.'

The record of contemporary art is to a large degree the record of Cassandras and Jeremiahs, of desolate prophets, of a prefabricated wilderness. From Schopenhauer to Proust, and the melancholy testament of the later Freud, evolving the mechanics of a racial will to death, we have had our omens and portents. The Lord has sent us enough plagues and pestilences to convince everybody but the Pharaohs of Detroit. . . . Just as the ancient peoples suffered all sorts of idiots and wretches for the sake of the holy spark that might animate a grotesque soul, so we should pay heed also to our local Dadaists and Existentialists. And even among the writers who are more securely rooted in the older tradition of the artist and in the folkways of the community, who are determined, like a J. B. Priestley in England or our own Sherwood Anderson, to give 'this democracy thing another whirl yet,' we have seen those recurrent cycles of doubt and anxiety, those literary 'running fits' to escape from the industrial and financial stretch-out of modern times.

'There is nothing short of the Alkali Desert that compares with the desolateness of the common American industrial town,' said another historian of our urban society, Lewis Mumford, writing in 1922, and in the later work of a James T. Farrell or a Richard Wright his gloomiest predictions were realized—not to mention the air-conditioned nightmare of Henry Miller's work, or that

take it from me kiddo
believe me
my country, 'tis of
you, land of the Cluett
Shirt, Boston Garter and Spearmint
Girl with the Wrigley Eyes*

of E. E. Cummings. In the studies of the Middle Generation itself, we have noticed many indications of the commercial values which spread, in the nineteen-twenties, from the business activities of our literary heroes to their domestic affairs and their secret fantasies of pleasure, until the realm of the unconscious itself was merely another standardized product, sensitive only to the stimuli of a money society. During this period, the economic inferno first fully glimpsed in *Babbitt* became a reality—and a blueprint.

Was it merely a question of the parable of the talents as against the parable of mercy, as John Chamberlain said in an early study of Dreiser? Wasn't it now a question of the Judeo-Christian ethics as against the daily practices of finance capitalism? 'Behold how good/ And how pleasant it is/ For brothers/ To dwell together in unity,' said the royal Hebraic bard. But wasn't it even better, perhaps, for brothers to dwell together in combines? . . . What was frightening, after all, was not the 'moral obsession' of the American man during the first post-war period, as Henry Mencken claimed, but the actual loss of this 'obses-

* From: 'Is 5' in *Collected Poems,* published by Harcourt, Brace and Co., Inc. Copyright, 1923, 1925, 1926, 1931, 1935, 1938, by E. E. Cummings. Copyright, 1926, by Boni and Liveright.

sion': the increasing immorality of the national life in the period of the boom, and a moral defection that was betrayed in the very series of vicious and irrelevant moral 'crusades' which marked the period. The national spirit would reassert itself in the years of the Depression and in the Second World War. But how much of this was due to the residual resources of the democracy? And which had become the actual, dominant cultural force in the democracy: the ethics or the practice?

For the nineteen-twenties also marked the coming of age of capitalism in America, now almost unrestrained by the last vestiges of Puritanism, the frontier code, or an older democratic ethos. And didn't Henry Mencken himself, the Logician of the Cartels, clearly express the prevailing economic rationale in his adaptation, at once harsh and brittle, of the Darwinian survival of the fit? In his alternate mood, we have seen how beautifully he also represented that historical vision of desolation which was to become a central vision of the epoch: the negation of all the ordinary elements of a natural life, the stress on sexual sterility and on a similarly sterile 'psychology' of fear and envy, the procession of dark jokes which lead to the 'triumph' of the New Order. We have seen the nature of liberty and truth for this solitary urban citizen speeding through a diseased American hinterland in his steel Pullman. . . . Here, certainly, is Conrad's sense of terror and darkness in the life of man, but where is that accompanying sense of the wonder and prodigality of life? For an evolutionary philosopher this is a curious climax to the nineteenth-century view of an ever-expanding universe; and now indeed it would seem that mind had reached the end of its tether, and the force of the universe had become the Antagonist.

In a sense, you could say that H. L. Mencken, like his

own Faustian prototype, is the 'villain' of this curious drama of the Middle Generation, while Sherwood Anderson is its hero. At least they represent opposite poles in the history of the temperaments which made up that generation. It is Sherwood Anderson who has preserved the account of an earlier native manner: confident, expansive, and stubborn in the face of danger. And it is H. L. Mencken who has developed the narrative of national folly and of personal superstition. 'I am the spirit that denies.'

Yet it is change in America which is the true villain of the piece, and Mencken's is in many ways the most illuminating of all these chronicles of change. And the inverted modes of his logic are familiar to us in an age of inversion. They are the stigmata of the disturbed personalities and the disturbed societies of our time. They are the endemic symptoms of the contemporary social maze and of the uneasy souls who cavort down blind alleys and pound against mirrors in the attempt to evade reality and cherish illusion.

In the work of the Younger Generation itself, over the period from 1925 to 1940, we will continue the record of the native literary mind in its years of tension.

THE END

Appendix

Bibliography and Acknowledgments

In the separate bibliographies I have listed the main works of each novelist in terms of the periods under which they are discussed in the text. I have also included a selected list of critical studies in each case. However, I ought to acknowledge a debt to several works which have been particularly valuable for the general background of this volume.

In general I have used Fred B. Millett's excellent handbook, *Contemporary American Authors,* for the biographical details in these studies and also for the bibliographies. F. J. Turner's *The Frontier in American History* is particularly illuminating on the historical pattern of this literary period. Ferner Nuhn's *The Wind Blows from the East* is a very interesting study of cultural orientation which has special significance for the writing of the nineteen-twenties. Alfred Kazin's *On Native Grounds* carries an admirable treatment of the historical and literary milieu of the novelists under consideration here. *After the Genteel Tradition,* edited by Malcolm Cowley, also deals with these writers in a collection of very useful essays, as does the volume called *Spokesmen,* by T. K. Whipple, a neglected and discerning critic. Joseph Warren Beach's *American Fiction: 1920-1940* is particularly good on questions of literary craft and historical influences. Dealing with an earlier period, F. O. Matthiessen's *American Renaissance* illuminates many of the cultural and artistic issues of the nineteen-twenties.

Any student of cultural history is indebted to Vernon Parrington, while in different areas the works of Van Wyck Brooks and of Edmund Wilson serve as a general guide and model for contemporary literary criticism.

M. G.

Bibliography

H. L. MENCKEN: 1880–1956

Ventures into Verse 1903
George Bernard Shaw, His Plays 1905
The Philosophy of Friedrich Nietzsche 1908
Men Versus the Man (with Robert La Monte) 1910

A Little Book in C Major 1916
A Book of Burlesques 1917
A Book of Prefaces 1918
In Defense of Women 1918
Damn! A Book of Calumny 1918
The American Language 1919
Prejudices: First Series 1919

The American Credo (with George Jean Nathan) 1920
Prejudices: Second Series 1920
Heliogabalus, A Buffoonery (with George Jean Nathan) 1920
Prejudices: Third Series 1922
Prejudices: Fourth Series 1924
Prejudices: Fifth Series 1926
Notes on Democracy 1926

Prejudices: Sixth Series 1927
Treatise on the Gods 1930
Making a President: A Footnote to the Saga of Democracy 1932
Treatise on Right and Wrong 1934
The American Language: Fourth Edition, corrected, enlarged, and rewritten 1936

Happy Days 1940
Newspaper Days 1941
Heathen Days 1943
The American Language, Supplement One 1945

Selected Studies by: Irving Babbitt, Joseph W. Beach, Ernest Boyd, V. F. Calverton, Gilbert Chesterton, Benjamin De-Cassères, Isaac Goldberg, Frank Harris, Lewis Kronenberger, Ludwig Lewisohn, Walter Lippmann, Fred L. Pattee, Burton Rascoe, Stuart Sherman, Upton Sinclair, Carl Van Doren, Edmund Wilson.

Bibliography

SINCLAIR LEWIS: 1885–1951

Our Mr. Wrenn	1914
The Trail of the Hawk	1915
The Innocents	1917
The Job	1917
Free Air	1919
Main Street	1920
Babbitt	1922
Arrowsmith	1925
Mantrap	1926
Elmer Gantry	1927
The Man Who Knew Coolidge	1928
Dodsworth	1929
Ann Vickers	1933
Work of Art	1934
It Can't Happen Here	1935
The Prodigal Parents	1938
Bethel Merriday	1940
Gideon Planish	1943
Cass Timberlane	1945
Kingsblood Royal	1947

Miscellaneous: The American Fear of Literature, Nobel Address (1931); *Cheap and Contented Labor* (1929); *Selected Short Stories* (1935); *Jayhawker,* a play (with Lloyd Lewis)

(1935); *It Can't Happen Here* (play, with John C. Moffit) (1938).

Selected Studies by: Sherwood Anderson, Percy Boynton, James Branch Cabell, V. F. Calverton, Henry S. Canby, Robert Cantwell, Floyd Dell, Clifton Fadiman, E. M. Forster, Granville Hicks, V. L. Parrington, Fred L. Pattee, Stuart Sherman, Carl Van Doren, T. K. Whipple.

Bibliography

WILLA (SIBERT) CATHER: 1876-1947

The Troll Garden	1905
Alexander's Bridge	1912
O Pioneers!	1913
The Song of the Lark	1915
My Antonia	1918
Youth and the Bright Medusa	1920
One of Ours	1922
A Lost Lady	1923
April Twilights	1923
The Professor's House	1925
My Mortal Enemy	1926
Death Comes for the Archbishop	1927
Shadows on the Rock	1931
Obscure Destinies	1932
Lucy Gayheart	1935
Not Under Forty	1936
Sapphira and the Slave Girl	1940

Miscellaneous: Ed. *The Best Short Stories of Sarah Orne Jewett* (1925).

Selected Studies by: Percy Boynton, Clifton Fadiman, Dorothy Canfield Fisher, Granville Hicks, Howard Jones, Louis Kronenberger, Grant Overton, Fred L. Pattee, Burton Rascoe, Stuart Sherman, Carl Van Doren, Edward Wagenecht, T. K. Whipple.

Bibliography

SHERWOOD ANDERSON: 1876-1941

Windy McPherson's Son	1916
Marching Men	1917
Mid-American Chants	1918
Winesburg, Ohio	1919
Poor White	1920
The Triumph of the Egg	1921
Many Marriages	1923
Horses and Men	1923
A Story Teller's Story	1924
Dark Laughter	1925
Tar, a Midwest Childhood	1926
Sherwood Anderson's Notebook	1926
A New Testament	1927
Hello Towns!	1929
Alice, and the Lost Novel	1929
The American County Fair	1930
Perhaps Women	1931
Beyond Desire	1932
Death in the Woods	1933
No Swank	1934
Puzzled America	1935
Kit Brandon, A Portrait	1936
Home Town	1940
Sherwood Anderson's Memoirs	1942

Selected Studies by: Ernest Boyd, Joseph Warren Beach, Percy Boynton, V. F. Calverton, Henry S. Canby, Floyd Dell, Nathan Fagin, Harry Hansen, Harry Hartwick, Granville Hicks, Ludwig Lewisohn, V. L. Parrington, Fred L. Pattee, Burton Rascoe, Paul Rosenfeld, Stuart Sherman, Louis Untermeyer, Carl Van Doren, T. K. Whipple.

Bibliography

F. SCOTT FITZGERALD: 1896-1940

This Side of Paradise	1920
Flappers and Philosophers	1920
The Beautiful and Damned	1922
Tales of the Jazz Age	1922
The Vegetable	1923
The Great Gatsby	1925
All the Sad Young Men	1926
Tender Is the Night	1934
Taps at Reveille	1935
The Last Tycoon	1941
The Crack-Up (Edited by Edmund Wilson)	1945

Selected Studies by: John P. Bishop, Ernest Boyd, Arthur Mizener, Paul Rosenfeld, Carl Van Doren, Alfred Ward, Edmund Wilson.

Acknowledgments

The illustrative passages in this book are reprinted by permission of the publishing houses and individuals listed below and are copyrighted as follows:

THE WORKS OF H. L. MENCKEN

Passages from:

Prejudices: Second Series, copyright, 1920, by Alfred A. Knopf, Inc. *Prejudices: Fourth Series*, copyright, 1924, by Alfred A. Knopf, Inc. *Prejudices: Fifth Series*, copyright, 1926, by Alfred A. Knopf, Inc. *Prejudices: Sixth Series*, copyright, 1927, by Alfred A. Knopf, Inc. *Notes on Democracy*, copyright, 1926, by Alfred A. Knopf, Inc. *The American Language*, copyright, 1919, 1921, 1923, 1936, by Alfred A. Knopf, Inc. *A Book of Burlesques*, copyright, 1916, 1920, by Alfred A. Knopf, Inc.

THE WORKS OF SINCLAIR LEWIS

Passages from:

The Job, copyright, 1917, by Harcourt, Brace and Howe, Inc. *Free Air*, copyright, 1919, by Harcourt, Brace and Howe, Inc. *Main Street*, copyright, 1920, by Harcourt, Brace and Company, Inc. *Babbitt*, copyright, 1922, by Harcourt Brace and Company, Inc. *Arrowsmith*, copyright, 1924, 1925, by The Designer Publishing Company, Inc.; copyright, 1925, by Harcourt, Brace and Company, Inc. *Elmer Gantry*, copyright, 1927, by Harcourt, Brace and Company, Inc. *Ann Vickers*, copyright, 1932, 1933, by Sinclair Lewis; reprinted by permission of Doubleday and Company, Inc. *It Can't Happen Here*, copyright, 1935, by Sinclair Lewis; reprinted by permission of Doubleday and Company, Inc. *The Prodigal Parents*, copyright, 1938, by Sinclair Lewis; reprinted by permission of Doubleday and Company, Inc. *Bethel Merriday*, copyright, 1940, by Sinclair Lewis; reprinted by permission of Doubleday and Company, Inc. *Gideon Planish*, copyright, 1943, by

Sinclair Lewis; reprinted by permission of Random House. *Cass Timberlane*, copyright, 1945, by Sinclair Lewis; reprinted by permission of Random House.

THE WORKS OF WILLA CATHER

Passages from:

O Pioneers!, copyright, 1913, 1941, by Willa Sibert Cather; reprinted by permission of Houghton Mifflin Company. *My Ántonia*, copyright, 1918, 1926, by Willa Sibert Cather; reprinted by permission of Houghton Mifflin Company. *The Song of the Lark*, copyright, 1915, by Willa Sibert Cather; reprinted by permission of Houghton Mifflin Company. *April Twilights and Other Poems*, copyright, 1923, by Willa Cather; reprinted by permission of Alfred A. Knopf, Inc. *One of Ours*, copyright, 1922, by Alfred A. Knopf, Inc. *A Lost Lady*, copyright, 1923, by Willa Cather; reprinted by permission of Alfred A. Knopf, Inc. *The Professor's House*, copyright, 1925, by Willa Cather; reprinted by permission of Alfred A. Knopf, Inc. *My Mortal Enemy*, copyright, 1926, by Alfred A. Knopf, Inc. *Death Comes for the Archbishop*, copyright, 1926, 1927, 1929, by Willa Cather; reprinted by permission of Alfred A. Knopf, Inc. *Shadows on the Rock*, copyright, 1931, by Willa Cather; reprinted by permission of Alfred A. Knopf, Inc. *Obscure Destinies*, copyright, 1930, 1932, by Willa Cather; reprinted by permission of Alfred A. Knopf, Inc. *Not Under Forty*, copyright, 1922, 1933, 1936, by Willa Cather; reprinted by permission of Alfred A. Knopf, Inc. *Lucy Gayheart*, copyright, 1935, by Willa Cather, reprinted by permission of Alfred A. Knopf, Inc.

THE WORKS OF SHERWOOD ANDERSON

Passages from:

Marching Men, copyright, 1917, by John Lane Company; reprinted by permission of Mrs. Sherwood Anderson. *Mid-American Chants*, copyright, 1918, by John Lane Company; reprinted by permission of Mrs. Sherwood Anderson. *Wines-*

burg, Ohio, copyright, 1919, by B. W. Huebsch, Inc.; copyright renewed, 1946; reprinted by permission of Viking Press. *Poor White*, copyright, 1920, by B. W. Huebsch, Inc.; reprinted by permission of Mrs. Sherwood Anderson. *Horses and Men*, copyright, 1923, by B. W. Huebsch, Inc.; copyright renewed, 1942; reprinted by permission of Mrs. Sherwood Anderson. *Sherwood Anderson's Notebook*, copyright, 1926, by Boni and Liveright; reprinted by permission of Liveright Publishing Corporation. *Tar, A Midwest Childhood*, copyright, 1926, by Boni and Liveright; reprinted by permission of Liveright Publishing Corporation. *Hello Towns!*, copyright, 1928, by Condé Nast Publications, Inc.; copyright, 1929, by Horace Liveright, Inc.; reprinted by permission of Liveright Publishing Corporation. *Perhaps Women*, copyright, 1931, by Horace Liveright, Inc.; reprinted by permission of Liveright Publishing Corporation. *Beyond Desire*, copyright, 1932, by Sherwood Anderson; reprinted by permission of Liveright Publishing Corporation. *Puzzled America*, copyright, 1935, by Charles Scribner's Sons. *Home Town*, copyright, 1940, by Sherwood Anderson; reprinted by permission of Mrs. Sherwood Anderson. *The Triumph of the Egg*, copyright, 1921, by B. W. Huebsch, Inc.; copyright renewed, 1942; reprinted by permission of Mrs. Sherwood Anderson.

THE WORKS OF F. SCOTT FITZGERALD

Passages from:

This Side of Paradise, copyright, 1920, by Charles Scribner's Sons. *The Beautiful and Damned*, copyright, 1921, 1922, by The Metropolitan Publications, Inc.; copyright, 1922, by Charles Scribner's Sons. *The Great Gatsby*, copyright, 1925, by Charles Scribner's Sons. *All the Sad Young Men*, copyright, 1926, by Charles Scribner's Sons. *Tender Is the Night*, copyright, 1934, by Charles Scribner's Sons.

The quotations from the work of T. S. Eliot are from *Collected Poems of T. S. Eliot*, copyright, 1930, by T. S. Eliot; copyright, 1934, 1936, by Harcourt, Brace and Company, Inc.; reprinted by permission of Harcourt, Brace and Company, Inc., and Messrs. Faber and Faber, Ltd.

The quotation from the work of E. E. Cummings is from *Collected Poems of E. E. Cummings*, copyright, 1926, by Boni and Liveright, Inc.; copyright, 1923, 1925, 1926, 1931, 1935, 1938, by E. E. Cummings; reprinted by permission of Harcourt, Brace and Company, Inc., and E. E. Cummings.

The quotation from the work of Zelda Fitzgerald is from *Save Me the Waltz*, copyright, 1932, by Charles Scribner's Sons, and reprinted by permission.

Index